One Who Came Back
The Diary of a Jewish Survivor

One Who Came Back
The Diary of a Jewish Survivor

Josef Katz

Translated from the German by Hilda Reach
Foreword by Herman Taube

 DRYAD PRESS
IN ASSOCIATION WITH THE UNIVERSITY OF WISCONSIN PRESS

Printed in the United States of America.
Cover photograph "Drancy (Homage to Georges)" by Muriel Hasbun
Text and cover design by Sandy Rodgers

Text is typeset in Bembo 12 points on 15

One Who Came Back: The Diary of a Jewish Survivor was originally published
by the Herzl Press and Bergen-Belsen Memorial Press in 1976. This new edition
includes a revision of the original translation.

The paper used in this publication meets the minimum requirements of American National Standard for Information Sciences — Permanence of paper for
Printed Library Materials, ANSI Z39.48

Dryad Press
P.O. Box 11233
Takoma Park, Maryland 20913
dryadpress@yahoo.com

One Who Came Back: The Diary of Jewish Survivor is distributed to the trade
by the University of Wisconsin Press, 1930 Monroe Street, 3rd Floor, Madison,
Wisconsin 53711-2059, www.wisc.edu/wisconsinpress

Library of Congress Cataloging-in-Publication Data
Katz, Josef, 1918-1990
  One who came back : the diary of a Jewish survivor
/ Josef Katz ; translated from the German by Hilda
Reach ; foreword by Herman Taube.– Rev. ed.
      p. cm.
  ISBN 1-928755-07-0 (alk. paper)
  1. Katz, Josef, 1918-2.
Jews—Germany—Lübeck—Biography. 3. Holocaust,
Jewish (1939-1945)—Latvia—Personal narratives. 4.
Lübeck (Germany)—Biography. I. Title.
  DS135.G5K36745 2005
  940.53'18'092—dc22

This book is dedicated to the memory of my dear mother, Emma Katz, and to the six million Jews who perished in the inferno of Hitler's Europe.

Josef Katz

⸺

As the widow of the author, I am deeply appreciative that my late husband's account of his experience during the Holocaust will remain alive through this book. I would like to thank my dear friend Herman Taube and publisher Merrill Leffler who worked so diligently to bring this book to life.

Irene Katz

During the German occupation of Central European countries, national borders changed from what they were before World War II; they shifted again at war's end and have continued to, most recently with the break-up of the Soviet Socialist Republic. This schematic map of Central Europe today identifies major locations that Josef Katz refers to in his diary: his home in Lübeck, Germany, labor camps in Latvia, and Stutthof and Danzig (Gdansk) in then-occupied Poland.

Contents

Foreword

Among the thousands of Jewish communities the Nazis obliterated during World War II, there was the small Jewish community of Lübeck, an old, imperial port city, a half-hour's drive from Hamburg. Historically, Lübeck was not hospitable to Jews; however, a Jewish community began to grow in the mid-19th century after the annexation of Moisling, a nearby Danish city where Jews first established themselves by the end of the 17th century. With the rise of Hitler's regime, the Jewish community was systematically decimated through arrests, emigration and deportations to the East — Josef Katz's family was among the last to be transported in 1941 and 1942.

Katz and his fellow prisoners were sent to Riga, Latvia, months after the Nazi Einsatzgruppen nearly emptied the Riga Ghetto, marching its Jews to the Bikerniek Forest and the Rumbula Forest several miles away; there they and Russian prisoners of war were forced to dig deep execution pits — over a period of ten days, 27,000 were murdered. Only 4,500 men and 300 women remained in Riga when the first of the German Jews got there.

Over the next four years, Katz would experience the most horrific and brutal human behavior the Nazis could design. Shortly after his liberation, he began his retrospective diary. It is searing in its detail. Beatings, shootings and hangings were his daily companions, let alone indescribable hunger and disease. From Riga, he was sent back and forth to other notorious ghettos in Latvia: Jungfernhof, Salaspils, Liepaja, Kaiserwald, Stutthof, then Danzig (Gdansk in Polish) from where he barely survived a final death march in Germany, January to March 7, 1945. While it may be comforting to say his survival reflects a triumph of the human spirit, he acknowledged, as have all survivors, that he was the beneficiary of one good fortune after another. "Once again," he writes of life in Kaiserwald in fall, 1944, "I have escaped death in a mysterious, incomprehensible manner."

In Liepaja, a Latvian city on the Baltic, the Jewish community numbered some 8,000 before the war. Less than 10 months before Katz arrived there, Liepajan Jews were rounded up and shipped to Skeden, a fishing village several miles away. Between December 15 and 17, 1941, 2,800 Jews were murdered. Marching raggedly through Liepaja's dark streets in October, 1942, he likened himself and his fellow slave laborers to the ruins in the Bahnhofstrasse. "We are a column of misery; with our ragged clothes and torn shoes, our unwashed, unshaved and exhausted faces, we look like derelicts and bums."

Random beatings by Nazi and Latvian guards over these years became routine. At one period in 1943 in Riga, he worked on a farm outside the ghetto. He and his friend Schweitzer were weeding a turnip field, working next to an old Latvian who was both skilled and well-fed. The previous day, Schweitzer had been beaten senselessly by a guard known as Harald the Dane for working too slowly. Schweitzer said he could no longer "go on with this life any longer. He is not going to go to work anymore and submit to [these] brutalities." Katz and others prevailed upon him to return. Harald came from behind the Jewish prisoners and kicked them as they were bent over weeding: " 'Get up, Jew!' he commands them. 'You were laughing at me, weren't you?' he says, constantly hitting them in the face with a thin reed." If a prisoner denied it, he was hit in the face with a fist.

" 'You did laugh. Why are you lying?' Then he gave his victim a good going-over with his cane so that he screamed in pain. 'Did you laugh or not?' The tortured man, hoping for relief, admitted that he laughed. But now the Dane said, 'Why are you lying? I know you didn't laugh. Take your pants down. You lied to me, you swine.' He continued beating him without mercy until the man was writhing on the ground in agony. I, too, have gone through this several times."

Schweitzer was sent to clean the latrine. Afterwards, he and another Jew were "forced to get into the container with excrement, embrace and say that they loved each other. The five SS men stood by, laughing. A few days later Schweitzer was taken to Riga where he died of internal injuries."

The systematic cruelty took its terrible toll on civility. Elie Wiesel and so many other survivors, Josef Katz among them, write about the inconsolable depths of depravity such cruelty and hunger — especially the unearthly hunger that no words or photos can truly convey — reduced them to.

The men lying here were members of the human race only in outward appearance. They had lost all civilization or humanity. Here everybody fought everybody else for a place near the stove, for a piece of potato peel, for the last possessions of a comrade who had just died. The pockets of the dead man were quickly searched, the lunch bag snatched from under his head and ransacked, and the blanket torn from his body. It no longer mattered how one lived, as long as one survived.

The potato "has become the greatest treasure we can still possess," writes Katz — one sentence after another serves up tales of utter degradation. "After the mass feeding the Kapos have their second meal. It makes my mouth water," he writes, "when I see them dig deep into the bucket and come up with ladlefuls of potato peels and meat scraps which they gobble up with relish. I have known for a long time that only the worst and most brutal kind of person can survive here. Everyone else is fated for the mass grave." And again, "But who is going to give up a potato here without a struggle? These people who are hardly able to stand on their feet are fighting and wrestling with each other; there is nothing human left in us anymore.

Given these details of macabre brutality, Josef Katz could have despaired over human nature and who would have dared to blame him? But *One Who Came Back* relates as well the unexpected acts of kindness and generosity of strangers, both Jews and non-Jews, including even a Nazi commander Kerschner in Liepaja and a Nazi guard in Lenta, a labor camp. "He never had anything against the Jews, he says. They never harmed him, and that's why he can't treat them badly now." When Katz and his fellow prisoners were finished and were being sent back to Kaiserwald, the officer said, "Good luck, boys. I did what I could for you."

Given the danger of such assistance, these seemingly small gestures were in themselves heroic and, in effect, said No! to such debasement of human beings. One more example: "Often an old woman visits the nursery," Katz writes of Kaiserwald in June, 1942. "She owns a chicken farm outside the camp. Lately, whenever she passes me, she drops a bag with dry bread crumbs. She collects them in the neighborhood for her chickens. I nod my head to show my gratitude. She probably saved my life with her stale bread."

Though Josef Katz wrote his diary-memoir shortly after his liberation, it remained unpublished for thirty years. When it first appeared in translation in 1976, the late Marie Syrkin of Brandeis University praised "its unpretentious candor and simplicity. Katz succeeds in giving a remarkably vivid picture of how life was endured in the ghettos and concentration camps of Nazi-held Latvia," she wrote. "Writing starkly and with understatement, the author conveys not only the Jewish tragedy but the psychology of survival." Since then, hundreds of other memoirs have been written — we now have an immense library of survivor accounts by men and women who have written of their ordeals. How many can we bear? What are we to do with them all? Isn't there enough terror in the world today? Why must we continue to revisit the past?

There is no simple answer. In a world that for many has been nothing less than a charnal house, Josef Katz's memoir represents what is enduring in the human spirit — the will not only to go on, but the commitment to live as best as we can, with generosity and compassion. There is no other way if we are to honor those who have been and suffered so terribly and those, our children, who are to come.

Herman Taube, Winter 2006

Introduction

Out of desperation, unable to understand the terrifying events I witnessed, I sat down shortly after my return to Lübeck in the early summer of 1945 to write this book. The first notes were written with a pencil as I did not own a typewriter. However, soon after our arrival in New York, with the first money earned, I bought a portable Underwood which hastened the completion of the manuscript.

This story is one of suffering, starvation, torture and anything else the sick human mind may devise. The dialogues I report here, from the day Hitler came to power until the moment I was freed from the last death camp, are true. Nothing was added, altered or changed, and every incident, every experience, every horror is exactly as it occurred and as I put it down so many years ago. At that time the gruesome details were still so fresh in my mind, so vivid before my eyes that I felt this book had to be written to release the pent-up tensions of those many years of tribulation. But even during those times of anguish, in the hours where resistance and the will to live declined due to inhuman treatment by our German captors, I found truly warm-hearted human beings who shared their last piece of bread, their last watery drop of soup with the dying friend next to them. In most cases it did not help because as soon as the will to live began to wane, physical resistance started to decline and it was only a matter of days until death occurred.

I completed these memoirs in the fall of 1946, shortly after my arrival in New York. For some twenty-five years this book was stored in the bottom drawer of our linen closet, always guarded by my wife, Irene, who hoped it would at some time see the light of day.

In my daughter's German class at U.C.L.A., during the fall of 1971, Dr. Ruth Kunzer gave a lecture on the literature of the Holocaust. Sensing her personal interest in this subject and knowing of my manuscript written so many years ago, Jeanne asked Dr. Kunzer if she would read my account of the Nazi period. She agreed and consulted with Dr. Ehrhard Bahr, Professor of Germanic Languages at U.C.L.A., who helped in bringing it to the attention of the publisher. Dr. Kunzer's kind and unselfish help made this book possible and I gratefully acknowledge her assistance. My thanks are also extended to Dr. Bahr for his encouragement as well as his personal interest in my book. Furthermore, I would like to express my sincere appreciation to Hilda Reach for her excellent translation.

Josef Katz, September 1972

One Who Came Back
The Diary of a Jewish Survivor

1

Lübeck, Germany

January 1933-December 1941

January 30, 1933. Many people are standing in front of Lübeck town hall. I am just coming out of school, the leather case with my books under my arm. I cross the market square and join the waiting crowd. I don't know what they're waiting for. A few minutes later several SA[1] companies march up to the town hall. Everybody screams, "Heil!" Several SA men enter the building and come out again a few moments later with a civilian in their midst. Somebody standing next to me says he is the Social Democratic police magistrate Mehrlein. Two SA men appear on the balcony of the town hall and hoist the swastika flag. People raise their arms and sing the German anthem and the Horst Wessel Song [Nazi party anthem]. In between, some old crones shout, "Heil!" The singing and shouting still ring in my ears after I have turned the nearest corner.

April 1, 1933. Boycott. Large yellow signs are plastered on all Jewish stores. SA men are posted in front of our small leather goods store in the Braunstrasse to keep our customers from entering. One SA man punches my brother in the face when he tries to walk into his shop. He comes home very dejected and says to my mother, "We Jews are finished now."

May 1934. We now have "race education" at school. Koepke, my teacher at the secondary school, is trying to be objective. After discussing the Nordic and Dinaric races, he mentions the Jewish race. He says the Jews are different. He doesn't say better or worse — just different. That's O.K. with me.

September 1934. After classes we play football on Buniams Field. They have made a rule that the students have to greet the opposing team with the Hitler salute. I don't raise my hand. After the game the coach comes to me and says I have to raise my hand like everybody else. I tell him that I'm a Jew. So he says I no longer belong on a German football field. My teammates ask me if it's true that we always drink Christian blood for Easter. When I tell this to my mother she takes me into her arms, strokes my face and says: "That is rishus.[2]"

Witzenhausen near Cassel

December 1935. I am here as a business apprentice at Kugelmann's. The store is right on the market square. We have two large show windows which we find smeared with anti-Semitic slogans every morning. Customers come into the store only rarely, and even then they sneak out the back way so nobody should see them.

When I walk through the streets, rocks and curses fly after me. Although I don't know anybody in the town, everybody knows I'm a Jew. At the commercial college the blackboard bears the legend: "'The Jew lives by lies and dies by the truth.' — Adolf Hitler, *Mein Kampf*." I tell Roeper, the teacher, that I can't work with that staring me in the face. He says it is educational material. I pack up my books and go home. Several days later my boss has to pay a fine because I left the class without permission.

We have a little vineyard on the shore of the Werra River. Sometimes my bicycle stands at the foot of the vineyard. Two German boys come pedaling along, throw my bike down and try to smash it. "We can do what we like with your bike," they jeer, "because you're a Jew." Afterwards I push my bike home.

Lübeck

August 1936. I am visiting in Lübeck. Allegedly Jewish judges in Poland have condemned German nationals. Protest demonstrations are staged. A crowd of teenage youths chases through the streets. Suddenly they stop before our leather goods shop and sing their hate songs. Some cry, "Get the Jew!" The crowd pushes forward and about 30 people press through the open door into the shop. Scraps of leather fly through the air, a bottle of black dye is smashed against the wall, and nails of every size are scattered all over the floor. From both sides men run behind the counter. They grab my brother and toss him into the seething mob like a rubber ball. Meanwhile I am standing in front of the counter and watch the rioting crowd, but they don't know me. With his hands held behind his back, my brother is led through the main streets of the town. The crowd has dispersed — I see that the contents of the cash register are gone. I find my brother at the police station, beaten black and blue. Zipper, a watchmaker, in his white coat, and Schachtel, another leather dealer, are also there. The three of them play Skat until they are sent home at night.

June 1937. I have left the apprenticeship in Witzenhausen to continue my training at another store in Lübeck. Hardly any young Jewish people are left in Lübeck. I buy myself a small canoe to get some exercise. The dock master raises difficulties about mooring the boat of a Jew, but when I slip a few marks into his hand he gives me a berth "until further notice." I am repeatedly stopped on the river. Every vessel has to fly the German flag, the harbor police say. So I only go canoeing at night to avoid being recognized.

November-December 1938. Josef, my department head, says things are looking pretty rotten. He doesn't like that affair with Grynszpan[3] at all. Something's in the air he says. When I take my girl friend home that evening, she says I'm imagining things. During the night on November 9th through the 10th, all Jewish stores and apartments are wrecked. My brother is arrested in the street. The Gestapo doesn't find me at home. My sister gives me 100 marks to escape. While I'm still with her I hear heavy footsteps on the stairs. I quickly dash up the two flights to the attic.

"Is Josef Katz here?" the Gestapo bellows at my sister.

"No, he isn't here," I hear my sister reply.

He says he has a search warrant. He opens and ransacks the drawers. My savings book and my mother's cash disappear into his pockets. My sister asks him whether he has any identification.

Shut up," he says, "or I'll smash your face in."

After he leaves I, too, leave. My goal is Hamburg. At the gate to the Lübeck railway station I see several policemen who scrutinize everybody walking through the barrier. There is nothing for me to do but take the streetcar to Schwartau. In the waiting room I order some food. I haven't eaten all day. The waiter turns on the radio. I just hear the news that Goering wants to make a billion marks out of Grynszpan. Two SA men sit down at my table. One tells the other that the synagogues all over Germany have been destroyed. There is no room for these Oriental structures on German soil. I put my sandwich in my pocket. I've lost my appetite. Then I take the train to Hamburg.

The next morning I get a telegram from my mother asking me to return home as quickly as possible; otherwise she will be arrested. I take the next train back to Lübeck. There I stay with my uncle in the Fischergrube. At four in the afternoon the doorbell rings. I look through the keyhole. Gestapo.

"Are you Josef Katz?" the man asks me.

"Yes."

"Get dressed." I take my coat and hat and wrap a scarf around my neck.

"You know Holzblatt?" The Gestapo opens the conversation on the stairs. I say "No," because I'm determined to name nobody and to know nothing. So he hits me in the face.

"Of course you know Holzblatt from the Huexstrasse," he says. "Why don't you tell me the truth?"

I make no reply. Silently we walk side by side through the busy streets of the inner city to the police station. Two old friends, Morgenstern and Selmansohn, are already there. We greet each other like old jailmates. A little later the "Grüne Minna" [green-painted police car] arrives and takes us to the jail in Lauerhof. The desk sergeant receiving us says we have been brought here for our own protection. I land in a cell with 12 other Jews. I arrive just in time for the warden to slop a salt herring and three boiled potatoes in front of each of us.

The next day Dr. Bade, one of the inmates, begins an interesting series of lectures on "English Democracy." We have a stimulating discussion. Every day we have one free hour. We walk in the prison courtyard, keeping a distance of about three yards from each other. An old German inmate leads the parade. I watch him give hand signals to a prisoner on the second floor. Dr. Bade tells me later that the two have exchanged the latest political news about the one billion marks and so on.

On December 20 I am released. My sister has made arrangements for my emigration to Shanghai. However, I decide not to go but to stay with my old mother, as the climate there would not be good for her.

Paderborn Training Center

April 1940. It is raining. Spring storms are blowing through the almost deserted streets of Paderborn. A group of Jews are sweeping the streets. All wear the yellow Star of David on the left breast. On the whole, this small Westphalian town has gotten used to the Jews. Now and then a few passing school children shout anti-Semitic remarks at us. Sometimes they sing the Jew-baiting song, "The Stars Are Shining." But I also see the opposite. One Catholic priest always removes his hat before the Jews. On the left side of the road walks the foreman of the Jews, an old street cleaner in a long raincoat and hood.

"Hey," he calls to me, "take care of the middle, too."

"The middle" is the horse manure.

"This is how you do it." He takes the broom from my hand and starts to scrape the street clean with the back of the broom.

"You German Jews in Paderborn," he says to me, "you still have it very good here, but the Jews in Poland have nothing to laugh about. Well, I'm not going to say anymore, but my son is a soldier there and I heard it from him when he was home on leave." He nods his head thoughtfully. The old man's remarks run through my mind all day. I feel very uneasy.

Berlin

October 1940. The Moetza [Jewish Council] in Paderborn has decided to send me to Berlin for a six-month seminar on Palestine so I can brush up on Jewish history. Two haverim[4] from each German Kibbutz group[5] take part in the seminar. Chief Rabbi Dr. Baeck[6] gives the opening address. The representatives of the Jewish community are on hand. Baeck says that in these times, when the house we live in threatens to collapse, we should sit down to observe the ancient Jewish tradition of study in order to understand the spiritual heritage of our ancestors. "We don't put our people into uniforms!" he cries. "Never forget that you are looking with eyes and hearing with ears that are centuries older than those of your fellowmen. Hamushim to'alu," he continues. "You must go forth well trained." We sing Hatikvah[7] and begin our work. Instruction starts in the Chorinerstrasse at nine in the morning and lasts until one o'clock in the afternoon. Then we go to the public kitchen in the Johannesstrasse for food. From two to six we have more classes.

Frequently there are air raid alarms in Berlin. I am living with a Jewish family near the Kurfürstendamm. We Jews are not allowed into the "Aryan" air raid shelters. We have to stay in the entranceway to the cellars. Sometimes the alarm lasts several hours and then I get to my classes dead tired.

After the Oneg Shabbat[8] on Saturday afternoon I go for a walk with Rosel Strauss Unter den Linden. Suddenly a tall man wearing a long grey winter coat with boots and spurs rushes towards us. "Jews," he hollers at us, "get the hell out of here!" He keeps following us until we turn into the Leipzigerstrasse and disappear in the crowd.

Paderborn

March 1941. After my return from Berlin I start to share my new-found knowledge from the seminar with the haverim, but the times are no longer conducive to learning. From all over Germany comes news of the deportation of Jews. The phone rings constantly. Parents are asking their children to come home and accompany them on the road into the unknown.

November 28, 1941. A telegram arrives from my mother asking me to return immediately. She has received her evacuation order. I obtain permission from the Gestapo in Paderborn to join the transport voluntarily. The Gestapo in Lübeck agrees to this arrangement by wire.

2

Jungfernhof and Salaspils, Latvia

December 1941-April 1942

December 1941. We go to the police station, another Lübeck Jew and I. I have the key to our apartment in my hand.

"I'm bringing the key to the Katz place, St. Annenstrasse 11."

"Let me have it," says the desk sergeant. He starts to write a name-tag for the key.

"Get to the collecting point," he shouts. "You know you must not be on the streets after eight. Get a move on!"

"Now we are homeless," I say to my companion when we come out.

"You can spin that out indefinitely," he says. "We are without a home, without rights, without honor, without protection, without work." We agree we have lost everything.

A lot of people have assembled at the collecting point. There is Mrs. Prenski with her three small children, eighty-four-year old Mrs. Cohn, Simson Carlebach, our cantor, and also the Catholic teacher from the Sophienstrasse. She says her parents were already baptized and she has nothing to do with this whole business. Altogether we are 90 Lübeck Jews. There is little Margot Salfeldt, a blonde girl of 14. Margot says she is glad she will be living among Jews, but she is worried about her mother who is over 50. I try to comfort her and tell her that at the place we're going there is sure to be work for everyone, also for her mother who can still do light housework.

"Yes, I suppose so," Margot replies, "but what is old Mrs. Cohn to do or Mr. Carlebach?" She thinks something worrisome is going on. My uncle is of the same opinion. He says he could understand their sending me to the East because I am young and strong, but he can't imagine what they would want to do with the old people there.

The next morning is luggage inspection. Three Gestapo officials have arrived. Everybody has to show his evacuation order and open his luggage. I notice the inspection is rather lax, as if the inspectors knew we would never see our trunks again. I read on the evacuation notice that persons not complying with this order will get up to ten years in prison. All movable and immovable property is confiscated. It is forbidden by law to remove anything from one's residence or to destroy any possessions. One hundred ten pounds of hand luggage are permitted. My uncle bought himself an iron stove at the last moment because he thinks it will be very cold in the East. We also take our sewing machine. My mother thinks she can maybe earn a little money by sewing.

Around eleven o'clock two large buses of the Lübeck transit line roll up. All ninety of us board them quickly. I am thinking it is probably the first time in their lives that Mr. Carlebach and Mrs. Cohn are traveling on the Shabbat. They are the last of the Lübeck Jews whose avot avotenu [remote ancestors] all came from Moisling, the old ghetto of Lübeck. The buses start up. A few curious bystanders in the street make malicious remarks. "Thank God we're finally getting rid of the damned Jews." An old woman on the other side of the street is crying.

Two special passenger trains are ready for us at the Lübeck railway station. They are heated. We slowly move out, and soon the towers of the old city have disappeared in the fog of the grey winter day. In Oldesloe, we are told, we will join a transport from Hamburg. The Gestapo agent who escorts us says we are going to Riga.

They are already waiting for us in Oldesloe. Chief Rabbi Carlebach[1] passes alongside the cars exchanging greetings here and there. He stops at my mother's window. "Hello, Emma," he says. "I haven't seen you for a long time." After they have spoken a few words, my mother says she can't understand what the reshaim [wicked ones] are planning to do with us in our old age.

"Whatever their plans, Emma, we have to hope for the best," says the Chief Rabbi, deep in thought. He presses her hand and walks on, stopping here and there with a friendly word for everybody. My mother tells me they went to school together. In the meantime, the Hamburg Jewish Assistance League has passed food to us through the train windows. Slowly the long train with twelve hundred Jews aboard rolls out of the station accompanied by the good wishes of the League members who remain behind.

At the next stop the doors of the compartments are sealed. Policemen in green uniforms, with rifles on their shoulders, have taken charge of the train. Now a new wind is blowing. We are forbidden to look out the windows or make contact with people at the station stops. I throw a few postcards to some friends out the window. The train rarely stops. We pass at a rapid pace through the fertile regions of East Prussia, through the Memel region into the vast flat stretches of Lithuania. Snow covers the ground. Every now and then there are a few wretched wooden shacks or small farmhouses, otherwise nothing but snow. There is only one set of tracks. At junction points we have to wait for oncoming trains to pass.

We have been en route for three days without being permitted to take on fresh water. Finally, in Dirschau, one person from every compartment is allowed to get out to fetch some. Here, for the first time, we walk in columns, guarded by the green-uniformed police with fixed bayonets.

The next morning the train rolls slowly over the badly damaged Dvina bridge into Riga. After four days of travel we have reached our destination. The train is switched onto a siding at the railway station of the suburb of Skirotava. Curious and worried, we wonder what will happen next.

It is quite light outside. Through the compartment window I see a company of Latvian SS[2] with rifles at the ready. An Oberscharführer [sergeant major] stands in front of them hollering, "Get a move on." One of the men walks from compartment to compartment unlocking the doors.

"Who is the transport commander here? Where is he? I want to see him. The compartment leaders, too."

"You are the transport leader?"

"Yessir."

A tall, thin man with a long flowing beard stands before Sturm-bannführer [major] Lange[3] and the other SS officers. With his fur-rowed face and stooped back, he looks like one of the Jewish patriarchs of old. It seems that the whole burden of past centuries was resting on his shoulders.

"Stand up straight when I'm talking to you," the Sturmbannfurer shouts at him. "What's your occupation?"

"Chief Rabbi," the Jew says clearly and proudly eyeing him from top to bottom.

"Ha ha ha! Chief Rabbi! Just see you don't open up shop here again. You hear, Chief Rabbi?"

No reply comes from the lips of the Jew.

"Did you hear me, Judas?"

Still no reply.

Suddenly the Obersturmbannführer's [lieutenant colonel] fist strikes the Chief Rabbi full in the face.

"There. And now let your crowd line up, Mr. Chief Rabbi, but quick. I want to see what we've got here."

The Obersturmbannführer's cane points to the line of compart-ment leaders. "Get going, bastards, or I'll make you fly."

Meanwhile, under the curses of the SS guards, the deportees are streaming onto the platform. The confusion is incredible. Children are crying, mothers are yelling, and shots are heard above the sharp commands from the SS. In front of me, a nurse is trying to help an old woman who fell off the train. Suddenly an SS guard beats her from the back with his cane. But the girl is brave.

"Aren't you ashamed," she screams at him, "to hit a nurse who is practicing her profession?" And again she says, "You ought to be ashamed of yourself!"

The SS guard lays off her and forces two old women to run with their heavy bags. In the meantime I have carefully lifted my mother off the carriage steps and slung her knapsack over her shoulders. We are right in the middle of the tumult. The pressure of the masses of people pushing from behind propels us forward.

"Hold on to my arm, Mother," I call to her. "Leave your suitcase here. There is no point in carrying it any further."

Slowly we are pushed to the exit and reach an open square in front of the railway station.

"Come here," an SS guard yells at me. "You, and you, and you." I find myself in a group of about 50 young people. I have to let my mother walk on without me. Slowly, the heavy knapsack on her back, she walks by my uncle's side. It is a procession of unspeakable misery. Mothers with screaming babies in their arms are loaded down with luggage. A man on crutches is wearing his decorations from World War I; maybe he thinks they will help him. One of the guards has already seen him, rushes towards him and yanks his Iron Cross, First Class, from his chest. The old man staggers, stumbles and falls into a mud puddle.

"Get up, you old swine," the SS shouts.

Helping hands stretch out to the old man and get him back on his feet. Leaning heavily on his crutches, he stumbles on, tears rolling down his age-worn face.

A mother with two children passes by me. The children are about six and eight. They are lively and gay.

"Mommy," the younger one asks, "where are we now? "

"I don't know, darling."

"But there is a sign over there, Mommy," the child says.

"I can't read it, Rosel. Now be quiet."

"And what is that over there?" the little girl asks a moment later, pointing her little hand at a body by the side of the road. The mother bursts into tears.

"Is he dead?" the child asks.

"Yes," the mother whispers. She, too, is probably seeing a corpse for the first time.

On the opposite side several Jews are busy digging a grave in the rocky ground with their bare hands. It is obviously meant for the dead man. An SS guard with a long cane is standing over them, driving them on to greater haste. The workers' hands are bleeding and there are beads of sweat on their foreheads — still the guard keeps whipping them with his cane.

"You swine, get busy," a voice hollers at us suddenly, when the miserable procession has disappeared from sight. "Quick, on the double! Get the bags off the platform and clean the train."

Our work begins. An SS guard with a heavy truncheon has stationed himself in the middle of the platform. He stands at the narrowest point where the platform is only about 26 feet wide. Everybody has to pass him with their heavy bags in hand. It is like running the gauntlet; there is no way of bypassing him.

I ditch this job and get busy in the empty train instead, cleaning the compartments. Cars drive up to take the luggage away. I help load them and stack the bags in the cars, away from the threats of the SS guards.

"May I ride with you?" I ask one of the SS drivers. "Maybe I can help with the unloading."

"Your column is over there," he says. "Just do your job and don't give me that stupid look or you're in for it."

I think we might get our luggage after all, if they're going to unload it wherever the transport will be put up.

Of course we are not fast enough for the gentlemen from the SS.

"Hurry up with that luggage or you won't eat for a week. Do you hear me?"

Nobody answers.

"You think you can sabotage this, you filthy dogs?" he cries and starts beating us.

One of the Jews has caught on. He starts screaming orders like the SS guards. "Load the bags, you there, and hurry up! The Oberscharführer would like to have the leather bag. But of course! Right away! The bag for the Oberscharführer. . . ."

One bag after the other disappears into the private SS car. Some German soldiers come along and ask the guards for one or the other of the bags and walk off happily.

"Hey, you," the SS guard says to the Jew who is shouting out the orders. "You are going to be my Kolonnenführer,[4] understand? And see that the work gets done."

"Yessir," the newly appointed Kolonnenführer says with a bow.

When night falls, the job is done. The last car takes us to the camp that houses our transport.

Jungfernhof

We drive through a gate guarded by Latvian SS into what once must have been an estate. Several large barns, a few service buildings and off by itself the big house, that is all that awaits thousands of people at Camp Jungfernhof. Several other transports have already arrived from various German towns. Everybody is running around in confusion. Saxons, Bavarians, and girls from Vienna promenading on the muddy roads as if they were in the Prater [Vienna's big amusement park]. Bavarians in their native costumes mingle with Latvian SS, who quickly make friends with the Jewish girls. And now here we are with our broad Hamburg dialect. There are Jews with long flowing beards, probably from somewhere in the East, and young Jewish women holding their children by the hand so they won't lose them in the commotion. Others push their babies in carriages. The total effect is of a disturbed anthill.

In the meantime a pitch black darkness has come on. All the inmates are ordered to their quarters. I enter the men's barracks, an enormous barn filled with thousands. Smoking stoves are surrounded by men. You flop down wherever you can find a place. In one part of the barracks prayers are being said. Up on a wooden scaffold someone sings Viennese songs and accompanies his singing with a guitar. A circle has formed around him. Everybody joins in the chorus. As I look for a suitable corner I see Chief Rabbi Carlebach cutting k'ria.[5] His brother [Simson] has died of a stroke during the march to the camp.

Near a stove two men are fighting over whose turn it is to heat his coffee. Noise and cries fill the air. One man wants a blanket; another does not know where to lie down. While all this is going on, an icy wind sweeps in from the open field. We can see our breaths. A man lying on one of the bunks is begging for some coffee. He is obviously a Viennese. "Please, please give me something hot to drink! I am freezing."

It is beginning to snow. The wind drives the snow through the cracks of the barn. The aisles are narrow, and the men away from the stove are standing wrapped in their coats, afraid to lie down because it is so cold and there are no blankets.

On top of the bunks I see a man with a novel cooking appliance: a piece of metal on four legs with a small spit underneath, which he feeds with tiny slivers of wood. It smokes badly, but he does not care. He says he hasn't had a hot meal in days.

A woman has come into the barracks. Every minute or so she calls, "Oscar! Oscar!" — probably her husband. But nobody answers.

In the middle of the barracks is an oven. People are lying on the bare ground around it.

We are allowed to go out only in groups of ten. All the time men are at the door, calling, "Who wants to go out? Who wants to go out?" When ten men have gathered, a guard escorts them to the latrine about a hundred yards away. As an emergency solution, many relieve themselves right at the door.

I don't sleep all night. It is too cold. I manage to get hold of a quilt, but every few minutes I have to shake off the snow. My warm breath melts it and that is very uncomfortable. I change my place several times, but it is the same everywhere.

Very early the next morning we are driven from the barracks. "Report to the railroad Kommando [labor detail]," they say. The new Kolonnenführer appointed by the grace of the SS is in charge.

I would like to sneak off, but I see my mother waving on the other side. There is nothing I can do. The Kolonnenführer turns us over to several Jewish policemen, and off we go, once again without coffee or breakfast.

As we march off, I see the camp for the first time in daylight. A huge mountain of luggage, stoves and sleeping bags rests under the sky, completely covered with snow. There is no room in the barns for all the stuff. Pieces of clothing, pulled from the trunks, are scattered everywhere. The muddy roads are deeply rutted from the trucks and strewn with rubbish. Crowds are everywhere. The one pump in the camp is surrounded by people trying to wash up a little. I see several women rinsing clothes in the icy water.

At the railroad station we have to work very hard. All day long we unload stoves and sewing machines. Our Kapo[6] drives us like mad. He screams and yells and threatens us with the SS if we don't jump at his commands. An SS guard gives him a piece of bread and butter. He must be doing a good job.

All the while our Kapo hunts through the trunks and knapsacks for valuables. Watches, rings and fountain pens he puts into a special sack. He says it is for the SS. In the evening I see him sneak the sack into the barracks. He kept everybody else from looking through the trunks, but we would not have taken other people's belongings anyhow. We are still counting on getting our own things, as far as they haven't been given to German soldiers. Only later do we find out differently. The SS has given orders for all leather suitcases to be set aside, along with all other valuables, such as fur coats, musical instruments, and typewriters. We all ignore this order. On the contrary, we try to smuggle the best pieces into the cars that go to our camp. When our Kapo notices this, he begins to scream until the SS guards hear him. He has to stay close now at all times and see to it that all valuables are loaded into the SS cars. He definitely has a sense of duty.

As a reward, he has permission to visit the women's barracks at night. He feeds his wife and two daughters the tidbits he has stolen from the trunks. All the other starving people hang around them and look on as Mr. Kapo enjoys the finest delicacies with his family. As long as he is in cahoots with the SS, there is nothing we can do about him. He can report any one of us and that means certain death.

That night, for the first time, I enter the women's barracks to visit my mother. She is lying on a thin layer of straw on the floor. The women are squeezed together like sardines. The air is thick with the smells from their bodies. Once this place was a horse's stable. The feed troughs are still on the wall. Now they serve to hold hand luggage.

Clotheslines are strung above the resting women. The wet laundry slaps their faces when they sit up. A nurse in a white uniform and a Red Cross armband moves among the crowd. My mother says she is taking temperatures and giving aspirin. At noon the nurse ladles out the soup and hands it to the sick women lying on the ground. Several people have already died, my mother says, and she doesn't know what is going to happen. Did I hear, she asks, that we are soon to be sent to a ghetto, and that we will be living in houses there?

It is just that the fences haven't been completed yet. My mother tells me that last night the commander had eight old Jews from Vienna taken from the men's barracks. They were led behind the latrines and shot. "I don't know what to think of all that," my poor old mother says. There is no wash basin for the women; they already have lice. An oven sits in the middle of the barn, but without fuel. My mother asks me for a blanket. It is strictly forbidden to go outside to the luggage — a guard is watching it. He is standing at the other end of the pile, joking with a few girls. I manage to get hold of a sleeping bag to make my mother a little more comfortable on the cold floor. Then I take her to the latrine which is several hundred yards away. I hold her by the arm so she does not slip in the dark on the icy ground. Most of the women do not take this walk anymore. They turn the corner from the barn and relieve themselves there. Because of the lack of solid food many women have diarrhea. They are lucky it is so cold. Otherwise epidemics would break out.

December 15, 1941. When we come back from work we learn that they are having a Chanukkah party for the children in the men's barracks. The Chief Rabbi has called all the children together to celebrate the Festival of Lights with them. Soon, amidst all the misery and suffering, the clear voices of many small children ring out. Then the Chief Rabbi stands in their midst. He is holding two small children by their hands. Before him on the stove the candles are lit, and the old familiar melodies we used to sing at home resound. What a contrast to the holiday at home when we sat in the circle of our family, played with the dreidel, and cracked nuts while the candles burned down. Here everything is cold and bare. The wind howls through the doors and the cracks in the walls. The men are pressing around the stove wrapped in their coats trying to recreate the holiday they used to celebrate under happier circumstances. The singing has ended. Dr. Carlebach begins to speak. He talks very softly, we all listen spellbound.

He is talking about miracles. How the oil lamp[7] had burned longer, much longer than an oil lamp normally burns. "Why," he asks, "why shouldn't another miracle come to pass even in these hard times? And isn't it already a miracle that we can gather around this warm stove, whereas yesterday there was only icy cold? Thank God, we have an understanding commander. He has promised to help as far as he can. Things will get better, my brothers! We must not despair; we must not lose faith in God. Hinei lo yanum v'lo yishon shomer Yisrael." [Behold, He that keepeth Israel shall neither sleep nor slumber. *Psalms 121:4*]

During the Chief Rabbi's talk there is complete silence in the barracks. Here and there people sob and wipe their eyes. After the closing prayer, the rabbi distributes small bags of candy to the children. Their eyes are shining as they leave the men's barracks, holding the hands of their kindergarten counselors.

The next day young girls and women are also called up for work. They have to carry luggage from the railroad station to the camp. Since the trunks are too heavy for them to lift, they tie ropes or straps to the handles and drag the trunks through the mud and the puddles all the way to the camp — almost two miles. Who cares in what condition the luggage arrives at camp? We have discovered that every day trunks are removed from the camp in SS cars. Somebody says he heard they are being shipped back to Germany.

I am told that yesterday the newly-named commandant went for a walk through the camp with his staff. He had ten old Jews dragged from the barracks and shot, one after the other. He did not want them to suffer, he said.

Many people are dying every day. They are carried out on stretchers and buried in a mass grave near a potato patch. It is said that in the very short time we've been here, two hundred Jews have been buried there already. Sometimes when I return from work at night, I see the Chief Rabbi leaning on his cane, walking slowly behind a corpse.

December 18, 1941. When we return to the camp tonight the order is given to fall in. Thirty names are read out; mine is among them. From the thousands of Jews in the camp I am among those chosen to go to Camp Salaspils, which is near here. We all know what that means. Our dear Kapo Mr. Kenschorek squealed on us: all those called have tried to stop his abuses. This is how he gets rid of troublesome people. The commandant is also present at the line-up.

"Listen, you Jews," he says, "tomorrow you'll be going to Salaspils to build living quarters for your families. Then you can all be together again. The faster you work, the sooner you'll be reunited with your loved ones. And another thing: don't forget to take king-size dishes so you can grab enough chow," he ends jovially.

In the evening I say good-bye to my mother. Again and again I try to make her believe we will soon be together again in the new camp. But she looks at me with such a sad expression as if she knew that this farewell is forever.

The snow grinds harshly under my feet as I slowly walk back to the men's barracks.

The next morning I see my mother looking for me. When she doesn't see me she disappears around the well-known corner. A few minutes later, marching in step, I leave the camp.

Salaspils

We slide rather than march. The fresh snow is frozen. The leader says we have to march about nine miles. It is the Latvian SS who guard us, all of them strong, bold, young. After a march of about two miles, the Kolonnenführer makes us halt in the middle of the road.

"Hand over your watches and rings," he orders, "or I'll pick you off like rabbits."

The other guards begin to frisk our clothes while the guard commander keeps his gun at the ready. They take everything they can find: gold cigarette cases, lighters, and wedding bands which they pull right off the fingers. I have pushed my wristwatch way up on my arm. When the guard searches me he finds nothing. He has three watches in his hand. He discovers a valuable gold watch on the Jew next to me, but the Jew refuses to give it to him. Only when the guard drags him to the gutter and points his gun at him does he hand it over. He tells me later it was a memento from his father.

We are glad when we get to the new camp. It lies in the midst of a pine forest, far from the view of other people. We new arrivals find a half-finished barrack, roofless and windowless. Next to it is a shack, hastily thrown together from a few wooden slats. A pipe sticks through the tarpaper-covered roof. A smell of cabbage fills the air. This is the camp kitchen for which we were told to bring along king-size dishes. Nothing else is in sight but snow, trees and sky. The Jewish Lageralteste[8] appears with SS Commandant Nickel. Our names are being recorded. After standing in the cold for two hours we are told to fall out.

We go for food, the cabbage soup I had already smelled. The cook juggles the ladle as carefully as if he were dishing out caviar. The soup is hot and one can drink it.

The roof is hastily finished that same day in the dark and the windows are boarded up. There is no light. We stumble and step on each other trying to find a place. I have settled on top of a stove with two men from Hamburg. The carpenters have built a box-like partition there — for what purpose I don't know. In any case, we have a warm berth and nobody steps on our heads or feet. It is difficult to get the hot coffee up there. This is our only nourishment. Some say you feel fuller after the coffee. Some eat the coffee grounds. Ernst Levi has got hold of several mattresses. It is hard to lug them up on our stove, but later we are bedded wonderfully soft and warm.

December 25, 1941. We haven't had any bread in three days. In the evening we get three lumps of sugar and black coffee. The Lager-führer [SS officer in command of a concentration camp] says it is not his fault; there are transportation difficulties. Some people start rummaging through the garbage in front of the SS kitchen for bones and potato peels, fried or cooked. I made my first barter deal. For a sports shirt I got a whole loaf of bread and two pounds of bacon. We three on top of the stove share it all.

December 27, 1941. The roof of the commandant's quarters is being laid. I am busy nailing down some roofboard when a new transport arrives. The deportees are all from the Rhineland. They pull their luggage behind them on sleds and baby carriages. At the entrance to the camp everything is taken away from them. We were still allowed to keep our belongings. Several children are among the prisoners.

"Everybody into Barracks Number One," says Einstein, the camp senior. "I don't care how you do it. Just get them in."

It is impossible to work on the roof in this cold. I can no longer hold the roofboard; my hands are stiff. After spending five minutes up there, I go to the barracks for an hour to thaw out. Anything else is impossible with the kind of food we are given. Only one who can avoid hard labor has a chance to get out of here alive. All those who have to do hard labor are lost. I can't shake off these thoughts. How can I manage to avoid outdoor work in this cold winter? I don't have an answer.

The roof is finished. Now we have to remove tree trunks to make room for the other 48 barracks which are supposed to go up. It is very hard work; the grounds are frozen solid. It is forbidden to light a fire to thaw the soil, and our stomachs are empty. We ask ourselves how long we can keep this up. There is only one thing to do: sabotage, shirk whenever possible. We all agree on a plan. The next morning we simply don't get up. We wait and see. Nothing happens. The Kolonnenführer missed us, but did not say anything. From now on we always remain behind. When the others leave for work in the morning, we pull the blankets over our heads so we cannot be seen so easily. Later the barracks slowly fills again, and nobody notices that we are still lying on our bunks. At noon we rise and line up for our cabbage soup, then we lie down again. At night we get our 300 grams of bread. This way we'll be able to survive without working.

They are looking for a glazier so I report to the commandant.

"Are you a glazier?"

"Yes."

"Then take a few other people and install the windows in the new barracks."

I am dismissed. I go to the printer and have him make me an armband with "glazier" on it. Nobody can drive me out of the barracks anymore, because I always have a pane to fit in somewhere. It so happens that I do know something about glasswork. In the plant nurseries where I used to work [in the old days] I always did all the glass work, so I have some idea. In addition, the windowpanes that arrive are all pre-cut. There is no putty, so I can just fasten them temporarily. The armband is priceless. I am immune. Whenever somebody wants me to do something, I am terribly busy and have no time. "Later," I usually say, "later." I have taken on an assistant, Robert Popper from Nuremberg. He knows as much about the glass business as I do. We lie together on our bunk and play chess. Around noon, when it has warmed up a little, we go outside, put in a few panes and breathe some fresh air. In the afternoon we make our little deals with the Latvians. For a jar of Nivea skin cream I get a wonderful Latvian breakfast: two slices of bread with butter and bacon. I trade a length of genuine English suiting at the smithy. I return to our bunk with two pounds of butter and a whole loaf of bread.

January 2, 1942. General roll call. Two Jews have escaped. We have to line up in the assembly yard in a quadrangle. There is one small open space. We are immediately surrounded by Latvian SS men with machine guns. The temperature is 20 degrees below, and a blizzard is sweeping over the dismal landscape. The camp leader arrives. He says that if the escaped Jews are not back by 12 o'clock, twenty of us will be picked at random and shot. Wertheim, the head of Barracks Number Two, says he will volunteer. Shortly before twelve a closed car arrives. Two youths in shirt sleeves jump out, followed by two guards, their guns drawn. The boys have to walk to the center of the quadrangle. Obersturmbannführer Lange appears. He especially enjoys shooting Jews on the Sabbath.

"How old are you?" he asks the taller one of the two.

"Eighteen."

"And you?" he asks the other one.

"Seventeen."

"Where are you from?" he asks them.

"From Hanover," they reply in unison.

"You know that attempted escape is punishable by death. Turn around."

Two guards come and blindfold them. The two boys stand there proud and erect like two trees, fearless in the face of death. The squad marches up, commands are shouted, shots follow, and two more young Jews have honorably gone from us.

We later learn that the two had managed to enter the Riga ghetto. They felt homesick for their parents and had to pay for the visit with their lives. They were caught by the Jewish ghetto police.

Today I cannot eat my lunch. Usually I greedily gulp down our watery soup, but my appetite is ruined. It is the first execution I have witnessed. Life is too cruel.

One thing is sure. Such crimes will not go unpunished forever, and even if the Germans are now standing before Stalingrad and Moscow, justice will someday triumph. But it is doubtful whether we will live to see it.

In this desperate situation I cling to the idea of revenge. If ever I get out of here alive I'll do nothing but shoot and shoot. Wherever I come across any of these bastards I'll shoot them down like mad dogs. These thoughts make it possible for me to endure — they strengthen my resistance.

We realize this camp serves only for the destruction of human beings. The later daily hangings hardly bother us any more. We are becoming tough and hardened.

The prices for the barter goods are falling steadily. The supply of clothing is too great and too few Latvians are working in the camp to buy them. Also, trading is getting more and more dangerous. Too many of the SS are running around the camp, sniffing and spying. One of them caught a Jew at the smithy cooking a few potatoes and shot him on the spot. Obersturmbannführer Lange has returned on a Sabbath. He saw a Jew standing near a stove warming himself.

"Come outside," he called to him. "Shake a leg." Lange then shot him, in the back.

January 15, 1942. Transports of sick inmates are being collected. They are to go to the Riga ghetto. Hans Laeser and his father are lying in a bunk underneath mine. The father wants to be with his wife. He tells the block senior that his feet are frozen and he wants to go to the ghetto. Hans, who is seventeen, volunteers to go with his father. The truck makes the trip every ten minutes, although it takes at least half an hour to reach there. But the people lose their heads and rush into disaster; they do not realize that the promised "ghetto" leads straight to heaven.

Hirschel, a businessman from Hamburg, always raves about his wife and small daughter. He has boils all over his body from the lice — the pus is running from him. It is disgusting how the lice crawl over the bandages. In addition, Ernst Levi, who is now working as a medic, says it is contagious. Hirschel is slowly wasting away. He knows he is dying. If I survive, he wants me to look after his Hannelore and give her his heavy gold watch. When Levi comes to change his bandages – they are made from torn sheets — Hirschel dies in his arms.

January 18, 1942. There is great excitement in the camp. The SS has brought in 15 young Jews from Riga. They are under heavy guard. The Latvian troops have been called out and the officers' quarters are sealed off. Nobody is permitted to leave the barracks. The 15 Jews are shot immediately. One of them was still alive after the volley of gunfire. He pleaded with the Jews from the burial Kommando to carry him to the mass grave along with the others. From there he wanted to try to escape. But he was reported to the SS. A guard arrived and killed him with a bullet in the neck. We learned that these 15 Jews had been working for an SS unit in Riga. They reportedly stole some bread and potatoes.

January 22, 1942. An automobile has arrived from Jungfernhof. Material for the barracks is being unloaded, including glass. One of the Jews hands me several pieces of paper with messages scribbled on them. One of the messages is for me. I read the hastily written words.

"My dear Josef, your mother died last night of a stroke in the arms of Chief Rabbi Carlebach. She recited the "Sh'ma Yisrael." [9] She did not suffer. In the afternoon she suddenly felt ill, and a short time later she was dead. She died like a pious woman, the rabbi said. She is well off. Regards from all of us. Your loving Aunt Linchen. P.S. I took her valuables. If you can come here sometime I shall give everything to you."

Early Spring 1942. The days are growing longer and so are the working hours. Spring is near. There are many advantages to that. We can leave the small, lousy barracks and stand outside to delouse ourselves. Although it is only February, the sun is shining warmly on our emaciated bodies. It is difficult for me to sit on a bench because the bones of my buttocks stick out painfully.

In the meantime Mr. Besen has been made executioner at Salaspils. It is his job to dispatch into the next world those whom the SS has condemned to death for trading. Besen is from Vienna. He is rumored to have participated in the Olympics in 1936. He is extremely well suited for his job. Every day at noon we are called up for "inside service." We march in step around the right corner to the open space where the gallows stands. Mr. Einstein, the camp senior, commands, "Eyes left!" Oberscharführer Nickel appears and reads out the sentence: "The Jew Hans Meier from Hamburg has been sentenced to die by hanging for attempted trading." While his sentence is read, the condemned man stands under the gallows. Besen helps him up on the stool. Einstein gives the order "Stool away!" and once again our number is reduced by one more. Sometimes there are several hangings in a row. A few days ago a Jew from Brno [Czechoslovakia] escaped. Nickel says if he doesn't return by tomorrow noon, ten others will be shot. The next day, as usual, we get the order to line up. We are all tense with uncertainty. Besen hangs two Jews in quick succession. Suddenly a car drives up. Obersturmbannführer Lange gets out, along with several other SS officers. He talks with Einstein in whispers. The two seem to be well acquainted. The senior of Block Number Three is called.

"Listen," Lange yells at him in his Wurtemberg dialect, "you send me ten Jews from your barracks right away, understand?"

The block senior hesitates. He can barely stand up, but he has to obey the command. Trembling, he begins to select ten Jews for probable death. It is obvious how he is struggling, trying to decide whom to pick from among the lined-up Jews. Suddenly Lange appears beside him.

"Look, Yid, get your ten men together quickly, or else." Reluctantly, several decrepit figures step forward from the rows of five. The Blockälteste[10] has deliberately picked only older people. He knows they are not going to live much longer anyway. Meanwhile, the ten Jews have lined up under the gallows. Lange, broad-shouldered, stands before them in his well-fitting uniform and highly polished boots.

"Where are you from, Yid?" he shouts at the man on the far left.

"From Prague," he replies.

"And you?" he asks the next in line. "Also from Prague?"

"Yes."

He passes along the line until he comes to the fifth man.

"Where are you from?"

"From Brno," the Jew replies.

"Come here," says Lange and, turning to Einstein who stands next to him, he asks, "The Jew who escaped was from Brno, too, wasn't he, Einstein?"

"Yes, Herr Obersturmbannführer."

All this time Lange has been shifting his gun from one hand to the other.

"Besen!" he now yells.

Besen comes running on the double.

"Besen, this one here gets thirty lashes on the ass, and then you bring him to me, understand? And see you beat him hard, or you'll get it yourself!"

Besen has taken a long leather whip in his hand. With the full force of a weightlifter he strikes the Jew lying on the ground before him. My knees turn to jelly; the victim's screams pierce me to the core. Lange counts out loud. When Besen is finished, he walks up to the unconscious Jew on the ground and shoots him.

Today I cannot eat my watery soup. My nerves are too shaken. At noon several cameramen arrive and take movies of the Jews getting their food. The Jews are not permitted to look into the cameras. They are also filmed while they work on the barracks.

When I lie on my bunk at night, I ask myself when my own turn will come. But there is no choice: you either trade or you starve. Trading seems to offer a better possibility of prolonging one's life a little.

Honig, a good friend from Lübeck, frequently employs me as a model for clothes. It is my job to sell stolen coats to the Latvians working in the camp. Sometimes he makes deals on commission, too; that means he makes barter deals for people who lack the courage to do so themselves. He then gets half the provisions. Honig speaks Russian and Lettish. Sometimes all I have to do is quietly drop the coat I have been wearing loosely over my shoulders. In the meantime Honig has settled with the Latvians on the price. Most of the Latvians are honest. They bring the promised food the next day and I get my share of it.

On March 15, 1942, we get the order to deliver our winter coats to the block senior. I manage to sell my coat quickly to a Latvian for 20 cigarettes. In camp currency, this is about two loaves of bread. The Latvians are getting rich this way. Gold watches and rings are paid for with two pounds of butter. But most of the Jews handed over their valuables right at the beginning on order of Oberscharführer Nickel. I wear my watch on my upper arm. In the early days, when we weren't familiar with camp life yet, Nickel said: "Your comrades at the front need your watches and rings." Later he made off with two big trunks full. He won't have to work for the rest of his life.

I accidentally find 550 marks in the pompom of a sofa roll but the Latvians don't want to sell anything for money. Nickel orders us to wear the Star of David on our chests and also on our backs — because we might try to escape, he says. Furthermore, in this lovely spring weather, he doesn't wish to see any more caps. Jews are to have their hair shaved off. He only wants to see bald heads, he says. We ignore this order. He kicks anybody caught disobeying and confiscates his cap. When Nickel talks to a Jew the man has to keep a distance of three yards so that Nickel won't get any lice from the filthy Jews.

But strangely enough, Nickel doesn't provide any washing facilities. Water has to be hauled from a spring about two miles away. It is intended exclusively for use in the kitchen to make coffee and cabbage soup. As long as there is snow on the ground we rub our faces with it every morning. That has been our entire morning toilette for the past several months. When the snow thaws, even this convenience is gone. Some use the breakfast coffee to wash with. There is nothing else. We got used to going to work on an empty stomach. The 280 grams of bread that we devour right after we receive them at night are hardly anything. At noon there is a rush on the kitchen where six long rows of inmates are lined up. Everybody tries to be on good terms with the cook, so that maybe he will scoop the ladle a bit deeper into the kettle and dish up a few noodles, a spoonful of groats, or some rotten red beets besides the plain water. After the meal we tell each other how much solid food we had. The cook usually does not remember us when our turn comes; he simply says "Next!" when we stand in front of him. Previously we bribed him with cigarettes or tobacco. The cooks generally rank high in the camp hierarchy. They are well-fed and elegantly dressed in this desolation of sand, snow and death. They can have anything they want in exchange for our bread or the other provisions intended for us. At night they play football with their colleagues from the clothing center. We look on and can hardly move.

A few days ago Kussies, the head cook, hit me on the head so hard with his crutch that I almost fainted. Stephan Weinberg, the camp tinsmith, happened to be standing right there and caught me. I was holding on for dear life to the cabbage I had picked off the floor. Later I gave the cabbage to Stephan. He washed off the sand and ate it.

Our situation is getting more hopeless all the time. The German armies have penetrated deep into Russia. They are certain of victory as long as they go on destroying indiscriminately. When half the camp inmates die off, new people from the ghetto are sent in who go to their deaths in the same way. At the end of March 1942, a large blue bus pulls up in front of Barracks One. All the sick people who want to go to the ghetto — and who doesn't want to go to the ghetto? — are to report immediately in front of the barracks. Their coats and shoes are taken away. They will be given new clothes in the ghetto, they are told. Einstein, the camp senior, stands in front of the barracks and beats the poor limping creatures with his cane. Some have frozen feet; others have large suppurating boils or ulcers. These diseases are caused by the rampant lice infestation. The Jews are piled helter-skelter on top of each other — so many miserable, suffering bodies — and they scream and cry. But who listens? The SS guard stands there with a leer on his face. Some say they heard a machine gun volley shortly after the bus left. Nobody ever saw these people again.

The bread truck is our only means of communication with the outside world. During the past few days the Jewish co-drivers have brought letters from the ghetto. They tell us a lot of luggage has arrived in the ghetto, all marked with addresses in Vienna. But there is no trace of the owners. We suspect [they are all in the] Hochwald.[11]

Unexpectedly we get the summons for general roll call. Everybody who can walk, Nickel says, has to unload luggage this afternoon. Everything has to be at camp before dark. Understand? Yessir.
When we arrive at the station, six railroad cars are waiting. A race is
on to get to them first and unload the luggage. I am marching near
the head of the column and am being pushed right into a compartment by the masses in back of me. The compartment is filled with
hand luggage. Who cares to whom they belong? Small suitcases,
handbags, toys, personal papers, food (in abundance). Round white
loaves of bread, marmalade, Viennese honey cakes, cigarettes — all
things we haven't seen in months. The men go wild. They rip open
the trunks and stuff the bread into their mouths with both fists. They
reach into the marmalade jars with greedy hands and then lick off
their fingers. Suddenly we get word that Lange has arrived. Soon
afterwards we hear three shots. Jews coming from the camp say that
Lange shot three Jews he saw looting. He found food on them. The
three are left lying on the road to the camp. Whoever is discovered
with food on him will be shot, Lange said.

Einstein the camp senior is suddenly there also. Beating a swath
through the crowd left and right with his cane, he approaches. He
looks like a big businessman in his long fur-lined overcoat, his legs
in fur boots. He now stands in the middle of the compartment and
drives us on to make haste. But the way we work, the contents of
the luggage always spill on the floor so that we can grab the provisions. "What do you have in your hand?" Einstein calls to me. I open
my hand and show him a pack of Viennese cigarettes. "Give it to
me!" he screams, and hits me on the back with his cane. The cigarettes disappear into the pockets of his overcoat. A box of Viennese
honey cakes falls out of a handbag, and I stuff it between my sweater
and jacket. It does not show at all, because I am very thin. Other edibles I hide in my boots and pants pockets. When Einstein turns away,
I dash from the compartment to carry all the stuff to my bunk. The
platform looks like a battlefield. Pots and pans and ladies' underwear,
family photographs and woolen blankets are scattered about in con-

fusion. I snatch a knapsack in order to carry the stuff to the camp because one must not go back empty-handed. The road to the camp, about a mile and a quarter, is also strewn with luggage. Opened trunks, bags, clothes, prayer books — everything is thrown about helter-skelter and nobody bothers to pick it up. Only edibles and medicines are of interest; the rest is of no value to us. Everywhere in the camp are Kapos, the Jewish trustees who see that everything gets delivered to the clothing center. Occasionally they make spot checks and frisk people. Whatever they find they keep. I succeed in sneaking into the barracks past a Kapo who is busy with somebody else. My bunk is directly under the roof. One cannot steal anything from there because anybody else climbing up would be noticed. With great difficulty I lugged a mattress up there and all the provisions are now stored under it. Beside me lie Aronstein on the right, Levi and Loeb on the left — all Jews from Hamburg. Aronstein is getting weaker all the time. He can hardly climb up to his bunk anymore. Because Levi is a medic, he gets an extra ladle of watery soup at noon. He tells me that Aronstein can't last much longer; our life is a matter of simple arithmetic. Four weeks without more food, he says, and one starves to death. People who barter for food and get caught are hanged.

This year Pesach [Passover] comes early in April. Loeb has traded his bread ration for a bit of white flour and is baking matzoth for the Seder night. Each of us gives him a piece of our bread at night as reward. Levi is the oldest among us; he conducts the Seder. We are lying on our bunks because we cannot sit upright. Loeb recites the Mah Nishtanah.[12] He cannot have said it differently at home; he pronounces each word so slowly and solemnly. We have saved our midday soup for this meal. We do not eat bread. The mood becomes quite solemn when we all pray together after the meal. Everybody talks about their homes and families, then we sing old songs from the Haggadah.[13]

Loeb is determined not to eat any bread for all eight days. On the fifth day I succeed in talking him out of it. He has become very weak. At noon we give him some of our soup; gradually he feels a little better. Schwartzkopf, another Jew from Hamburg, really does not eat any bread all that week. Several days after Pesach he dies.

The barracks measures approximately 200 feet by 33 feet and houses 600 men. The bunks, arranged in six tiers, are near the walls to the left and right, with a third row in the center. On each side there is an aisle about five feet wide, in which the men crowd each other when they get up in the morning and again when they make coffee at night. Since there is no chance to eat our sumptuous dinner sitting down or even standing up, we all lie on the bunks with our cups of coffee and dry bread. Each bunk is about five feet wide. At night, when all five bunk occupants are present, we can lie only on one side, because there is no room for any other position. Most of the Jews have diarrhea due to the lack of solid food. The latrine is about ten yards away from the barracks. The men can't hold their bowels for that long. They soil their bunks. A sickening stench develops from the dirty blankets, dirty underwear and the dead who are found in their bunks in the morning. During the last few days we have had twenty to twenty-five deaths in our barracks every day. It is strange how quickly people die. In the evening I am still talking to Mr. Stockhausen. I don't notice anything unusual about him. When I go to look for him the next morning to bring him a couple of razor blades, men are already dragging him from his bunk, dead. Peiser, the barracks doctor, comes, shines his flashlight into his eyes, and pronounces him dead from heart failure. Aronstein, too. When I wake up one morning he lies dead beside me. The night before, he was still telling me about his wife and fourteen-year-old daughter who, he thought, are at Jungfernhof. Ernst Levi calls the burial Kommando. Aronstein is carried outside — completely dressed, just as he was found. In the beginning, when we did not have so many casualties, we had a minyan[14] for everybody and recited the Kaddish [prayer in memory of the dead]. While the dead were carried from the barracks we chanted "El molei rahamim [God full of compassion]." Now that has stopped. There are too many deaths. The cantor says he cannot sing so much. Outside the SS engineers have blasted a huge mass grave. There the corpses are carefully piled on top of each other by a specially selected detachment. These men get double rations for their labors, but sometimes they become infected and die.

A new transport from the Riga ghetto has brought my uncle and two cousins from Duisburg. After a very short time my uncle falls ill: heart failure. One evening my cousin Leo comes and asks for a few potatoes for his starving father. I give him my last six potatoes I got that afternoon for a pair of scissors. They were all the Latvian had left. A little later I go to the next barracks to visit my sick uncle. Leo is sitting on his bunk, his legs dangling, eating the potatoes with the skin. His father is already unconscious, he explains by way of apology, and can no longer eat.

The next morning we carry our uncle outside. Leo and I walk in front and two from the burial Kommando in back. I have a strange feeling. It is as if the dead were carrying the dead. It is a long funeral procession that moves under guard slowly to the mass grave. Afterwards Leo takes my arm and we stumble — more than walk — back to the camp.

They say Nickel has given orders to send all the sick and weak people to the [Riga] ghetto to recuperate. I rather doubt this is true. Until yesterday they destroyed Jewish lives with every means at their disposal, and today they want to send us away to recuperate. Ridiculous! By now we are all agreed this is just another "transport to heaven." When Einstein, the camp senior, announces Nickel's command, nobody wants to go. The people selected by the doctor for this transport all hide. The Jewish Kapos have to drag most of them to the transport cars by force. But this thing looks different. The big shots — block seniors, that is — go along. The cars are open, the names of the departing inmates are listed, and medics go to deliver the invalids to the ghetto hospital. The incredible happens, the transports are kosher. We know this because when the first car gets back we find a message on its floor which says, "Have arrived safely in the ghetto." Ernst Levi says they apparently want to conserve our working power. He thinks they need us as slave labor. From now on they will destroy us with work, not with pointless hangings. This view makes sense to me, particularly when it turns out that those who recuperate are immediately sent to work again. Nobody returns to Salaspils. They even say all the Jews will be sent away.

The newly completed barracks are filled with Latvian prisoners. We are not permitted to talk to them. They perform totally unproductive labor. Several hundred prisoners, paired off two to a stretcher, carry sand from one pile to another. They keep going around in circles, chanting a monotonous sing-song. Their guards are Latvian SS volunteers. At night they come into our barracks to trade. It is very dangerous to deal with them. Mostly they take the stuff without paying for it. They enjoy shooting out the electric light bulbs in the barracks. Einstein talks to Nickel with the result that the Latvians are no longer permitted to enter the barracks.

Goetz, the block senior, asks Levi if he wants to go to a nursery with him as a gardener. After all, he is a gardener by profession. Levi agrees, and I volunteer because Goetz needs ten gardeners and another hundred Jews to build a sports arena for the SS. We feel it cannot possibly be worse anywhere else; we can only improve our lot. The next day three SS cars arrive. Soon we are miles away from the death camp of Salaspils. We know that eighty percent of all the Jews have remained behind in their lonely burial grounds at the edge of the woods. It is April 20, 1942, a lovely spring day. All of us in the open truck feel as if we had been returned to life once more.

3

Riga Ghetto and Liepaja, Latvia

April 1942-November 1943

April 1942. We drive through Riga, past the ghetto. A high double barbed wire fence separates the Jews from the outside world. There are signs everywhere saying it is forbidden to make contact with the inmates. The guards will use their firearms. The people in the ghetto wave when they recognize us as Jews. I am happy about this show of sympathy. It is a greeting from what seems like a better world to me. The SS take us to one of the most beautiful parts of Riga, the suburb of Kaiserwald. A former student hostel situated directly on Lake Jugla now accommodates us. We sleep on straw on the floor. The main building lies on a hillock surrounded by a beautiful park. Oberscharführer Wolters takes charge. As soon as we have put our knapsacks on the ground, we are told to report for work. Wolters says anybody leaving the premises after work will be shot for trying to escape. He says as far as he is concerned there are no sick people, only healthy ones. What happens to them, you know. We will work from six in the morning until twelve noon and then from one to six. He wants to see work, or else. He gives us this speech from the flight of stone steps leading to the front of the house, standing there like a general, smug in the feeling of his power. I am wondering what he was in his civilian days, perhaps a minor civil servant or a bank clerk.

We ten Jews report to the gardener. He is a Baltic-born German. The SS supplies him with Jews, and he in turn supplies the SS with fruit and vegetables. The nursery is beautiful. There are magnificent tulip beds of all colors. It is a feast for eyes that have missed beauty for so long.

Levi is immediately employed as a professional gardener in the greenhouse, while the rest of us do planting and weeding. On the third day Levi says, on behalf of the group, we are always hungry because our rations are not sufficient. The gardener replies that he can do nothing about it. The Chinese can live even on a handful of rice.

I volunteered for the plant nursery because I thought that where something is being grown there is bound to be something for us to eat. But the first lettuce is cut, the first young carrots are gathered, and there is nothing for us workers. The gardener watches very closely that not one head of lettuce is lost for the SS. Only when his back is turned for a while do we have a chance to pull some carrots, to grab a bit of raw lettuce, or to pop a few peas into our mouths. Even this little bit helps us because it is fresh green food.

Our regular rations are very meager. As in Salaspils, we are supposed to get 280 grams of bread at night; at noontime we get the usual watery soup. It is impossible to survive for any length of time doing the amount of work required.

Ten Jews are occupied with cleaning the interior of the house and with kitchen work. They get extra rations which reduces our own rations considerably. The supplies for the Kolonnenführer are also deducted from our share. Sometimes the bread, which is inferior to begin with, is moldy, then it is made into bread soup; the green scum is skimmed off the top and we no longer have any control over how much we get.

Our foremen are like the SS. They drive us and beat us; they say they have to do it because otherwise they will get beaten themselves. Today the gardener called us all together. "Here," he says, pointing to a vine, "a red tomato was sitting right here. Whoever took it had better step forward right now." Nobody moves. He says if we don't report the thief by tonight, he is going to inform the SS. He keeps threatening us, but when he realizes the futility of his words, he starts beating us with the horsewhip he carries in his hand. We clear out of the greenhouse as fast as we can. I suspect Levi took that tomato, but he doesn't say a word. He only winks.

When we leave the nursery at night, everybody carries a box of melilotus plants under his arm. Melilotus is a weed, somewhat similar to spinach in taste. We cut it fine, cook it with a little salt, and eat it like that. We also eat nettles, but they taste very bitter, and our stools, always thin because of the lack of solid food, turn green from it. Under the nettles we sometimes hide real spinach, carrots, or some outer leaves of cabbage. For a time all goes well, but then the gardener catches Sasha and beats him unmercifully. It is all over. We cannot take anything out of the nursery anymore.

The cucumbers in the greenhouse are ripe. Heinz Lorge from Cassel and I decide to "organize"[1] a cucumber. We want to trade it with the "inside service" for some bread. Heinz has the job to go into the greenhouse and hand me the cucumber through the open-air vent. I intend to disappear with our prize as fast as possible. But we are unlucky. The gardener just turns the corner when I am about to hide the cucumber under my jacket. He breaks it over my head. The Oberscharführer, who just happens to pass by, also beats me. I can still feel it eight days later, but if you want to survive, you have to take chances.

There is no more to be had from the nursery. We begin to trade the last of our clothes we brought from Salaspils to the Latvians of the neighboring barracks. Levi sells his second pair of shoes. He says one can easily go barefoot now, and who knows whether he will still be alive in the winter? Under the present circumstances that makes sense to me. Heinz has traded his last shirt. A Latvian pointed to the shirt Heinz was wearing. So Heinz took it off and gave it to him. In the summer one does not need a shirt.

The camp is surrounded by a fence made of boards over six feet high. We have loosened several to pass the articles for the Latvians through the gap in the fence. They give us the promised provisions in return. I have just handed over my last three handkerchiefs to the other side when suddenly Oberscharführer Wolters is standing behind me. I was supposed to get half a loaf of bread and half a pound of noodles for them. Wolters asks my name, that is all. The case seems to be settled. The same night he catches another Jew with two pounds of butter. Sigi had been trading with the gardener's wife. Wolters saw him come out of the gardener's house with the package.

The next day Wolters calls me. He walks me to the barracks of the Latvians, close by the fence. I am to tell him whom I traded with. We go from room to room and Wolters looks at me hard, but of course I don't recognize the Latvian.

May 18, 1942. Sabbath. I am just watering the cabbage when an SS car drives up. A few minutes later they call me and Sigi. Wolters asks Gimlich, the deputy of Ghetto Commandant Krause,[2] whether we should take our baggage. "Those two won't need anything anymore," he replies. We are seated between two SS guards. Their guns rest on their knees. The guard on my side lights a cigarette.

During the ride I face the fact that my life is finished. I am sure we are being taken to Salaspils, that in two hours' time the "inside service" will be called up to witness the execution, and all my dreams of freedom will be over. How pleasant is the warm sunshine and how good it feels to ride in an open car! It is hard to believe I shall no longer be alive two hours from now. The Latvians we are passing take no notice of us at all. I feel like screaming. Don't they see two innocent young people are being taken to their deaths? How strangely clear my thoughts are! I have a vision of all my brothers and sisters whom I shall never see again. My heart refuses to believe it, but here I am sitting in a car guarded by the SS; therefore I must be doomed like all the others I saw dying in Salaspils. The car stops at a railroad barrier crossing the road. Almost immediately Gimlich, the driver, starts up again. Everything goes so fast. Couldn't he have stopped there for just half an hour? Every minute is precious. Well, Josef, at twenty-three you've reached the end of the road. What crazy plans you had! You wanted to be free. Why are you so surprised now? Didn't it ever occur to you that you, too, would have to die? It is over, definitely over. But my mind refuses to accept the idea. Maybe a miracle will happen, only it is hard to believe that. You know, Josef, that trading is punishable by death, and you still believe in miracles? I sit in the car and stare at the floor. I am not afraid, but I am not brave either. I am no hero. My knees are shaking when I leave the car in the ghetto. I was so lost in thought I didn't even notice when we drove through the ghetto gate.

Two Jewish Kapos are ordered to take us to the ghetto bunker. They stand at attention before Gimlich. When I realize I am in the Riga ghetto, my courage returns. Maybe you will live after all, I tell myself, particularly when one of the Kapos shows me the warrant for my arrest. I read "duration of custody indefinite." That means they're not going to hang me today. The Kapos try to console us. You'll get a few lashes on the ass, that is all. Tomorrow you'll be taken to see Krause; you just tell him the truth and then everything will be all right. These and similar phrases accompany us on the way to the ghetto bunker. An iron gate closes and we are doubly imprisoned.

Through the barred window I see people steal past the bunker. Some throw a sympathetic glance at the prisoners, but immediately turn back to their own thoughts. Only one young girl stops and talks to us when the Jewish Kapo turns away for a moment. She returns later to hand us a few slices of bread through a broken pane. She tells me she is living in the "Hanover house" with ten other girls. She tries to comfort me, but she does not seem to have much faith in her own words.

Ten other Jews are in the bunker with us. During a body check, food they had stolen from the army supply center was found in their possession. We are all very downcast. We believe we'll all be sentenced to death.

Theft of army provisions is always punishable by death, but the ten Jews say they have been in the bunker a week and have seen Ghetto Commander Krause only once.

Monday morning, very early, Sigi's name and mine are called. The Kapo says we are going to be released, but first we would get ten lashes from the police chief. Our affair is too unimportant, he adds.

The police chief has a powerful arm. He says he received the order from Obersturmbannführer Krause and has to comply with it. He also has to report to him afterwards. Although our buttocks burn, we are happy to have gotten off that easily. The other ten Jews are taken out to the cemetery a few days later and shot. Krause does it himself, we learn afterwards. He goes from one to the other and shoots them in the neck.

Afterwards, he likes to go to the sandbox where Jewish children are playing and give them chocolates and candy. A few children call him "Uncle Krause." Some time ago he shot ten women, one after the other. They supposedly had stolen clothing from the army supplies. One woman pleaded with Krause on her knees; she had a small child. He kicked her and then shot her.

A few days later we are taken back to Kaiserwald. Now very hard times are coming. During my absence, all the Jews have been deloused. My knapsack, too, was sent to be deloused but was not returned. Now my only possessions are what I'm wearing: a pair of short pants, a shirt, a pair of torn socks and a pair of worn-out shoes, that is all. No razor, no towel — nothing. The camp barber only shaves people who give him 100 grams of bread. In this boundless misery all friendship ceases. I tear off a long strip from my woolen blanket and use it around my feet and as a towel. Despair is taking hold of us. At night, several Jews leave the building, although a guard is constantly patrolling it. They climb over the fence and go begging.

June 1942. Two Jews from Hanover are caught outside the fence. The next day they are taken to the ghetto. A few days later they are shot for attempted escape.

Wertheim, our camp senior, has been arrested; he smuggled news of us to the ghetto by the bread truck. They also found a poem on him with the lines: "A grim fate wills — many must die at Salaspils." Wertheim is a leader type, tall and blond, the embodiment of the look the SS likes. He clicks his heels with a vengeance. When he stood in the cemetery and heard his death sentence, he took his ring from his finger and handed it to one of the guards with the request that it be given to his parents. Then he clicked his heels smartly once more and made a sharp about-face to the wall. Krause came and finished him off with his usual shot in the neck.

When we leave our barracks in the morning, it seems as if a herd of cattle was put out to pasture. Everybody goes looking for mushrooms or sorrel to appease the sharp hunger pains. Often an old woman visits the nursery. She owns a chicken ranch outside the camp. Lately, whenever she passes me, she drops a bag with dry breadcrumbs. She collects them in the neighborhood for her chickens. I nod my head to show my gratitude. She probably saved my life with her stale bread. The Oberscharführer had a big argument with the gardener. As a consequence, we are no longer permitted to enter the nursery. Our work now is to break rocks or push carts.

Wolters is lying in the grass on the edge of the building site, sunning himself, while we are under his watchful eye. We are lucky this kind of work does not last long. One night Wolters announces we're all going to the ghetto. Only later do we realize why we are sent back to the ghetto so suddenly.

Riga Ghetto

July 1942. Transports of Jews from Berlin reach Riga. Selection is held at the station. Ninety percent of the arrivals are sent to the Hochwald and thus to their death. Those assigned to live are sent to the camp we have vacated, in order to get used to the new conditions.

The ghetto has given us a lively reception. The streets are crowded with laborers returning from work. Our car is surrounded by people. Everybody wants to see the new arrivals. The news travels fast through the ghetto that the Jews from Kaiserwald have arrived. Some of us find our relatives. I see children embracing their mothers, brothers who find their sisters. They are happy. Together it is easier to bear this life. But for most, the loss of loved ones becomes a certainty. Nobody awaits me. Only a few acquaintances come and want to hear the news and find out where we come from. That is all.

Our cars stop in front of the administration building. I notice there is no SS. Two ghetto policemen are stationed in front; they bar our entry into the five-story building. A medic with a Red Cross armband escorts us to the delousing center. The atmosphere is quiet. Nobody screams; everything proceeds in an orderly fashion.

A woman with an armband marked "Social Service" appears. She inquires who has relatives with whom he can stay. All the others are assigned to the various groups in the ghetto. Since there is no Hamburg group, I am sent to the group from Hanover where I have to register. I am told I shall get my food ration card there.

After a trek over shaky little bridges and through twisted back lanes I finally reach Berliner Strasse. Here, I assume, the survivors of the transports from Berlin are residing. A man carrying a large knapsack filled with wood shows me the house where I have to report. On the left is a sign, "Labor Recruiting Agency of Hanover Group. Jewish Council — one flight up."

"I would like to register," I say after having entered the waiting room. I am handed a card with many small numbered squares.

"Your food ration card," says the woman who took my personal data. "And here is the address of the housing registry. They will show you to your lodgings there."

I walk past miniature gardens planted in the sandy deserts of the courtyards to the address I was given. An old man opens the door and asks what I want. After I tell him, he says that he doesn't know where to put me up. Then he remembers there is space in House Number 2, on the fifth floor, in the place of a teacher by the name of Erlanger and his wife. Erlanger is not enthusiastic about his new lodger; neither is his young wife. But we quickly become friends. We all know you have to put up with a lot of things in the ghetto.

It is a narrow attic. Through a vent in the roof a little fresh air blows in. A small stove smokes badly. Erlanger says it is the damp wood his wife brings home from work. I'll get used to it, he says. In the middle of the room stands a wobbly table with two equally wobbly chairs. Erlanger and his wife sleep along the left wall. I lie on a mattress near the other wall. I can't sleep at all that first night in the ghetto — the bedbugs bother me too much. Erlanger is up much of the night chasing bugs with a candle. The many black stains on the wall show his efforts have been successful.

The next morning I report to the Arbeitsamt.[3] They ask what my trade is. "Gardener," I say.

"At the moment we have no job for you in your field. Come back tomorrow and we will assign you to a labor Kommando."

Erlanger advised me the day before to go immediately to the clothing distribution center which is located upstairs in the Ghetto Administration Building. He said I would find bed linen and the necessities of clothing there. However, a ghetto policeman turns me away and sends me to the Jewish Council which has to confirm that I arrived yesterday. A long line is waiting there. Some people wear torn old shoes and hope for another pair. Others make requests for clothes which Mr. Fleischel, the Judenälteste,[4] has to approve before the garments are released by the agency. Fleischel is seated behind a large desk. After I tell him what camps I have already been through, he approves everything I need. Fleischel makes quite a sensible impression on me. I learn only later that he was converted to Catholicism. He conducts Catholic services in the ghetto. Some people from Hanover claim to know he was once a leader in the Nazi Motor Corps. I hear many Jews resent the fact this man holds such a high position. But Krause put him in his job, so there is nothing to be done about it. The clothing agency is a regular bureaucracy.

"Do you have a clothing card? Have you ever received any clothes from us before? What is your name? Do you have an application signed by the Judenalteste? Let me see it. Go and wait. You will be called."

After I have signed several forms confirming I own nothing except what I'm wearing, a large door opens; this is the clothing chamber. Mountains of clothes and shoes are piled up. Everything is here. Some of the employees are busy unpacking trunks from the Berlin transports. They give me a light sports jacket and a good pair of pants, a work suit, and a change of underwear. When I finally get back to my attic, I am happy and cheerful. I haven't owned so many barter goods in a long time.

With my ration card I go to the distribution center of the Hanover group. It is a long room with a counter and a decimal scale. In front of the counter are many boxes — they are filled with large fish heads; there are several other boxes with tiny fish about an inch long. In a corner of the store a man is busy raking cabbage leaves into a pile. A piece of horsemeat hangs on a hook. A small shelf on the wall holds a few loaves of bread. Colorful packages of ersatz coffee complete the picture.

"Do you have a bowl for the fish heads?" the man asks me.

I say that I don't want any. The man behind the counter wants to know how I'm going to take my cabbage leaf ration home. He produces a sheet of newspaper from under the counter and rolls up two pounds of cabbage in it. I also receive 90 grams of horsemeat neatly wrapped in wax paper. He takes a loaf of bread, cuts it in half, and weighs out exactly 1260 grams. With 90 grams of suet and 90 grams of oatmeal I now have the total weekly ration.

Back in my attic, I immediately eat half the bread. It is just wonderful to have a full stomach. In the evening Erlanger passes his fish heads through the meat grinder. He says it makes a delicious spread; don't I want to try it? I decline politely. I can't eat it; I always have to think of those large fish eyes. Sometimes, Erlanger says, he cooks a fish soup. His wife brings a few potatoes from her Kommando; then we have a good dinner, he says.

The next morning at the Arbeitsamt I receive 100 grams of bread — an extra ration for hard labor. I am assigned to the harbor Kommando. Several thousand men have assembled on the large open square. There are various labor Kommandos. Some Jews are employed at the railroad and in the SS hospital, others work for the Reichskommissar[5] at the castle, or load wood for the SS Kommando. Another Jewish unit is occupied with the transport of provisions for the German troops at the front — a well-fed Kommando, but the work is dangerous. Large numbers of women work in the army supply center. All the dirty clothes coming from the front are sorted and disinfected here. Under mortal peril the women hide some clothes on their bodies and smuggle them into the ghetto. Other Kommandos, who are in contact with the Latvians, trade the clothes for provisions. One woman was shot for stealing a pair of gloves. A man from the army supply center was found with a package of sugar on him and was also killed. In spite of everything the Jews are not deterred. Hunger is stronger than all threats.

Every Kommando is led by a Latvian escort. A Jew stands at the gate. He calls out the name of each Kommando. As we march past him, he counts the number of workers. We move past the administration building, where several SS cars are parked, and out the ghetto gate.

I have been assigned to a tough Kommando. We have to unload wet, freshly-dredged gravel from the barges. Army trucks drive up and remove the gravel which is used for military installations. I am told this command is good for trading as we are in touch with many Latvians.

When the barge is empty, a tug arrives. We ride the barge out on the River Dvina to the dredge. There is an interesting scene right on the Dvina: as soon as our barge is secured alongside the dredge, Latvians simply pour out of the holds. A lively trade starts with the Jews. Everything is being traded, from pants buttons to ladies' coats.

Ladies' underwear and stockings are particularly high-priced articles. Some of the Jews have to get almost totally undressed in order to bring their barter goods to the light of day. We can only carry a knapsack or an empty paper bag with us when we march out of the camp. Krause is supposed to have said that even if he were to send his Jews out into town stark naked, they would return in "top hat and tails."

When the barge is full, trading comes to an end. The provisions have been hidden on our bodies, but it is difficult to work when you are loaded down with all those groceries.

Our working day ends at four o'clock. Many start the trip home with an anxious heart. The risk of inspection upon return is great. Camp police are stationed at the ghetto gate and sometimes search every single worker. Women are occasionally taken to the administration building where they have to get undressed. Today everything goes well. Unhindered, we march through the gate. Everyone hurries toward his sleeping quarters.

As soon as I reach home I begin to cook. I make oatmeal soup. I got the firewood in trade for a 100-gram hunk of bread. Wood is a very valuable commodity. Many Jews who have an opportunity to carry wood into the ghetto live on it. They go from door to door, "Who wants wood? Who wants wood?" Some accept cooked meals in exchange. I add a few breadcrumbs and suet to the oatmeal and water to thicken the soup.

In the evening I go for a walk. I meet many men and women, singly and in pairs, relatively well dressed. Some still wear their own clothes which they brought with them from Germany. Girls in bright summer dresses stand at the fence separating the German and Latvian ghettos. They are waiting for their Latvian boyfriends who may enter the "German ghetto" only with a permit from the police chief. The Latvian boy friends are very popular. They have good connections in town and bring in plenty of butter and bacon. For butter and bacon one can get anything in the ghetto. Almost every girl has such a friend; they are called Iska and Joffe, or Abrashka and

Chaim. It is easy to start a conversation and an understanding is quickly reached. There even are some ghetto marriages which are recorded with the Ältestenrat [Jewish ghetto council].

Between the fences, in the center, is the Bergstrasse, the main street of the ghetto, which I slowly ascend until I reach the ghetto gate. To the left of the gate, still in the ghetto, is the hospital. The beds have white sheets. The patients are looked after by professional nurses though there are usually no medicines. Aufrecht,[6] a Jew from Cologne, is chief doctor and surgeon. The rations at the hospital are the same as in the ghetto. People with stomach trouble get the same black bread and a rhubarb-leaf soup for lunch. I hear that only a few people leave this hospital in good health — hospitalization is mostly synonymous with death. In many cases Aufrecht has to abort the results of intercourse, since Jews are forbidden to have sexual relations. There is an alarming number of such "appendectomies."

Opposite the ghetto, there is a large, imposing building. In big gold Hebrew letters I read Linas Hazedek.[7] The former Jewish hospital, it is now the place where flea-infested clothing is disinfected.

Labor Kommandos are returning to the ghetto. At the gate their Latvian escort hands them over to the guard, who counts them. The number is correct. Move on! All the men try to disappear as fast as possible from the main street as the danger of inspection is the greatest here. On the side streets and narrow lanes they quickly vanish from sight. One man continues on the main street. Just then Krause emerges from headquarters.

"Come here! What do you have in your knapsack?"

"Wood," replies the Jew.

"Let me see."

The Jew unpacks his knapsack and empties it right in front of headquarters. Jewish police have already arrived, but today there are no arrests. It is really only wood. Krause walks on.

When we return to camp the next night, we can already see from a distance something is wrong in the ghetto. A long line at the gate

is moving slowly. The atmosphere is tense. The road defies description. Dozens of loaves of white bread, pounds of butter, bottles of
liquor, potatoes — everything a man could wish for is lying in the
mud. Bank notes are flying about in the breeze. They are all thrown
away, trodden into the ground by the workers, for if any of these
items should be found on a person during inspection, he won't live
to enjoy them.

I have traded twenty cigarettes which are hidden under my
cap. A quarter-pound of butter is stashed on my back under the
belt. I have to smuggle these things in — otherwise I won't eat
tomorrow.

The SS picks some of the workers at random. All those that look
too heavily stuffed they frisk, but only briefly, because the crush at
the ghetto gate is too great. They have to hurry. I arrive home safely
with my butter. Erlanger gets half of it and he gives me some bread.
The next day I hear that several women had been arrested. Their
heads were shaved and signs were hung on them: "We traded. He
who trades gets this treatment." They had to stand in front of headquarters for several hours. Now they are in the bunker. Nobody
knows what will happen to them.

A sign at the Arbeitsamt says, "Lecture on 'Faust' by Professor
Weil, for many years lecturer at the University of Vienna. Sunday
afternoon, Hanover House Number Two, 4 o'clock." Only a small
circle of people has gathered. Professor Weil recites several passages
from Faust and analyzes them afterwards in a very interesting manner. Then there is a short discussion. Weil is an old man; he coughs
a lot and on the whole makes a very decrepit impression. At the
end, each of us leaves a little something on the chair — a few potatoes, a piece of bread.

In the ghetto I also hear lectures on Jewish history. One teacher
speaks on the period from the destruction of the Temple to the present. It is a lecture series held at the school organized by the Berlin
group. Here a large circle gathers regularly because the speaker is fas-
cinating and instructive and knows how to hold his audience.

Leiser, the Ghetto Elder, himself puts on Jeremiah by Stefan Zweig. There are some outstanding Latvian artists in it; they even have costumes. Tickets to these performances are hard to get and have to be ordered weeks in advance at the Arbeitsamt. I hear they always play to packed houses. Even Krause is supposed to have seen and liked it. Unfortunately, I don't have a chance to attend a performance because it is always scheduled during the hours when I'm at work.

Next to the sign announcing the Faust lecture is another notice: "The Jew Josef Strauss from Dusseldorf has been sentenced to death for trading. The sentence has been carried out. The Chief of Police (signed) Haar."

The Jewish ghetto police always appear to me like puppets. A few days ago, I saw Police Chief Haar walking in the Prager Strasse. Two Jewish policemen approached him, snapped to attention, made their report, gave a military salute and walked on.

A strange story is being told about Haar. Eye witnesses swear that Haar once saved the life of Ghetto Commander Krause. They say a Latvian guard took aim at Krause, and Haar jumped in front of him and knocked the gun from the guard's hand. For this, Krause named him Chief of Police.

I have been assigned to a new Kommando. The harbor Kommando has been dissolved. We are told the installations have been completed. In the heavily bombed part of Riga, mainly near the Dvina Bridge, I break rocks with about 200 other Jews. It is a monotonous occupation and particularly difficult in the driving rain. We are permitted to take wood from the rubble into the ghetto. I always chop it up small enough for the oven. That way I get more bread for it.

September 1942. One evening I find a message from the Arbeitsamt: "Report to the Administration Building at 4 P.M., to load wood for the SS. Duration of absence: approximately 14 days. The Hanover Arbeitsamt, (signed) Steg."

I go to the Arbeitsamt and tell Steg I've hardly been in the ghetto for two months and ask him to let me stay for the time being. He says he especially picked people who've been to Salaspils for the wood-loading Kommando because they have a lot of food there and I would return round and fat.

That night ten people arrive at the administration building. Two SS Unterscharführer [lance sergeant] drive up with a small medical truck that has room in the back for one patient. We ten are all pressed into that space. At the railway station two more SS await us. We are going to meet our Kolonnenführer just before Leningrad, about 250 miles from here.

A passenger compartment has been reserved for us. We travel like human beings. We brought along supplies from the ghetto for two weeks; they are stored in the luggage rack above our heads. The ride is endless. The train stops at every small station. Occasionally the Unterscharführer, sitting in the compartment next to ours, throw a few cigarettes over the back of his seat into our compartment; sometimes they give us some bread, too.

We pass through a monotonous landscape, all flat country without any elevation, pasture land on which cattle are grazing. Then again untilled, fallow fields.

In the evening we arrive at Schwanenburg and are told we have to spend the night here. The SS guards find an empty hut by the side of the station and lock us inside for the night. We are given some straw by a neighboring farmer. All night long we sit squeezed tightly together. It gets cold early here in the north, and the icy air penetrates through the cracks in the poorly fitted boards.

At the first light of dawn the journey continues, this time in an open freight car. The scenery changes. For several hours now we have passed through wooded country. To the left and right of the tracks, as far as the we can see, there is forest, nothing but forest. The forest appeals to me; it calls up peace, safety, and walks with friends in the distant past.

One of the men reminds us that today is Yom Kippur.[8] "For us, every day is Yom Kippur," another man says laconically. In the late afternoon, we arrive at the terminus, Schiguri, a small village about 60 miles from Leningrad.

"You'll remain in the compartment overnight," the taller of the two SS tells us. "Tomorrow a narrow-gauge railway will take us to our destination. And remember: anybody leaving the compartment after dark gets shot. This is the war zone," he adds by way of explanation, "and you know that for every one that escapes, ten others will get a bullet. Remember that!"

We make quick contact with Russian railroad workers. They approach us, ready to trade. One of our group has already made a few good deals with the conductor of the train while still en route. Now our business is thriving. One of the Russians points to my shirt.

"Klever," I say, meaning bread.

He shakes his head, tries to explain something to me. Finally he has an idea. "Cock-a-doodle-do!" he crows several times. Everybody laughs. "Skolko? [How many!]" I ask. He gestures with his hands: twenty. "Karosho, tovarishi [Good, Comrade]," I say. When he returns with twenty eggs, I give him my shirt. I now eat eggs — which I haven't seen in a year — in every conceivable variety. Some I drink raw, others I boil soft or hard in my pan. We cook in front of our compartment on two bricks. One man is always on the look-out so that we aren't surprised by the Unterscharführer. Trading continues merrily. Here, way out in the backwoods, we at least get good prices. One man tries with all the languages at his disposal to sell his old coat. He mostly talks with his hands. Finally the Russian buys, gives him two pounds of butter, three eggs and a large loaf of coarse black bread. For him today is no longer Yom Kippur.

The Russians are good-natured, helpful people. They point to the yellow stars we are wearing; they want to know what it means. "Ivreh [Jew]," we tell them. "Ivreh karosho [Jews, good!]" they say and start to name Jews who are in Russian politics: "Litvinov, Kara-masov, toshe Ivreh [also Jews], Ivreh karosho." Then they point to the forest: "Partisan tom [Partisans over there]," they say, "and we are good friends with them."

The night is cold and uncomfortable again. It starts to rain. We pull our blankets over our heads and longingly wait for the morning.

For several hours now we have been traveling through the most beautiful forest. Here and there are gaps that have been cut among the dense trees. The timber lies piled up near the tracks. Our job will be to load it. At noon we reach our destination. We are put up in the hayloft of a barn belonging to a small, solitary farmhouse. This farmhouse, a barn, and a stable with several head of cattle are the only places of habitation in the middle of the forest.

Shortly after our arrival, we are forced to run, over ruts and tree roots, to our work site.

"You've loafed long enough. Now we're going to show you what's what."

Two men each are given two poles to hold. The logs are piled high on top and then carried about fifty yards over dense underbrush to the tracks. The loads are very heavy, because it is freshly cut lumber. In addition, we have to endure vicious treatment from the SS who stand over us, armed with their canes. Here in the forest they are kings; they can do with us as they please. The shorter one, in particular, has it in for me. He notices I am not quite as husky as my comrades. It amuses him to add several more logs onto the poles so that I almost collapse under the load. When a badly arranged pile slips off the poles, he is immediately on hand and works us over with his polished boots. It is slave labor in the extreme. The loading onto the freight cars cannot be watched quite so easily. So, fortunately, we get a little rest doing that, particularly since one of the monsters goes off hunting every now and then leaving us under the supervision of his pal. We are longing for the day when we can leave this place which the SS has turned into a living hell.

After finishing our job, we realize the cause of the mad hurry: our masters wanted to gain time to sell our labor as potato pickers to the farmers a few miles away. The two SS are right behind us, watching that not a single potato is left lying on the ground. Considering the haste in which we are driven to work, potatoes inevitably fall. When they do find one, they call us back, point the tips of their no longer shiny boots at it and kick us in the pants as we bend down to pick it up.

Often the good-natured peasants give us something to eat, while the SS men, their sacks and pockets crammed full, walk behind us. Before we leave, I quickly sell my second pair of pants to the peasant woman for four pounds of butter, two large coarse loaves of bread, and as much fresh milk as I can drink. I don't know where to put all that butter. I haven't had such rich sandwiches in a long time. But one cannot eat so much fat for long; it becomes disgusting. I decide to apply for a new pair of pants from the Council in the ghetto. I'll tell Fleischel that I tore my old pair at work.

I feel a lot better on the return trip. We leave the forest at dusk, lying on the loaded timber wagons, dreaming. A few Russian prisoners join us and start to sing. All is peaceful around us. My knapsack with the butter is under my head; I am covered with my blanket. It is a wonderful trip through the silent forest and I am sorry when we reach Schiguri where an empty train section is ready for us. Our cars are attached to a train full of soldiers on leave from the front. The next morning we arrive at the main station in Riga. Only after we have safely disappeared with our knapsacks in the narrow side streets of the ghetto do we breathe easier.

Sunday morning. Children are going for walks holding their parents' hands. Others are standing around in the main street waiting for relatives to return from work with the labor Kommandos. On the way to my quarters I see Jews digging garbage pits; others are chopping wood to cook their midday meal.

In the afternoon I visit several friends. Stefan is very pleased to see me; we were good friends in Salaspils. A few boys and girls are together. They're dancing to a record player. Who knows where they got the modern dance records? To celebrate my return, Stefan brings out a bottle of vodka which he smuggled into the ghetto under great danger and we drink a toast to our freedom. A very cozy atmosphere develops. People warm to each other, and for a few hours forget the hopelessness of their situation.

Jungfernhof

October 1942. The next morning I am assigned to the "SS Service" Kommando. Our party loads the wood from the freight train onto the waiting cars. It is shipped to Jungfernhof, where the SS is building a supply depot. I enter Jungfernhof after an absence of ten months. I am amazed at the exemplary order I find here now. Neatly-bordered walks and attractive shrubbery lend a friendly appearance to the camp. In the spot where the luggage had been piled up a field with cabbages is ripening now. The Jewish inmates of the camp are occupied with harvesting the potato crop — they are all healthy, strong people. A few Jewish drivers return from working in the field, their wagons piled high with potatoes. The horses are led to the watering troughs. Labor Kommandos return from the fields. It is noon. Suddenly Sasha, a comrade from Paderborn, stands before me.

"Hello, Josef! Imagine finding you here! I thought you were dead! I remember you went to Salaspils, and not many return from there. Come on! Tell me what happened to you! But first I want to get my soup. I'll be back soon."

Later we sit on two boards, our backs leaning against a pile of lumber. While Sasha is spooning up his soup, I tell him quickly what I have been through.

"Well, Josef, there is a lot for me to tell you, too. When you left the Jungfernhof, the Jews here fed themselves from the provisions they had brought, but these were soon used up. We did not get any food from the SS, but they found a solution. You must have heard about it. It is called Dvinamünde" — a place supposedly located just where the Dvina flows into the Baltic Sea. I'm sure you know about the closed blue trucks which appeared here on Thursday, March 26. A commission arrived, with Krause and Lange at the head. They had a selektion.[9] About 400 people remained — all the others were taken to this Dvinamünde, which was supposed to be a fishing village. Until the trucks came the Jews were locked into the large men's barracks. Then the trucks departed every fifteen minutes. Chief Rabbi Carlebach was supposed to be the camp senior together with Kehlmann.[10] The evacuated Jews were told they were going to work at the fisheries. Fish nets, too, would be manufactured there. My parents went, too," Sasha tells me. "I volunteered, but Seckt, our commandant, did not let me go. My eighteen-year-old sister went with them. I was the only one left behind from my family. Josef, could you ever have imagined such a thing? I would never have thought it possible, but what is to be done? We are quite comfortably off now. Ever since that Aktion[11] nobody has been shot anymore. The other day Seckt caught one guy trading. He said he already had thousands on his conscience; one more wouldn't make any difference. But he let him go."

"Sasha," I say, "I have a request. Please show me the mass grave. My mother is buried there and I want to recite the Kaddish."

We walk past the large men's barracks, which now serves for the storing of agricultural equipment, to the open country. Sasha stops at a potato field.

"If you walk about twenty yards into the field, you'll get to the grave. The ground there has settled a bit."

I walk past potato plants already turning brown and arrive at the place. I see potatoes, nothing but potatoes. It seems as if they thrived particularly in the dip. I recite the Kaddish.

On the way back to camp Sasha tells me that about seven hundred people are buried there.

Work in the SS service Kommando is very hard. Everything has to be done on the run; every SS man has to be saluted. They are continually after us with, "Quick, isn't the train empty yet? You swine are moving like snails. You, there, get on with it or you'll catch it! Yid, you've been loafing around on the john all morning. Get going or else!" And their whips crack.

October 14, 1942. Sabbath. As usual, we report for roll call in the morning. We are standing in the square, waiting to be picked up by the SS. Suddenly a column of SS, armed with machine guns, marches into the ghetto. The Latvian Jewish police is called together. They are locked up in the administration building. SS men are posted at every street corner. The whole ghetto is surrounded by Latvian SS. All work Kommandos leaving the ghetto are searched for weapons. Several arsenals have supposedly been discovered in the Latvian ghetto. All Jews who are found in possession of barter goods or other forbidden articles are led under guard to the Latvian parade ground. There they are made to kneel in the dust, their hands above their heads. The SS is particularly after Latvian youths, but I also see many old men on their knees as I march past. When the German ghetto, too, has been searched without result, all the Jews who were herded together on the Latvian square are led from the ghetto under heavy guard. Later their clothes are returned from disinfection and delousing. Meanwhile, horrible scenes are taking place in the ghetto. The Latvian Jewish police, about fifty men, all very young and strong, are taken to an open square in the ghetto. A grave has already been dug, but the Jews are determined to fight for their lives. With their bare fists they attack the SS men and are shot down fighting. The SS is supposed to have had a few wounded also. One of the Jews hides out in a chimney. He is discovered when he steps out later; he is killed like the others. The Latvian ghetto is put under German-Jewish administration; a German Jew is put in charge of the Latvian Arbeitsamt. The elite of Latvian Jewish youth has been wiped out. The next day life in the ghetto is back to normal. The labor Kommandos march out as usual. Ghetto life in all its hopelessness continues.

With the cold temperatures now setting in, the poor nutrition, shoddy clothes and worn footwear are doubly felt. Lice are invading the ghetto, for without soap and sufficient warm water nobody can keep clean under these working conditions. Many people die a "natural" death from malnutrition. For all these reasons I am quite pleased when I get the order to report to the parade ground for departure to the labor Kommando in Liepaja on October 22.

Liepaja

Slowly a small company of about 160 Jews, men, women, and children, move toward the railroad station in Riga. Loaded down with their last possessions, they walk through the deserted streets of the town. It is cold. The women have drawn their threadbare shawls tightly around their heads; their hands are buried in the pockets of the men's trousers they are wearing. On their backs they carry knapsacks with their bare necessities. They were permitted to take only one change of underwear and two pairs of stockings. They were told they would be inspected by the SS as they left the ghetto. It was only a scare. Still, after the latest incidents in the ghetto we have all become a little more cautious.

Three freight cars are ready at the station. We are packed 60 people in each car, the doors sealed from the outside. As he locks the doors, the guard says, "Remember: ten for one."[12]

It is terribly crowded in the car. People swear and complain in various languages — there are Latvian, Russian, Polish, Czech, and a small number of Lithuanian and German Jews. It is a mad Babel. In one corner some people begin to sing Yiddish songs, always with the refrain, "Girlie, lift up your little dress, show what you've got." A few Viennese Jews show admirable endurance and keep on singing their postillion song. Everyone yells or sings above the rattling and creaking of the freight train — it is a hellish racket. Several Russian Jews sing patriotic Russian songs; everybody joins loudly in "*Mosiva, Mya, Lubimaya* [Moscow, My Beloved]." It seems to me that everybody's morale is lifted, for in the distance, still far away, is the Russian front. The nights are horrible. We sit closely huddled together to get warmth from each other's bodies, for a cold draft comes from the doors and through the cracks in the walls. A girl from Vienna sits next to me. After we've been talking for a while she tells me she was raised as a Catholic and went to a convent school in Vienna. She was already baptized as a child. By the light of dawn she shows me the small cross she wears on a chain around her neck. I am not bothered by all the chastity vows of her church. She sits close to me and warms me. As far as I am concerned, she can belong to some Moslem sect; we still understand each other. She cuts my bread and spreads it with suet. She offers me some hot coffee from her thermos bottle. The trip is quite pleasant. Only the Litvak [Lithuanian Jew] sitting on the other side of me is a bother. He uses too much garlic and onions, and their aroma does not fit in with my heightened spirits. In this manner we ride for two days and two nights; in between we stop for hours at small stations where the compartments are opened so we can relieve ourselves. This is a far cry from hygiene. We are all glad to finally reach our destination and stand up, for our backs hurt from all the sitting.

We march through the still-dark streets of Liepaja. Most of the houses in the Bahnhofstrasse have been destroyed. For the first time I see the ravages of war. A Czech Jew who walks beside me says the houses are like our lives: destroyed, and what's left is ruins. This applies to us also. We are human ruins, he says. We are indeed a column of misery; with our ragged clothes and torn shoes, our unwashed, unshaved and exhausted faces, we look like derelicts. Even the guards walk slowly and quietly on the sidewalk, no longer yelling and driving us on as usual. They, too, are worn out.

As we approach the ghetto, we meet more and more Jews on their way to work even at this early morning hour. On their chest and back they wear the Star of David. I notice they are allowed outside the ghetto without a guard. Only a Jewish Kolonnenführer is with them.

Soon we reach the ghetto, which is surrounded by a high barbed wire fence barring anybody from entering. Large signs announce it is strictly forbidden to get in touch with the inhabitants and trespassers will be shot. The streets have been swept and the ghetto makes a clean impression. There is nothing to remind us of the poverty of Riga.

As soon as the Jewish inhabitants notice the new arrivals, a lot of activity begins behind the fence. After a short time they hand us hot coffee through the spaces in the barbed wire. Some distribute their breakfast sandwiches among us, which are spread with butter and cheese, a luxury that is quite taken for granted by our hosts. My eye is caught by a young girl, of middle height, slim and graceful in her movements. She runs back and forth behind the fence handing several cups of hot coffee here and there, as though it was her job every day to serve refreshments to poor, homeless Jews. Her features are serious and sad, bespeaking some deep sorrow.

"Would you like a cup of coffee?" she says to me in fluent German, after having talked in perfect Russian with a Russian Jew a moment before. I am captivated by the deep glance from her brown eyes which seems to want to penetrate me.

"You are a German Jew?" she continues after handing me a cup of coffee. I nod. Then, her long-restrained resentment bursts forth.

"It is you who brought all this misery upon us," she says fiercely, "and now you're even coming here to steal our peace."

I want to reply to these accusations, but she disappears into one of the neighboring houses. What happens then takes my mind off her. Everyone entering the ghetto gate receives a number; at the same time we are divided into various labor groups and housed in a separate building. The rooms are quite livable — a few army cots, an oven, table and chairs make up the furnishings. I share a room with two boys from Vienna, one from Cologne In the courtyard, one of them discovers an old shack filled with kindling and soon a bright fire is burning in our small iron stove. Our Kolonnenführer — Einstein, our camp senior from Salaspils — appears to relay an order from the ghetto commander, Police Sergeant Kerrscher. For the time being, he says, all Jews from Riga are forbidden to enter the Latvian ghetto.

Einstein appears quite harmless to me. He has lost much of the arrogance of the camp senior. He came to the ghetto with a letter of recommendation from SS Commander Nickel. They wanted to get rid of him, so they sent him to Liepaja as a Kolonnenführer for the German Jews. When he comes to our room for the second time, a bucket of water accidentally falls from the transom of the half-open door on his head. Silently, without shouting or beating anybody, he hurries away.

The native Latvian Jews bring us soup, bread, and potatoes in large milk jars. Every minute there is a knock at the door. Pretty young girls stand outside and ask if we want to have something to eat, or whether we need any clothes. "Don't be ashamed to tell us what you need," a tall blonde girl tells us. "Whatever we have, we'll share. Today you come to us, tomorrow we may come to you. In Skeden,[13] where 9,000 Liepaja Jews are buried, everybody is equal anyhow." She gives us some warm milk and leaves.

The Liepaja ghetto is a women's ghetto. Seven hundred women and two hundred men survived the pogroms during the German invasion. Many of them went into hiding and stayed alive — almost accidentally, as Chaim tells me. Chaim is a young man from Leningrad.

The next morning we start at the sugar refinery, where we work in three shifts. Everybody else is busy unloading the sugar beets from the freight trains into water-filled channels. From there the sugar beets float to the refinery where they are cut into thin slices and carried on a conveyor belt to the large five-ton vats in which the sugar is extracted by heat. The remaining pulp is loaded onto trucks and shipped to freight cars, to be used as cattle feed. The liquid is boiled down to a syrup. At the end of the conveyor belt the crystal-clear sugar runs into the waiting sacks.

Dressed only in sneakers and gym pants, I work the beet press together with two Latvians. It is our job to fill the beet slices into the vats. We work without interruption for eight hours until the next shift comes and relieves us. We have to work at top speed. The Latvians treat us decently.

During the first few days none of us takes any sugar back into the ghetto; we have to get the feel of the situation first. We soon find out the Jews occupied in the refinery supply all the others with sugar, although, of course, that is strictly forbidden. A few days later a Latvian Jew is caught stealing sugar. The directors of the refinery report him — erroneously, as they say — to the S.D.[14] instead of the ghetto command. The next day he is arrested in the ghetto, and a few days later he dies. Our Latvian Kolonnenführer finds a way out. We start bribing the Latvian guards posted at the exit of the refinery — with stockings and underwear, sometimes with money — and from then on each one of us carries several pounds of sugar from the refinery without difficulty. In the ghetto the sugar is sold for 40 marks per pound, or traded for butter and other supplies. Since the ghetto provisions are much better than in Riga, we lack for nothing.

The press where I work is also very nutritious. The thickened syrup can be drawn into glasses and bottles from a faucet and although one cannot drink a great deal of it, the syrup supplies food and energy. Work at the refinery has another advantage: after our shift we can take wonderfully warm showers which leave us relatively clean and refreshed. We have a ten-minute run over an open field to the railroad station, then a twenty-minute train ride, and finally a half-hour march from the station to the ghetto.

Something unexpected occurs in the ghetto every day. A woman returning from work has been arrested in the street. She leaves behind two small children aged four and six. The next day, I am just going on the afternoon shift from four to twelve, when a car with S.D. men drives into the ghetto. They call for the Ghetto Elder Israelit, once a wealthy businessman, and his deputy, Kiganty.

"Israelit!" the notorious Hanke of the S.D. yells at him. "Bring me the two Rubinstein children."

I see Israelit disappear into a house nearby and return immediately with two warmly-dressed children on his right and left hand. As soon as the children see the three S.D. men they start screaming and yelling.

"Uncle Israelit!" they plead. "Uncle Israelit, please, we don't want to go away from here."

Brutal hands seize the children and throw them like rubber balls into the open car.

Several Jews working for the S.D. report later that the mother, naked, her two children on her arms, was led to the place of execution and they were shot.

November 1942. A field kitchen has been set up in front of the house in which we live. Thanks to additional gifts of potatoes, meat, and other food from the Jews of Liepaja, we now enjoy a really hearty, nutritious soup when we return from work. On top of that, we receive supplementary rations for hard labor. If one is careful during the allocation of potatoes, which are plentiful in the ghetto, he can carry several bucketfuls to his room without a word of protest from the good-natured Latvian distributor. At the "shack," as the Latvian Jews call their grocery canteen, we receive 180 grams of butter, 90 grams of sugar, and 2500 grams of bread every week. Supplementary rations, meat, and potatoes are used for the communal soup kitchen.

On the whole, hardly anybody lives on these rations alone. Everybody trades and hustles after additional food.

I already noticed in Riga that the sleeping bag I received at the clothing center is made out of coat material. I sell it to the ghetto tailor and get another blanket from him, as well as butter and as many potatoes and other kinds of food as I need. Later I learn the coat material was given to Ghetto Commander Kerrscher.

The economic situation in the Liepaja ghetto is completely different from that in Riga. Latvians are officially permitted to visit the ghetto in order to have their clothes made by first-rate Jewish tailors. Jewish cobblers make shoes to order not only for the Latvian inhabitants of Liepaja, but also for the high-ranking officers of the army and the SS. It is said that upon receiving a pair of excellent, well-fitting boots from the Jewish shoemaker, the German town commander of Liepaja patted him benevolently on the shoulder and said: "Jew, you may live as long as you like."

Because the Latvians can come into the ghetto, the Jewish artisans get everything they need and even supply a great many other Jews with their necessities. Most of them have known each other from before the ghetto days and there are bonds of friendship between them. All payments for the custom tailoring are given to the ghetto commander.

Now we may also go into the Latvian section. Kerrscher has given us permission to move freely through the ghetto. One evening when I'm on my way to the "shack" to get my rations, I see the girl who received me so kindly at our arrival. She is busy chopping away at a large block of wood. I walk over to her and ask if I can help her since she was so very kind to us when we arrived. Her first response is a gesture of refusal with her hand. After a moment, she says, "We here in Liepaja are used to doing our own work."

"Why are you always so unfriendly and rude?" I ask her, irritated by her tone. "You don't know me at all — except that I'm from Germany."

"Yes," she replies. "I don't know you as an individual, but you Germans in general are the cause of our misery. "

"I can understand your hatred of the Germans," I say, "I also hate them with all my heart, but you can't include in your hatred people who share your misfortune."

I take the axe from her hand and finish chopping the wood. She stands beside me, watching but without replying to my words. Then

we each take an armful of wood and carry it into the house. There
is an unspoken agreement between us now. We have worked
together, so now she sets the dinner table for both of us. For a short
time we sit facing each other in silence. Then she starts the conversation again.

"It's not your fault that you were born in Germany," she says.
"You can't help that. But I suspect in you character traits of our
murderers and oppressors. It cannot possibly be otherwise, since you
went to school with them, visited the same movie houses and the-
aters. You look like a Yekke,[15] so that makes me feel I am talking to
a German. That you happen to be Jewish is purely a matter of education. And furthermore," she adds sarcastically, "it was probably only
Hitler who turned you into a Jew. If he hadn't told you that you
were Jews, all of you would have been assimilated by the German
people in a short time, and there would have been no more Jews left
in Germany. What kind of a Jew is it," she adds with a smile, "who
doesn't even speak Yiddish?"

I listen to Mucia attentively, because everything she says is true,
at least in part, but one cannot generalize. My parents' home in
northern Germany was strictly Orthodox, I tell her. In the after-
noons I went to religious school and learned some Hebrew, too,
though that was the extent of Jewish life in a community that
numbered only several hundred Jews. And what happened before
Hitler I can hardly remember.

"Here," she tells me, "we had about 12,000 Jews before the
Germans came. I went to the Jewish high school, attended the
Jewish theater and saw movies with Jewish content. Everybody
around me spoke Yiddish. Liepaja was a Jewish town until the Germans came. Our men and boys fought for days defending the
town. Many of our people died — the city's devastation tells all.
They sent Stukas [Nazi dive bombers] over and broke our
defenses. Then the Germans arrived with their thoroughness and
exactness. The first thing was we had to wear a star in front and
back. The curfew came next. Anybody found on the street was

arrested and never seen again. Every day they asked for a different identification card. The Germans would stand at the bridges and arrest everybody with insufficient identification. A strange carriage drove through the streets of Liepaja — a sleigh with cheery jingling bells which picked up people and took them to Skeden, and you know what happened to them there. They told the Jews they were going to be evacuated. Everybody was to take provisions for three days, but the trip lasted barely half an hour. Fantastic things happened, I tell you. There was an old man standing in the Muehlenstrasse here. He saw the carriage riding by. 'Hey!' he called to the driver and the guards sitting in front. 'Yesterday you picked up my whole family. Please take me along too, I want to join them wherever they are.' So they did him the favor. A woman who is still living in the ghetto was taken to Skeden. Shortly before the entrance to the fenced-off area, everybody started to scream. The horses got out of control, the guards were busy looking after themselves, and she escaped.

"I could go on for hours, but I see it is almost ten o'clock and you have to hurry to get home. If you're on the streets after ten here, they'll put you in the bunker. Keep well. I'll see you soon." I wish her good night and leave.

Einstein often comes to our room to talk to us. In these surroundings he appears totally different from the man he was in Salaspils. This former tyrant now seems like an ordinary piker. We often have talks together, and he tells me he used to manufacture shirts in a small town in Wurttemberg. "If I ever get out of here," Einstein says, "I'll go back to making shirts." When I remind him of the vicious role he played in Salaspils and tell him how many Jews he has on his conscience, he becomes restless and uneasy and starts to scream, as he used to do in Salaspils. "What do you know?" he yells. "I don't have anybody on my conscience. I have saved many people's lives." When he talks like that we all laugh at him and he leaves us, furious, his fists clenched. But Liepaja is no extermination camp. Even Einstein has noticed that.

December 1942. We are lucky the work shifts change every week. Otherwise the night shift would be unbearable. It starts at midnight and lasts until eight in the morning. Nobody can sleep during the day. There is constant noise and tumult in the house; nobody is considerate of anybody else. Furthermore, the nights are very cold. Several of us have frostbite on our hands and feet. Dr. Weinreich[16] the ghetto physician informs us the transport from Riga has too many patients. Every day he has to report the number of sick people to the ghetto commander. We, too, brought a doctor from Riga, Dr. Hirschfeld. I hear that he will declare anybody sick who brings enough bacon and butter.

December 10, 1942. The night is very dark as we march back to the railroad station from the sugar refinery. Our column consists of about 30 Jews. The Kolonnenführer, as usual, walks at the right side of the group, but this is a very difficult march. The streets and fields are icy, and it is almost impossible to keep in step. We are sliding and skidding rather than marching. Many of us have already made intimate contact with the icy ground.

The train, as usual, is late and we have to wait in the open field for about an hour with the wind biting in our faces. Around one o'clock the train finally comes chugging along. Just to get on and get back home is the fervent wish of every one of us, but things are to turn out differently, as they have so often before, since we've been in the hands of these unpredictable forces. Half an hour later we arrive at Liepaja, form three lines and start our march back to the ghetto. It is an eerie march through the pitch-black streets over icy pavement accompanied by the clatter of our wooden sandals. The moon is hidden by dark snow clouds. Only from time to time a guard's spotlight flares up and goes out again as soon as the guard recognizes the marching Jews. We hardly talk to each other. We are all tired and exhausted; everyone is deep in his own thoughts. We have covered the greater part of the way and are just crossing the bridge over the Baltic when misfortune strikes. Somebody suddenly shouts "Halt!" An arm reaches out of the dark into the rows of marching men and a fist strikes the man in front of me who returns the blow. A shot rings out and immediately afterwards the column breaks into a run. We gather at the ghetto gate to hand in the numbers we were given when we left for work. Eight men are missing. They obviously did not succeed in escaping. My friend, a Czech, is among the missing. Usually we walk side by side, but this time fate decreed otherwise. We had often talked about the stars which are particularly clear on certain winter nights. His thoughts in general were up with the stars. He believed firmly in his future liberation. It is written in the stars, he once told me.

We have no sleep that night. Anxiously we await the morning that will tell us about the fate of our people. It comes with alarming promptness. At eight o'clock the ghetto commander calls the roll. He says he has just been notified that the eight missing men have been shot for refusing the command of the S.D. to stop. There is nothing he can do, he adds. After all, we know that he hadn't given the order. That was the end of the morning assembly. Again eight people have gone to their deaths, among them my star-gazing friend.

A few days later Mucia, my friend from the ghetto fence, invites Ossie, a twenty-two-year-old Viennese Jew, and me to come over to Sachs, where we can have a little get-together. "It is always very cozy there," she says, "and there will be several other girls. You'll have a nice time."

Nothing in Sachs' place is reminiscent of the ghetto with its well-furnished living room, a couch, two armchairs and coffee table. A small table lamp throws a dim light on the members of the family sitting around the table. Taubchen and Bessie, two young girls, are introduced to us, and soon we are all engaged in a lively conversation. The main topic, of course, is our situation. We are all agreed there is little chance to survive these times. "If it were up to Kerrscher," says Mucia, "they would not touch a hair on our heads, but he is only a puppet. The SS collects the Jews and all he can do is look after the departing car, as he did with the two Rubinstein children." Meanwhile the table has been set. We are served black tea and potato pancakes. We change the subject; we discuss the theater and famous actors. We recount the great cultural achievements of little Latvia before the outbreak of the war. They had everything here: Russian, German, American, and English movies. The cultures of East and West met in the Baltic states. It is strange that we Jews always tended more toward Western culture. German was the main subject in school. We read German books, of course, also Gogol, Dostoyevsky and Tolstoy, but generally we were more familiar with German writers than with the Russians. "Just look at the Russian films," says Rosel, a tall blond girl who in her vivacious manner now almost alone dominates the conversation. "Most of them were plain propaganda films. And yet there's one I'll never forget." Rosel gets very excited. I can see how she relives that film. "Josef, do you know the movie Cirk? But how could you know Cirk? You can't have seen it in Germany. I will tell you the story. Somewhere in the world," she begins, walking about the room, "a black man marries a white woman. The child from this marriage is a mulatto. Wherever the family goes it is rejected, made fun of. The film shows how they travel all over the world, persecuted and scorned everywhere. And you should hear the music from the film." She starts singing the lullaby from Cirk, her clear voice rising softly and tenderly in the room, moving us, stirring us. "And then they come to Russia," Rosel continues the story. "There, everybody welcomes and applauds them. 'We don't care whether you are green, brown or yellow. The main thing is: you're a human being, a human being.' " After that, Ossie sings:

I have no country, I have nothing in this world.
My destiny is unknown, the blue sky is my tent.
I can't be happy, I know no sunshine.
Why am I so alone in this world?

I have no country, I have nothing in this world.
I wander from place to place and stay where they let me.
I cannot be happy, I know no sunshine.
Why am I so alone in this world?

Rosel shows us her photo album and her pictures from school. She points to this classmate or that and says, "He is still alive, and she too. These are all dead." There is a picture of a whole class, boys and girls about sixteen years old, and their teacher. "They're all lying in Skeden," Rosel says by way of explanation. All this blossoming youth! "Here, look at Fanny." She points a finger to a picture. "She fled naked from Skeden. They were shooting after her, but she was lucky. Now she is here in the ghetto."

That evening I go for a walk with Mucia; that is, we walk up and down the same street, always the same way. The snow crunches under our feet; the night is cold. I put my arm around her. There is only peace and quiet around us. The guards making their rounds about the ghetto do not disturb us. They, too, seem to be deep in their own thoughts. Only from time to time they knock their boots against a fence post in order to shake the snow from their soles. A few straggling laborers are still walking home, but soon the street is empty, deserted. We hardly talk. We dream of things which will never come true. Suddenly I see a shooting star.

"Make a wish, Mucia, quick!" I call out. "I'm wishing for freedom. What about you?"

"I wish to die a natural death," Mucia replies "because there will be no more freedom for us."

I am appalled. I was not prepared for such an answer. I try to talk her out of it.

"Mucia, you know from our history that the Jews have always gone through hard times. But it has never been possible to destroy our people entirely. Some are sure to survive the massacre. Maybe we will, too, you and I."

"You are a dreamer, Josef," she says. "In the first place, nobody has ever used such modern methods to destroy human beings, and secondly we have already been destroyed. We who are walking here are already survivors. The Jewish people, the great mass of them, is already buried in the Hochwald or in Skeden. Also I cannot understand why I should live when all my acquaintances and friends from school had to die. It is not possible, Josef. You know yourself how thorough the Germans are. They are just as reliable in murder as they are in producing their technical inventions. Do you believe in nissim [miracles] Josef? I no longer do. I must tell you something else: they are digging new mass graves in Skeden, and in my opinion it is not hard to guess whom they are intended for. Believe me, only a miracle can save us, because never before has a people been so helplessly faced with destruction as we. The other day a woman in our house broke her leg — it happened on a street in the inner city. Immediately an ambulance came from the fire department. She was carefully bandaged and taken to the hospital, where she was well treated and cared for. Two days later the same car came from the fire station; carefully, the same men carried her into the car. They took her to the S.D., and you know the rest."

We walk on silently, side by side. My mind is busy trying to find a way out of this wretchedness. All kinds of ideas come into my head, various ways of escape, but I reject them all and can reach no decision. It seems impossible that a girl like Mucia should die. For what reason? And why should I die? My thoughts are going in circles, and I hear Mucia's voice, "the graves are dug already, Josef, and it is not hard to guess for whom."

"Do you still have your watch, Mucia?" I break the silence. "I think it's time I took you home. We won't have to use the subway here."

Mucia tries to smile, but she doesn't quite succeed.

"The Germans took my watch the second day after their arrival," she says, "but I know it's time."

"Take care, Mucia, and sleep well, and promise you'll dream of happier things than we've talked about. All right?"

"I'll try, Josef. Good night. And you sleep well, too."

And Mucia quickly goes off to her room.

We're told that with the end of the sugar production season we're through at the refinery. The labor Kommando is going back to Riga. Since the middle of December we have not been employed at the conveyor belt. We all have to work outside during the cold nights loading peat for the refinery's heating system. It is difficult to have the December storms whistle around your ears with no chance to drink anything hot. Therefore many of us look forward to going back to Riga.

One morning when we return from work to the ghetto, Israelit, the ghetto elder, meets us at the gate. We have to decide immediately whether we wish to return to Riga or remain in Liepaja. The harbor administration needs a labor Kommando of Jews to shovel coal. If there are not enough volunteers, he'll have to choose the men. The list has to be given to the commander immediately. I make up my mind quickly. I imagine pleasant evenings at Sachs' apartment, walks with Mucia, but I certainly don't look forward to the cold winter nights on the ocean. After a conference, Kekanski, the elder of the Jewish Council, agrees to try and get permission for every group remaining behind to send a deputy to Riga for some clothes. What little we were permitted to take is torn, so we cannot work at the harbor without replacements. The commander approves the suggestion and on December 22, the 96 Jews returning to Riga are accompanied by one deputy each from the Latvian, Lithuanian, and German sections. I am not enthusiastic at having been appointed for the German group, but I cannot do anything about it. However, the trip is more pleasant than I expected. After the ghetto commander bids farewell to Einstein, saying he hopes to have made life in Liepaja as pleasant as possible, the small company leaves the ghetto, accompanied by the blessings of the remaining Jews. The trip is tolerable. Our two cars are attached to the night train to Riga. The next morning we arrive, but we cannot leave the station ye, since we must await an escort from Riga. Meanwhile the Jews working for the railroad station share their hot soup with us. They say they have enough to eat. They obviously enjoy sharing their food with us.

Riga

Several horse-drawn carriages arrive from the ghetto. We load our luggage on and start a slow march through the snow-covered streets to Riga. There is no inspection. Everybody breathes easier because our knapsacks are filled with sugar. We all know that one pound of sugar costs eighty marks in the ghetto.

We are stopped in front of the administration building. Ghetto Commander Krause appears. Behind him, with quick mincing steps, comes Ghetto Elder Leiser. Krause, his clumsy legs in a pair of boots, looks like a butcher. A cruel smile fills his face as he walks slowly past our column, scrutinizing every one of us. I feel a cold shiver run down my spine when he stops before a Jew, points to his knapsack and says: "Well, did you do some nice trading, eh?" But he passes on without asking him to open his knapsack. Our escort from Liepaja reports to him that he has the order to return three men to Liepaja. "What?" Krause says, "do you think these are tourists on a pleasure trip?" Leiser nods his head approvingly. "This is no travel club," Krause finishes. A Jewish policeman solicitously opens the door to the building, and the guard at the door gives a military salute as Krause disappears from sight.

A few minutes later I stand at the door of Ghetto Elder Leiser and knock.

"Come in!" he calls out in his rasping voice.

Leiser is seated behind a large executive desk. He is wearing a grey tweed sports suit with matching tie and his hair is slicked down. He eyes me suspiciously over his glasses.

"What do you want?" he asks.

"I am here on behalf of the German Jews who are remaining in Liepaja," I start out. "We're requesting more clothes and shoes. The clothes we had are worn out from the hard work in the sugar refinery."

"Why don't you come right out and say that you sold all your stuff and now have returned for more trading items?" he barks at me. "Do you think I am too stupid to know that? Where would we be if everyone came running and demanded clothes for his group of fifteen people? Anyhow, you still seem quite well dressed," he continues. "How come you have clothes, and the others don't?"

"This is all I have," I reply, "and you'll understand that one cannot work at the harbor, shoveling coal, like that." I try to explain that we need warm clothing for the night shift at the harbor. Furthermore, there is a file in the clothing center which shows what each of us has received so far.

"Do you have a list of what you need, and the names of the people?" he asks, in a somewhat more conciliatory tone.

I hand him the list hastily drawn up on the train.

"There, you see!" he screams. "You have fifteen people and you ask for seventeen toothbrushes. That leaves two to sell, right?"

I think that Krause himself would not talk any differently.

"Forgive me, Mr. Leiser, but I made an error there. Of course I need only fifteen toothbrushes. Kindly forgive the oversight."

"You seem to be riding high," he continues in his sarcastic manner. "Here you come and even try to chisel me."

He's acting the wrathful judge now, treating me like a criminal. He still studies the list.

"Of course," he starts again, "everybody needs a suit and a pair of shoes. Wouldn't you like that? I shall talk to Mrs. Fromm from the clothing center. Nobody who ever received any of the listed items before will get anything else. As far as I am concerned, you can run around naked in Liepaja. You should not have sold your stuff!"

With that I am dismissed. I am not quite sure whether I was talking to Krause or to the Jewish ghetto elder, but I feel convinced that the bell will toll for this gentleman, too.

Upstairs in the clothing center, things are a little more pleasant. The usual bureaucracy reigns here. File cards are pulled out and checked against my list. Meanwhile a messenger arrives from Leiser, telling me our train will leave tonight at one o'clock. It is already three-thirty. I've neither had a meal nor have I advanced the matter of our clothes. So I first dash downstairs to the food supply center. After listening to my story, they let me have about 400 grams of bread and 20 grams of margarine. "I don't suppose you are interested in these," the man says, pointing to rotten red beets lying on the floor.

Meanwhile, in the clothing center they have made some progress. I am handed signed slips stating the items I may receive for every single person. The choice goes fast. I am given some bags too, and at six-thirty I am standing with three well-filled trunks in front of the administration building. The luggage is deposited with the police guard, and now I am free to look after my own affairs.

When I arrive at Erlanger's, the whole room is already crowded. Everybody is waiting for me. The news spreads all around the ghetto that tonight somebody is going to Liepaja. Everybody has all kinds of messages for me. "Haver, can you take this letter for me?" "Haver, years ago a family named Yankelsohn was living in Liepaja. Do you know if they're still there?" My ears are humming. Soon all my pockets are filled with little notes, and still more people arrive with more requests.

Erlanger warns me not to take too many letters, for there is a death penalty for smuggling mail. I ask Erlanger to lock the door from the inside so I can sleep for a few hours. At twelve o'clock somebody bangs on the door and asks whether Katz is there. He has orders to take me to the administration building, since I must not be out alone in the streets at night. My two companions are already present. A few minutes later a heavily laden horse carriage rolls out of the ghetto gate. We follow slowly behind through the dark, deserted streets of Riga, accompanied by a Latvian guard.

Liepaja

Our return to Liepaja is greeted with great rejoicing. Our luggage is immediately taken to the ghetto and distributed. Half of the ghetto dwellers are assembled in our room. Everybody is talking at once:

"Haver, do you have a letter for me? Haver, did you meet Yankel? I am sure he sent his regards . . . ."

Soon my pockets are empty. My head only begins to clear when I sit in Sachs' room and drink hot tea. Nothing has changed in the ghetto during my brief absence. But there is talk the Germans are planning to liquidate the ghetto. Some say all the Jews will be sent to Riga. Others are skeptical. Rosel says they are getting Riga mixed up with Skeden. Mucia has come, too. She looks very tired. She tells me she works all day at the wood saw, cutting wood for the wood-fueled vehicles. It is nerve-wracking, she says, trying not to cut your hands. I say good-night early and go to bed.

January 1943. For several days now we've been busy unloading coal. Our shift is from six at night to six in the morning, a damned long time. The Jews are always sent down into the boat holds to shovel coal from the bulkheads to the middle of the bunker so that the crane can grab hold of it. The bunkers below are only dimly lit — the shadows of the workers and those leaning on their shovels are reflected on the bulkheads. The whole scene appears dreamlike and unreal; only the voice of the Latvian foreman who throws small chunks of coal at us and the freezing cold call us back to reality.

It takes little imagination to feel we are back in the days of the Pharaohs. In the mornings we smuggle large pieces of coal to the ghetto, for heating material has become very scarce. We now sell coal instead of sugar; it is well paid, half a mark per pound. Everything depends on the guard at the exit from the harbor department. If he is in a good mood he lets us pass without inspection; if not, we have to get rid of the coal. Sometimes the whole harbor street is covered with it.

I already have my steady customers. Every night before going to work, I visit Mrs. Feivelsohn. It is not strictly business between us: if she has something to eat, I get a share; if she has no food, she gets the coal anyway. Mrs. Feivelsohn has two small children, ages three and five. Her brother works in the slaughterhouse. He supports the entire family.

One morning when I've just gone to sleep after an exhausting night, a man comes rushing into our room.

"Haverim! Haverim!" he cries. "The ghetto is surrounded by the SS. Fifty of them have come inside. Get up, Haverim, get dressed. We're in big trouble!"

We refuse to be alarmed and go back to sleep. The homes of Latvian Jews are being searched. Everything valuable the SS find they take with them, then leave without arresting anybody.

That night I go to Mrs. Feivelsohn again. She puts a large plate with fried liver in front of me and starts talking.

"This morning," she says, "when the SS surrounded the ghetto, I thought our last hour had struck. I took my children and dressed them in their woolen socks and their best little dresses. I thought they should be nice and warm when they go to their deaths."

The liver on my plate is getting cold. I tell her I only just ate and have no appetite, and then I leave. I cannot bear to listen to her any longer.

The next few days are very quiet. We're working in the harbor. Many ships cannot make their way into the harbor because of the strong wind. So we have a few slack days, get some rest and put our things in order. We never know when we will be called back to work. Sometimes there is a call to the ghetto at seven o'clock at night, and we have to march out to work half an hour later. A large freighter has arrived from Germany with a load of cement. The Latvians work there during the day; at night, the Jews.

When we arrive, the foreman says 5,000 sacks of cement have to be unloaded by tomorrow morning. He doesn't care how we do it, but there'll be no rest until we're finished. This cement loading is unhealthy work. Soon we're covered from head to toe with fine cement dust. We are itching all over our bodies. The stuff gets into the pores of your skin. Three cranes are working. I am down below in the hold with twenty-four others piling the cement sacks on the pallets. We hear the Latvian command: "Sargas, Sargas [Careful! Careful!]" The winch starts turning and slowly pulls the load upward. We are in touch with German seamen, although they are strictly prohibited from talking to us. A man from Lübeck is among the sailors on board. He comes over and asks my name. It turns out he knew my whole family. He used to buy leather in our store.

"Shit," he says, "not only for you, but for us, too. Or do you think it's fun to sail this tub on the lousy Baltic? Yesterday two of our boats went down. Believe me, we have to stick our asses out the same way as you. But it can't last much longer anyhow. The end's in sight."

When an officer appears on the scene, he vanishes. Later he returns. He says the officer is a big Nazi; you have to be very careful around him. One day we'll rip his ass for him. He asks whether I need anything. I tell him how things are with us. He takes me into his cabin, gives me everything he has — bread, cheese and butter. I give him an address in Lübeck. If he comes back he might bring me some clothes from there. He promises, but I am never to see him again. His boat runs into a mine – whatever became of him I don't know. We only finish our work at 11 o'clock the next morning. Dead-tired, we march back to the ghetto, wash up a little and drop into bed — until the phone in the administration building rings and calls us back to work.

February 1943. I have temporarily knocked off from work in the bunker and am sitting in the warm engine room opposite a German cabin boy, perhaps seventeen years old. You can sit fairly comfortably on the ladder in the engine room; the hum of the machines is soothing and the atmosphere is conducive to sleep. The cabin boy gives me a cigarette and we both smoke. He talks about this and that. He says I speak a very good German. "You've been kicked out of Germany," he says. "Why do you hang on in this world? You know you've been buried alive. You'll never get out from where you are now. Sooner or later you'll all be knocked off."

"I don't know if I'll ever get out of this," I reply. "But one thing I know for sure: the last word hasn't been spoken yet."

He asks me how I mean that, but I am afraid to explain it to him; it is too dangerous.

We Jews are used only for the hardest and unhealthiest jobs. Several boats have arrived with potash. We have to fill it into sacks down inside the holds. After work we look like snowmen, white from top to toe. The Latvians watch us and laugh. They load the filled sacks above the deck into the waiting trains. On the whole, the Latvians tell us, there are far fewer boats than usual. It has to do with the political situation. The Germans have had heavy losses, one of them says, then looks around to see if anybody is listening. Radio Moscow said yesterday the Germans are going to mourn their lost battle of Stalingrad for three days. Soon they're going to suffer a defeat that will make them mourn forever.

Such news lifts our spirits, gives us new courage and hope and fills us with new self-confidence.

A Jew has had an accident during the coal loading. He was standing on a pile of coal when it suddenly slipped; he fell and hit his head against the iron crane. In the middle of the night we take him to the city hospital. Four men carry him on a stretcher. When they return, they say his head wound was stitched up immediately and that there is a chance he will survive. A few days later I get permission from the commander to visit him. For the first time in a year I am walking alone in the street. Kerrscher, the ghetto commander, gave me a permission slip to walk the shortest route to the hospital by myself.

Marching in a column, you don't feel it so much that you have to walk in the middle of the street instead of on the sidewalk.[17] But walking by myself I feel excluded from human society. The streets are poorly paved, and the puddles and garbage make it hard to walk on the cobblestones. I wonder how it feels to be walking up there on the sidewalk. I am thinking constantly it must be lovely. When I come into a small side street where nobody sees me, I cannot resist. Only a small part of the way I walk on the edge of the sidewalk, but feel as though I am committing a crime, and so I quickly get down again and walk on through the mud and dirt.

Everybody is very nice at the hospital. A nurse shows me to the haver's room. She tries to talk with me in Latvian. I reply with a few words of broken Russian. Apparently my linguistic talents amuse her for she laughs at every word I say. Still, she spoke to me as one human being to another.

My haver is fine. I'm pleased to find him so fit. He says they treat him well; apparently they feel sorry for him. The same nurse brings him everything he wants. She told him she did it out of kindness. The other Latvians in his room always share the gifts their relatives bring them. The doctor tells him he can return to the ghetto in a few days. We are all pleased when he actually shows up. It is a miracle the S.D. did not get him.

March 1943. Rumors abound that we shall soon be removed from Liepaja. The foreman at the Arbeitsamt said the Jews are no longer needed. So we wait daily for the order to leave.

In the evening I visit Mucia. I find her in bed, her whole head bandaged so that only her face is free. She seems to be asleep, but suddenly she gives a start, opens her eyes, and a smile of recognition lights up her features.

"I was lucky, Josef," she whispers. "A piece of wood hit me on the head during work. It is just a small flesh wound, the doctor says. Don't look so worried; it's really not bad. Take this book and read to me. It is Erich Kaestner; in Germany it is prohibited, I'm sure. This is the only book I took with me to the ghetto. Please read 'If We Should Win the War.' It is my favorite."

I read the whole poem to her, and several others, and Mucia listens attentively until she falls asleep with a smile on her face. The order to leave for Riga has come. In two hours we have to be ready to go. Kerrscher says he has to send us off today. I quickly pack my few belongings into my knapsack and walk over to Sachs' to say goodbye. Rosel presses a few medicines into my hand. She also gives me the addresses of some relatives overseas. "If you should live, Josef, write to them that you saw me here, and tell them about us."

I promise that to her and then I go to Mrs. Feivelsohn.

"Here, my yingele [boychik]," she says, "I made you a few sandwiches when I heard you had to leave. Keep well, my yingele, and send me a letter with the Jews who'll come here from Riga to get their clothes deloused."

I am sorry I have to leave here. Mrs. Feivelsohn is a good Jewish woman. Mucia has not yet returned from work when I go to say goodbye to her. Rosel says she will be back any moment. I am just putting my knapsack on my back when Mucia comes in the door. "Here, Josef, take this as a farewell present, but open it only when you are in Riga." Then she kisses me on the cheek and runs away. I am never to see her again.

Riga

As soon as we arrive in Riga, we are permitted to go to our living quarters. The first person I see is Einstein, our camp senior from Salaspils, in the Berliner Strasse. He wears a wide armband marked "Living Quarters." I tell him that I'm on my way to see him because my sleeping place at Erlanger's is occupied. "I know," he says. "But I have something suitable for you. However, it is with three old women in one room." He's sure I will get used to that. "Come on," he says and leads the way to Berlin House No. 2. When we arrive on the sixth floor, he calls, "Mrs. Kiewe, Mrs. Kiewe!" One of the doors opens and a woman of about fifty appears. "I'm sorry," says Einstein, "but I have to put this young man into your room. Nothing else is available — no use protesting," and he cuts off any reply she might have made. "This is it. I have no choice, and that's final." With that, Einstein departs. Meanwhile I have entered the kitchen behind Mrs. Kiewe. Through the open door I see a small room. There are two beds on the two long walls opposite each other, and an aisle in between. "I don't know what we're going to do," says Mrs. Kiewe, "and I wonder what Mrs. Engel is going to say." I try to reassure her and tell her that somehow we will arrange everything until I can find something else. Mrs. Engel has appeared in the meantime, and a little later her sister comes in. We agree the three women will go to bed first at night, and I will stay in the kitchen until they have undressed.

Mrs. Kiewe is already becoming a little more pleasant. She starts putting clean sheets on my bed, while Mrs. Engel says that now at least they have somebody to chop wood for them. Then they ask if I want to have dinner with them. I politely decline.

The next morning I report to the Arbeitsamt. The man asks if I want to work as a gardener in the ghetto plant nursery; they still need someone. A few days later I start. It is only a very small garden; Richard Horn, the former chief gardener of the German hakhshorah,[18] Kibbutz Winkel, leads the group consisting of three men and three women.

April 1943. I've fallen on hard times because my job does not bring me anything as yet. A lot of vegetables and lettuces have been sown, but they grow very poorly since we have no fertilizer at all. When the first lettuce is finally ready, Krause, the Ghetto Commander, and Leiser, the Ghetto Elder, get their share, a share goes to the hospital, and the remainder is distributed among us. I trade mine for some bread, and I bring several heads of lettuce to Mrs. Kiewe, who is pleased like a child. She hasn't eaten fresh lettuce in a long time.

Altogether, Mrs. Kiewe is a very kind woman. Somehow, she identifies me with her son in England. "If I'm good to you," she says,
"maybe somebody will be good to my boy." Sometimes when I
return from work she sits in front of her son's picture and cries. "I'll
never see him again," she says and dries her tears. Mrs. Kiewe darns
my socks and washes my shirts. Whenever I have something to eat
she gets her share of it.

The middle of April I get an invitation to see Fleischel, the
Ghetto Elder. When I arrive, about twenty young men are already
assembled there. Mr. Fleischel gives a short speech in which he says
that with the kind assistance of Leiser, the Ghetto Elder, he has
managed to create a home for single young men. All those present
have been chosen to live there and he hopes we will be happy
about it. On April 20, he himself, together with Leiser and other
leaders of the Jewish ghetto, will open the home in the Moskauer
Strasse.

The home is really well furnished. All the beds have white sheets.
There is a communal bathroom and a social room. For the festive
opening, old carpets have been laid everywhere and a large round
table, with chairs around it, stands in the middle of the social room.
Meanwhile, we twenty have moved in. We are all filled with pleasant anticipation and have designated somebody to speak a few
words. They say there is going to be coffee and cake donated by
some big shots in the ghetto. Mrs. Kiewe has specially washed my
only white shirt for the occasion, and so we all stand ready and await
the gentlemen. The first to arrive is Frankenberg, the [Jewish] police
chief of the Latvian ghetto. He sits down noisily on one of the
chairs. Several nurses from the hospital show up. Council Elder
Plessner from the Cassel group is also there. Slowly the room fills.
Police Chief Haar is in conversation with "Living Quarters" Einstein. Beside him sits Samuel, the elder of the Dortmund group; he
is talking with Mrs. Cohn, the head nurse.

All the officials from the Arbeitsamt are present; each has
brought a small package. There is quite a bit of noise. We're all

waiting for Mr. Fleischel and Mr. Leiser. Suddenly a door opens, and I think I don't see well: a large black fur collar appears and a slim figure slithers through the open door like a movie star, Mrs. Fleischel. She is followed by her husband and Leiser. Everybody is quiet. Mr. Fleischel starts talking. He says he doesn't want to miss this opportunity to thank Mr. Leiser and all those volunteer helpers for their cooperation in creating this home. Particularly Mrs. Fromm of the clothing center deserves his thanks for supplying the linen. He thinks everybody will agree if he names this house in memory of our homeland, Herrenhausen," he says, "after the beautiful castle in Hanover, the home town of many Jews who are now living in the ghetto." Meanwhile Mrs. Meier, the cleaning lady, has made the coffee. All of the men unwrap their little packages and share the cake among themselves. They exchange a few polite words and then some say good-bye and leave. A few cake crumbs remain on the table. One of our haverim then tries to make his speech, but his words are drowned out by the music of the ghetto orchestra. Mr. Fleischel leads his wife out to the floor; Leiser dances with Mrs. Cohn. A few ghetto artists sing some songs, and then the celebration is over. It was a very amusing evening.

Mrs. Kiewe has a friend, a young man of about twenty-five, who visits her from time to time. She knows him from Berlin, from a time when he was still well off. Now he is in poor shape. Mrs. Kiewe tells me his story. On a Sabbath in the spring of 1942 young men who were found in the street, about fifty of them, were loaded onto a truck and taken away. Only three of them returned and those three nearly insane. They had to dig mass graves in the Hochwold. When they came to their place of work in the morning the graves were filled with bodies and covered only with a thin layer of sand. All around the graves lay personal papers and possessions which the victims had thrown away as they went to their death. Every day those men who were no longer strong enough to work were shot, and then the Kommondo was replenished from the ghetto. This labor detail was called Krause Two. Krause One, which performed the same duties, did not have any survivors. "I'm helping the poor devil wherever I can," Mrs. Kiewe says, "but there isn't very much left of him."

Several soccer teams have been formed in the ghetto: Prague and Dortmund teams, as well as the Berlin, Hanover, and Vienna clubs. The ghetto police also play and there are two special teams for the Latvian ghetto. They play on the field where the Latvian police were shot last year. Although the field was cleaned, there still are a few uneven spots, but these don't bother the players too much. Police Chief Haar kicks off. Berlin, Hanover and Vienna are playing against Dortmund for the ghetto championship. I play too but find it hard. I last played in Paderborn under quite different circumstances. Since then I have been to Salaspils and Kaiserwald — it's no wonder I don't play as well as I used to. Dortmund wins, just barely. The soccer field is surrounded by several thousand spectators; everybody yells and encourages the players. If the field weren't so bad one could imagine we were someplace out in the free world. The Berlin, Hanover and Vienna teams wear white pants and white shirts, while the Dortmund team wears blue and white. On this Sunday afternoon there is life in the ghetto. But it sometimes happens that there are gaps among the players — people who were sent to an Aussenkommando[19] or shot during the past week. In this case another player fills in. The best team is a Latvian group which boasts several former international soccer stars. But the Sunday passes quickly and on Monday morning work starts again.

Next to our garden is a small meadow. I work in the morning and in the afternoon; when I'm done, I lie down in the warm spring sunshine. The children from the Dortmund group with their kindergarten counselor always come here to play. They play ball or "Ring-around-the-rosy." The ghetto children are clever. Some of them go to the fence in the afternoon and wait for their parents. They take the provisions smuggled in by their parents and disappear as fast as their little legs will carry them.

May 1943. It is five o'clock in the afternoon. I'm just setting out small tobacco plants when the messenger boy from the Arbeitsamt comes running. I'm to report to the office right away.

"You'll leave immediately," Steg tells me when I get there. "Pack your things, the car is waiting. We need a gardener and there is nobody else. There are fifteen Jews already where you're going."

"Not so fast," I think to myself. I first go to Mrs. Kiewe and give her the news. I also want to get my ration card, for today is bread distribution. There is a knock at the door. "Come in," calls Mrs. Kiewe. An Oberscharführer enters and asks me whether my name is Katz. "Yes," I reply. "Come on, then," he says. In front of the house stands a small delivery truck, with a closed tailgate. The Oberscharführer opens the door and points his right thumb to the back, indicating that I should get in there. Suddenly a bag which others have packed for me at "Herrenhausen" flies after me into the truck. Fleischel himself appears and throws two blankets and an old summer coat after me. Before the door closes, Mrs. Kiewe hands me two sandwiches, and off we go, out of the ghetto, over the Dvina bridge in the direction of Mitau. I feel very uneasy; the whole thing happened too fast. I look around in the small truck. Ah, I notice the Oberscharführer has been shopping. There are cigarettes, liquor and tobacco. He also took a Jew with him, I think. Through a small window I can look outside to the road; I see a sign "Mitau — 6 kilometers." We drive over two bridges into Mitau. The truck stops. Again I get the signal with the right thumb; this time it means that I'm to get out. The Oberscharführer precedes me into a barracks-like structure and opens a door for me. "Tomorrow I'll come to get you," he says, and then I'm left on my own. I look around the room. About 100 army cots have been set up, all vacant at present. I appear to be the only occupant. The door opens, a few Dutchmen come in and ask me where I come from, and where I'm going. I tell them what I know. "Oh, Baloschi," says one of them, "Shit, shit, shit." He explains to his neighbor that he worked in Baloschi, an SS farm, on the construction of a greenhouse. They leave, but return a few minutes later with butter, cheese, marmalade, and many other edibles. "You can use this in Baloschi," explains the man who spoke before.

The next morning at seven there is a knock at the door. I didn't sleep all night anyhow, and am fully dressed. Again, the door of the delivery truck is opened, we get in and soon we reach the open road. A sign indicates we're going towards Liepaja. After a ride of about one hour the Oberscharführer starts greeting people crossing our path with horses and carriages. I assume we must be near our destination. He seems to be well-known here. Soon the car turns right, drives over a short dirt road, then a sign: "Baloschi SS and Police Farm."

"Get out and start moving," an unfamiliar voice commands. I get my stuff together and walk behind the SS man. "Hannauer, Hannauer!" he starts yelling. An older man comes running. "This one," the SS says, pointing to me, "starts work in an hour. Show him where he will sleep." I enter a chicken house. A few army cots, a table made from bare slats of wood, and two wobbly benches are the sole inventory. Straw hangs down from the ceiling and the walls are covered with chicken manure.

"Up there is a free cot," says Hannauer. "You've had lousy luck. Twelve hours of working like a horse and nothing to eat. Well, you'll find out. I'll get you in an hour. Dress lightly, it is warm today."

When I unpack my bag, I see that half my things are missing, but that can't be helped. Hannauer comes to get me, walks me to the chief gardener, and asks him what I'm supposed to do. "Cut lettuce," is the reply. Suddenly Levi, the medic from Salaspils, stands before me. "Josef, you here? That's tough luck, poor devil. You better get to work now. Big Willi is coming, a real nasty customer."

Most of the lettuce I cut is overgrown. Levi tells me that nobody in the SS here knows anything about gardening. "And they want to grow vegetables . . . well, you'll see!"

The lettuce is washed and carried to the waiting automobiles.

At noon there is about a quart of very thin pea soup. All fifteen Jews eat together in our chicken house — ten men and five women. In the afternoon we have to weed the strawberries. "The field has to be cleared today. Work carefully and don't pull out young shoots or you'll be sorry, you bastards."

We work and work, but the weeds hardly grow less. Every now and then Big Willi appears, carrying his hazelnut cane with which he constantly hits his boots, and drives the lagging workers on. He digs the toes of his boots into the piles of weeds looking for shoots accidentally pulled out. He finds something in a pile belonging to an eighteen-year-old Jew from Vienna and hits him in the face with the full force of his fist.

I'll fix you, you son of a bitch!" he says. Levi tells me Big Willi must be from somewhere in Upper Silesia because he speaks Polish too. Around ten o'clock at night we finish the field; hungry and exhausted we go to sleep. At six in the morning a bell rings, and at six-thirty everybody has to report to work. The ranch has about a thousand acres; besides us Jews there are ten Russian prisoners of war and several deported families working there. In the morning we get 300 grams of bread and about a pint of skim milk. After that come the work assignments.

"Can you handle horses?" somebody yells at me from the side.

"No, Herr Unterscharführer."

It is Little Willi, as I later learn from Dr. Franz Schweitzer, a Jew from Nuremberg. Little Willi is a peasant's son from Schleswig-Holstein.

"Well," says Little Willi, "then you'll have to learn. Come here."

Before my eyes he starts hitching a horse. "That's how you do it. You attach the bridle here and the reins there. Do you understand?"

"No, Herr Unterscharführer."

"What? Oh, you don't want to understand even when I show you." He hits me in the face. "Do you understand now?"

"Yes, Herr Unterscharführer."

"Now you drive the hay to the barn. You know where it is?"

"No, Herr Unterscharführer. I don't know where to get the hay, either."

He seizes the reins of the horse and mounts.

"Come on," he calls to me.

There is nothing for me to do but run after him. He rides up a steep road to the barn where a cart is standing. "There is the hay," he says. "You better carry six loads if you know what's good for you, Yid."

With great effort I finally get the horse hitched. It always tries to get away from me. All the time I'm thinking how I can get down that steep path with the full load. In the end a Russian prisoner gives me a hand. He leads the horse at the head and I pull back on the reins. On the way to the barn I meet Little Willi who asks me how many loads I have taken down already.

"What, this is only the first one, you son of a bitch," he screams. "You're going to drive those six loads if it takes all night."

The horse simply does not want to move. Every hundred yards or so he stops and refuses to budge. All my yelling is of no avail. He just stands there looking at the scenery. In desperation I grab him by the reins and try to pull him forward. But I haven't got enough strength to pull the horse. So I start beating the shit out of him. Suddenly the old nag starts up with a jolt, I almost fall off the cart, and then the harness rips. It's enough to drive you nuts. By noontime I have finally moved one load of hay. In the afternoon things go a little better. I drive another four loads, but then I've had enough. When Little Willi asks me how many loads I've done, I say six. "Then knock it off," he says.

That's how it goes now, day in and day out, from early morning until late at night. There is no Sunday in Baloschi either. The Russians only have to work half a day on Sunday, but the Jews are kept busy all day long.

It happens that Big Willi drives us out of our chicken house even earlier than usual on a Sunday morning and sends us out into a pouring rain to thin out the cabbages. The next day he throws out all the extra cabbage plants. At noontime he walks past us, grinning mockingly. Obviously he enjoys our misery.

The worst of the lot is the Oberscharführer who brought me from Riga, a Czech Baron von Kurau. Mrs. Shapiro, who with her husband and daughter belongs to our group of fifteen and who works in the kitchen of the main building, keeps telling us how the Baron stirs up Big and Little Willie against us. "You have to wallop these bastards more," he always says. "They're just a bunch of lazy dogs." After that the two Willis outdo each other trying to please their lord and master.

The one who suffers most from them is Dr. Schweitzer. He is a chemist who has never done any physical work, and now is supposed to plant onions like an experienced gardener. He can't do it, no matter how hard he tries. Often Big Willi beats him ferociously. I get the feeling that they agree in the main building whom they're going to pick on the next day but mostly it is Schweitzer. They feel he is mentally superior to them, that he is an intellectual. Shapiro from Bamberg is also a teacher, but he adjusts better, and he is more adept at farm work than Dr. Schweitzer with his long, almost delicate fingers. Schweitzer tells me one evening he owned a big factory in Nuremberg He left a large collection of valuable old books with a friend in Germany. Later, when he is free again, he is going to complete his collection. Sometimes I ask him about his studies, what universities he went to and where he got his doctorate. Franz can talk so well and interestingly that we almost forget the cruel conditions under which we are working. He studied in Erlangen and when the Nazis came, he got his doctorate in French in Paris. "One day, Josef," he often says to me, "when this nightmare is over, you must come and visit me." I promise him. But mostly he feels dejected and beaten, in every sense of the word. And then he says he'll never get out of here, never.

The spring season makes our lot doubly hard. The gentlemen of the SS have decided to set up a vegetable farm in Baloschi. Six giant greenhouses are under construction and 2,000 glass frames are being built over compost heaps. One could imagine they're building for all eternity. But the reports we get from the Dutchmen about the Eastern front say that the Germans are engaged in "victorious retreat" from all points. A large new horses' stable is also being built. The Latvians working there say by the time the stable is finished the Russians will probably be there.

For weeks now we have done nothing else but set our tomato plants — 40,000 of them have to be planted. At 6:30 in the morning we go to the tomatoes and stay there until 8:00 at night. A Russian prisoner of war has escaped. Consequently our chicken house and the Russian barracks have been fenced with barbed wire. The Russians tell us, "Jurka gone, Jurka damoiy [home] to Kazan." He was a clever boy, this Jurka. We used to walk back from working in the fields together at night, and in his broken German he would give me the latest reports from the front. I don't know where he got them. His final words always were, "Germanski kaput," and he would stamp his foot hard on the ground as though to crush all of Germany.

Two new SS have appeared on the farm — Hans, a tall German from Hamburg, and Harald, a Dane. Both of them are absolute barbarians. It is Hans' pleasure to chase me from my bed several times a week at 12:00 at night. Suddenly he shouts through the open door, "Katz, Katz, get up, you lazy bum!" Half asleep, I jump out of bed, throw on my old summer coat and step into my torn shoes. Outside, Hans throws the reins at my head. Before I know what I'm doing I am sitting in the driver's seat. The stallion, eager to get home, jolts ahead and we gallop toward the stable at a fast clip. Sometimes I think I must be dreaming when I find myself riding through the countryside at midnight. Once arrived, I quickly unhitch the horse, put some hay and oats in his manger, and hurry back to bed. "Bed" is an exaggeration: it is a simple straw sack with innumerable fleas which keep me awake all night although we change the straw every few weeks. In the morning we always shake the fleas off the blankets.Very often I lie down in the hayloft with several others because it has become unbearable in the chicken house. But when Big Willi learns of this he puts a stop to it.

The first retreating cattle transports arrive. We drive the cattle from the railroad station, which is several miles away, to the farm. There are also several hundred geese, though no shelters for the animals. Schweitzer and Weiss have to guard the geese. At night they are locked into a stable that is much too small. Mrs. Shapiro says they are already sick of roast goose — she is speaking of the SS in the main building.

It is fortunate that vegetables are growing on the farm. We pull carrots and cut the kohlrabi. Usually we eat our fill of the raw vegetables right in the field, for the food we're given is totally inadequate.

One day when we return to the farm from weeding in the field, Schweitzer says he cannot go on with this life any longer. He is not going to go to work anymore and submit to the brutalities of Harald, the Dane. The next morning I am called out to weed the turnip field. What goes on here is too cruel for words. The man on the right wing is an old Latvian farm worker, skillful and quick at his job, and well-fed. We Jews work behind him. Everyone has two rows of weeds to clear. The Dane walks in back of us, cane in hand, constantly driving the Latvian on to greater haste. Consequently, we Jews simply cannot keep up with him, least of all Schweitzer, whom we persuaded with great effort to report for work. Schweitzer is right: it is impossible to work under such conditions. If we don't keep in line with the Latvian, we are beaten and kicked. Obviously the Dane is a pervert. He makes us take our pants down and beats us fiercely with his cane. If somebody screams, he goes on beating him until he stops. It gives him a satanic pleasure to torture us. He knows we are out in the open field and our lives are in his hands. Nobody hears our screams and moans. He has devised a new method now: he approaches us from behind and kicks us in the ass. Since we're working in a bent-over position, we fall forward. "Get up, Jew!" he commands then. "You were laughing at me, weren't you?" he says, constantly hitting you in the face with a thin reed. "No, Herr Rottenführer [corporal], I did not laugh." "Will you stand straight when you talk to me?" he says, standing very close and hitting you in the face with his fist. "You did laugh. Why are you lying?" Now he gives his victim a going-over with his cane so that he screams in pain. "Did you laugh or not?" The tortured man, hoping for relief, admits that he laughed. Now the Dane says, "Why are you lying? I know you didn't laugh. Take your pants down. You lied to me, you swine." He continues beating him without mercy until the man is writhing on the ground in agony. I, too, have gone through this several times.

At noon Schweitzer says he is not returning to work under any circumstances. They can do with him what they like. The Dane's first question when we return to work is, "Where is Schweitzer?"

"He is sick," Hannauer reports. "We shall get him well quickly," Big Willi joins in.

Schweitzer is lying in bed, asleep. Apparently he took a sleeping pill. The two men beat him up, tie a rope to his foot, and drag him behind them through the filth of the farmyard to the watering place. They throw him in. The cold water revives him, and he climbs on all fours out of the water, but again the two beat him like madmen. When we come back from work at night, we find him near the well barely breathing. Rosel Stern, a girl from Nuremberg, nurses him with the few means at her disposal. Hans comes into the stable and sees Rosel is trying to help Franz. The next day the gentlemen from the SS have devised a new torture. Schweitzer, who can barely walk, has to clean the latrine with Rosel. Afterwards, the two are forced to get into the container with excrement, embrace and say that they love each other. The five SS men stand by laughing. A few days later Schweitzer is taken to Riga where he dies of internal injuries.

Late Summer 1943. The summer passes and the hay is harvested early. Wherever the work is hardest and the dust thickest, that's where they put the Jews. We bring in the fresh hay and load it in the barn. No Russian or Latvian works there because it is too dusty. The Latvian drivers also enjoy torturing the Jews. One pitchforkful after the other is lifted without interruption. When I'm working in front I always let half of the load drop; that infuriates them and then they start using the same curses as the SS.

The wheat harvest is easier. We pile the sheaves and load the wagons. For a free man it must be a wonderful job, but here the pleasure is destroyed by the driving and bullying from the fiends. The potato harvest is horrible again. Two harvesting machines are working. As soon as we have gathered the row assigned to us, we immediately have to jump to the other side and do the next row, and this keeps up from morning to evening. The Dane walks behind us and watches that not a single potato is left lying on the ground. He pokes his cane or the toe of his boot into the soft earth and is devilishly pleased when he finds a potato. "Ah, you're sabotaging!" he screams. "For every potato I find you'll get a beating, you swine," and then he makes good his threat. In the evening he likes to make us march back to the farm singing. He himself marches at the head of the column, like a general. Usually we sing "Ich hatt einen Kameraden" [Once I Had a Comrade]. He doesn't know we're all thinking of Schweitzer.

September 1943. It is beginning to get cold. Our shoes have long since worn out; we tie rags around our feet, as we saw the Russians doing. We don't have any warm clothing either, nor gloves for the early sugar beet harvest. In the morning when we get out to the field, it is covered with frost. We tear pieces off our blankets and make gloves out of them. We no longer have any socks, or soap, or razor blades. We look like wasted derelicts, neglected.

Only now do we learn from the Dutchmen that Italy has surrendered a long time ago. We hear the English are fighting in Sicily. Who should have told us? The Russians, too, have had no contact with the outside world, so that we no longer know about political events. "In six months you'll all go home," the Dutchmen say. Suddenly the Dane disappears. Mrs. Shapiro overheard some talk in the main building. The Dane was thrown out of the SS because he is a homosexual. That is no news to us.

There is less work, the harvest is finished, and we hope to return to the ghetto soon. We are now all working in the wood shack, chopping wood for the winter. Tall Hans from Hamburg has had a new idea: every morning at four o'clock he makes two Jews clean out the cowshed before normal working hours start. "After all, you rest while it's dark," he says. Hannauer asks Big Willi to bring some clothes and shoes for us from the Riga ghetto. "You're still covered," says Big Willi and walks on. The Oberscharführer who brought me from Riga has been promoted to Untersturmführer [from sergeant-major to second lieutenant] for his outstanding work in managing the farm. That event is properly toasted in the main building. We all agreed that these men will be able to sit out the war for a long while yet, behind the lines.

November 1943. November and we're still here. It has turned bitter cold, and there is no stove in our chicken house. At night we get so cold under our thin blankets we're afraid to lie down. Everybody has a cold and some have fever, but there are no sick people here at Baloschi — only workers and corpses.

4

Kaiserwald, Latvia

November 1943-Fall 1944

November 1943. In the middle of the month during a labor assignment, Big Willi suddenly announces that in half an hour a car will pick us up. "You and you," he says, pointing to Levi and Shapiro, "you and your wives stay here." We're all glad to escape from this hell, but only because we don't know what lies ahead of us. A truck arrives, a cow is loaded on, and the Jews sit on the sides of the open truck around the cow. "Those," Big Willi says to the driver, "go to the ghetto." He grins so broadly all over his fat face that I suspect right away something is wrong here. "You know where to take the cow." During the drive the cow refuses to behave decently. It is unpleasant to have such a traveling companion. She has diarrhea, Hannauer says.

In Riga, the cow is first delivered to an SS hospital, then the car drives past the Dvina River to the ghetto. We soon reach the Moskauer Strasse. There is no light in the ghetto. We don't see a soul. The ghetto lies dead and deserted. We shudder. There is still a guard at the gate who lets us pass. A few Jews are standing in front of the administration building. They appear to be waiting for something.

"Where do you come from?" asks Leiser, the Ghetto Elder, who has stepped from the building. Hannauer explains the situation to him.

"You continue right on to the Kaiserwald concentration camp," Leiser says.

We ask him to let us spend the night in the ghetto after we have learned the ghetto was cleared on November 2.

"Not a minute longer than necessary," Leiser says. "Shut up," he yells at me. "You'll get clothes and shoes at the camp."

An acquaintance from Hamburg tells me that since the end of October no labor Kommandos have left the ghetto to work outside. On November 2 there was a general roll call. Every Jew had to appear before Krause and give his name, age and his last Kommando. Krause decided with the usual gesture of his thumb: one way meant they had to get into the waiting trucks, the other way they remained on the assembly square.

"Do you know where the transport went?" I asked him.

"You are rather naive," he laughs bitterly. "Well, some go a little sooner, others a little later, but we all go the same way."

A truck with two trailers has arrived. Ten guards, all with rifles over their shoulders, jump off.

"Everybody line up in five rows, on the double," commands the Kolonnenführer. "Keep in line, Yid, so I can see where you're standing!" he screams at one of us. Then he commands, "Attention! Caps off!"

A Hauptscharführer [captain] has stepped out of the administration building. The Kolonnenführer reports 88 Jews ready for transport to Kaiserwald. The Hauptscharführer gives the signal.

"Caps on! Move!" the Kolonnenführer commands. "Get on the trucks, but fast!"

In the meantime it has become dark. After only a short ride the watchtowers loom up, and searchlights illuminate the double barbed wire fence. The whole camp seems daytime-bright. There is the usual "Caps off!" command, and then the complaint of the Kolonnenführer: "That doesn't work well enough yet. We'll first have to practice awhile. This has to go in one move." So we stand for half an hour at the gate of the concentration camp and practice. Then the Kolonnenführer reports to the guard at the gate; he gives the command "Forward march!" and we march past several barbed wire fences inside the camp until we reach the living quarters.

A figure in a blue sailor suit, his Kapo cap at a jaunty angle, appears before us. "Well, then, men," he says, "we don't stand on ceremony here. Hand over whatever you have in valuables, money, personal papers, addresses, pictures, et cetera. Whoever fails to do so will regret it, take it from me. He can reserve his seat in hell already. Did you get that?"

"Yes," we answer.

"Your luggage all goes on one pile. Nobody is to take anything with him, understand?"

"Yes," we answer.

"I didn't get that 'Yes,'" the camp senior says. "I guess you need practice. Do you get me?"

This time our "Yes" is louder.

"Still no good," he says. "If that doesn't improve you can stand here for several hours, without any food. Did you understand that?"

"Yes!" we shout with all our might.

"That's much better. Tomorrow morning we'll go on practicing."

A few other wild-looking characters have appeared on the scene. Their Kapo caps are hanging over one ear; they seem ready to beat us up any minute, but they only form a cordon around us to prevent anyone from escaping. "Now get going into the barracks," a strong-looking guard orders. "Move your asses or I'll do it for you." Everybody jostles and shoves to get to the barracks first because the Kapos are pushing from behind. Before I know what is happening, somebody is frisking me from top to bottom. Until now I've managed to hold on to the picture Mucia gave me as a farewell present in Liepaja and the addresses Rosel gave me. Now I drop everything, for I see the men in front of me are beginning to undress. The stream of people in back constantly presses us forward. "Take your rags off," somebody yells at me. "We'd like to get finished today. Throw everything on the heap over there!"

Only now do I see what is going on here. Close to us is a room with several showers. For a minute we stand under the cold water, then several Jewish doctors command, "Open your buttocks!" Then comes the command, "Get out of here!" and the next lot comes in. The adjoining room is icy cold. Everybody stands around naked, wet, and freezing. Suddenly somebody throws underwear and a shirt at my head, somebody else presses a pair of pants and an old jacket in my hands, a third party hands me a pair of wooden sandals and a pair of baby socks, and I'm outside again, "dressed up like a count," as one Polish Jew says. If it weren't so deadly serious, I could laugh until I cry. An old man is standing in front of me. He is desperately trying to hold up a pair of pants miles too big for him. He could fit into his trousers twice. He could almost wear his jacket as a coat. He asks everybody, "Haver, do you have a piece of string?" Nobody does. I receive a pair of boy's pants. They only reach to my ankles, but at least they fit tightly at the waist. With it I get a brown checked sports jacket which fits tolerably. I can walk quite well on the wooden sandals. At least they're better than my old torn leather shoes.

"Everybody fall in!" comes the order. We are led from the living quarters to another barracks. I read "Office and Labor Kommandos." Somebody takes my personal data: place of birth, nationality, race. Then he issues me a number. Well, I think, what a coincidence: in Liepaja I was No. 579, and here I am No. 13079. Almost the same sum of the digits, and the same 79; that must be a good omen. Although I am not superstitious, I feel reassured by my number. A man has to cling to something.

Everybody who is registered can move on. We are led back to the living quarters. "Hannes, Hannes!" the Kapo leading us yells. "New arrivals for your block." A tall man stands before us, his shirt sleeves rolled up, his blond hair slicked down; he is the prototype of a German. "You certainly picked a fine bunch of clowns, X,[1]" he says to the Kapo leading us. "I don't know where to put all these Easter bunnies," X replies. "By order of the Obersturmbannführer, all the new arrivals are to go to Block One."

Everyone presses after the German into the barracks. He climbs on a bench to call for attention. "Listen to me, listen to me!" he screams above the din in the barracks. People standing near him call out, "Quiet! Quiet! Quiet for the barracks senior!" The blond barracks senior says, "we've had 30 new arrivals. I don't want to find anybody lying on his bunk tonight like a question mark. Otherwise there will be trouble. I appeal to your sense of solidarity."

The yelling starts again. "Who has some bread? Who wants to buy herring? Haver, do you have some butter?"

"How much?" asks another.

"Eighteen marks."

"That's too much. I was just offered butter for 16."

The salesman moves on. "Who wants butter?" we hear him call from the next table.

"Do you sell bread, too?"

"Yes, you can have a quarter pound for 6 marks."

"Six marks for that small piece? You must be crazy. I'll give you 4.50."

"All right. It's a deal." The buyer takes the bread, takes a knife from his pocket and starts to eat. From another pocket he gets a butter dish and starts to butter his bread.

I walk around the barracks looking for friends. At one of the tables I see Honig, whom I last saw in Salaspils. We are glad to see each other. "There is room in my bunk," says Honig. "You can move in with me." I am glad to have found a place to sleep because I am dog-tired. "You look bad," he says, "where have you been all this time?" I tell him what happened to me during the past six months. "That's nothing," says Honig. "The worst is yet to come."

I lie pressed between a doctor from Dunaburg [Dangavpils, Latvia] and Honig, squeezed like a sardine. Since there is no room for our clothes, we roll up our stuff like a parcel and tie our belts around it. The shoes have to be placed in front of the bunks in a straight line. I can hear somebody read the war bulletins from a newspaper. Zhitomir has been attacked. Somebody says the Germans are now really running themselves into the ground. Unfortunately so are we, someone else adds. Then I fall asleep. We are awakened by the bell. "Everybody up! Everybody up!" the barracks service is calling. "Aren't you out yet, you clowns? I guess I have to teach you how." This is the voice of the barracks senior. Everybody gets up as quickly as possible, for anyone found on the bunks is beaten without mercy. Bare-chested, we have to go to the wash-room about fifty yards away. God help you if a Kapo finds you fully dressed in the washroom: your next stop is the sick ward. Most of the men don't wash at all. Honig says it is better to be dirty than to catch pneumonia in the drafty washroom. Therefore, many men wash while on outside work duty. The coffee tastes of saccharin; we drink it from saucers. Only the Kapos have their own mugs.

"Everybody out! Everybody out! Roll call! Roll call!" A minute later the bell sounds. "Stand at attention! Eyes left! Caps off!" the commands ring out. The Rapportführer[2] inspects the ranks with a sideways turn of the head. "Caps on! All labor Kommandos report! All arrivals report to the assembly place at seven o'clock."

It is now almost six o'clock. Dawn is just breaking. At four the bell rings to get us up. It is a very long day, I think. Suddenly Stefan, my friend from Salaspils, stands before me. "Josef, when did you get here?" I tell him that I arrived last night.

"You look bad, Josef. Are you sick?"

"Yes. That cold shower did not agree with me. I think I have a fever."

"I tell you what," says Stefan. "You go to the sick ward right away and ask for a medical excuse, but don't lie down there. Sometimes the whole sick ward is evacuated and you know what happens to the sick people. When you have your excuse come back to my bar-racks, then we'll see."

About 30 people are lined up in front of the sick ward. They are called in groups. A medic takes their temperature; everyone with over 101° is excused from work. In my case the thermometer reads 102°.

"Do you want to stay in the ward?" the medic asks me.

"No," I reply. "Maybe you can give me a few aspirins and I'll feel better." He gives me two tablets and I walk over to Stefan with a note saying that I am to be excused from work for two days. Stefan is a kind soul. Right away he gives me some food; he even has prepared some hot coffee for me.

"When you've finished eating, you can lie down behind the stove. I'll put the screen in front, so the SS don't find you when they come in."

"Who of all the people who went to Salaspils with us is still alive?" I ask him. "Do you remember the march? How they stole your boots and your shaving kit as soon as we arrived, and you always used mine?"

"How well I remember," says Stefan. "But of all those people I believe only you and I are still alive. Loeb was here once," says Stefan, "but he went to Dundangen, and that is supposed to be worse than Salaspils. Usually people come back here like skeletons, and then another car stands ready, and off they go to the Hochwald. I was told they're building barrack parts in Dundangen. The people live in tents with only a little straw on the icy ground. The SS crap into the brook from which the Jews fetch the water for their soup. I'm telling you, Josef, compared to that, Salaspils was a paradise."

In the workroom activity has started; everybody is hammering and banging away. I lie down behind the stove. The warmth feels good, the aspirin takes effect, and soon I'm bathed in perspiration. Stefan comes from time to time and dries me off. I ask him whether he has a job for me in the workroom. "Get well first," he says, "and then we'll see." Outside, the Polish Kapos are overseeing the new arrivals who are ordered to push carts on the double: about 500 yards away from the camp is a large pile of sand, which has to be carted to the camp. Stefan says they want to plant shrubbery here. Obersturmbannführer Sauer struts about among the workers. He is wearing a long grey leather coat, high boots, and spurs. He doesn't say a word to the workers; he only drives on the Polish Kapos with a few words. "If the Jews don't work any better, I can't use you any longer." That is all the incentive the Kapos need. They start hitting about them like mad in order to please their lord and master. It is clear to me that if I have to do this kind of work, I will not live to see the spring. It is impossible to survive under such working conditions. Stefan says when I'm well he may have a job for me in the

interior service. They are looking for roofers. He will talk to Naehte, the chief roofer. Naehte arrives; he is a tall, strong man — at his
first word I can tell he is from Cologne. "Yes, of course, you can
work for me," he says, "as soon as you're well. In my shop you don't
get worked to death; we go slow. Now that it's starting to snow, we
can't do any work anyhow, so we have to find a way to kill time."

At night I watch the labor Kommandos return from work. At the
gate to the barracks the Kolonnenführer tells the guard the number
of inmates. The guard verifies the count, and they march off to the
barracks. A few minutes later trading is in full swing.

The women's camp is separated from the men's by a double
barbed wire fence. Men stand nearby, talking with their wives or girl
friends. Occasionally an inmate throws something to the other side,
although that is strictly forbidden. Skulls painted on the fence warn
anybody not to approach the barrier. Suddenly I see Rosel Sachs
from Liepaja. "Hello, Rosel," I call out, "what are you doing here?"
Rosel is not surprised to see me; she says she has been waiting for
me. "Where is Mucia?" I ask.

"Mucia was sent to work at the A.E.G.[3] like almost all the other
young girls. I am the only one left here from Liepaja."

"Where are Mrs. Feivelsohn and her two children?"

"They were taken away only two days after our arrival here, as
well as all the older people. I'm sure you remember crazy Sophie
who lived opposite you; she is gone too." I wonder whether, in the
end, Mrs. Feivelsohn dressed her children in their best and warmest
clothes.

"Josef," Rosel says, "you know some Sundays you get permission
to visit the women's camp for two hours. Will you come and see me
then? Jacob comes, too; he is a political prisoner, you must meet
him." Rosel tells me she is in the back part of Barracks Three. Then
the bell rings for roll call. Quickly everybody takes his place in the
five lines. Only the Rapportführer keeps us waiting. When he comes
he says to X, "What kind of a lousy line-up is this? You better practice this tonight for a few hours." Roll call is quickly over. "Every-

body stay in line," is the order. Several names are read out. All those called have to report to the office in the morning.

"People who try to go on the labor Kommando instead are going to be very sorry," says Schlueter, the office clerk. "Everybody move."

The whistle blows again, three times. "Everybody fall in quickly! March, march! Aren't you in line yet, you clowns? This has to go faster, and what kind of a line is that? One can see you didn't serve in the Prussian Army." Fall in, fall out, for the next two hours. It is almost nine o'clock when we're finally permitted to go to the barracks to grab some bread. I am assigned to Table No. 2. There is one loaf of bread for every four men. Everybody watches carefully to see that it is divided fairly. At the next table a noisy fight has broken out. One claims the bread was not sliced equally. Sometimes there is a spoonful of thin marmalade as a spread. At table we discuss the probable fate of those called up to report to the office in the morning. The pessimists say they will certainly be taken to Dundangen; others say they're only forming a new labor Kommando. From our table, too, one man was called up; he says he doesn't care anymore. Whichever way it goes, we're all finished anyhow.

In a corner in the back somebody starts singing a slow march. "Think not that you tread the final road. . . ." [4]

"To bed! To bed! Everybody go to sleep!" the block senior calls out. "Into the sack, you deadbeats."

"Foot inspection," somebody calls a few minutes later. It is the block senior. Everybody sticks their feet out of the bunks. "I want to check whether your sweaty dogs are clean." Many people now start washing their feet with saliva. Those found with dirty feet are driven out of the bunk and have to run barefoot over the assembly square to the washroom to wash their feet. The whole thing is a madhouse.

December 1943. Early one morning a truck arrives with 50 almost totally starved people. Most of them can no longer even walk; they are carried by the medics to the sick ward. The others stagger on the same path leaning on the arms of friends. The truck drives off with the 50 people called up yesterday. The pessimists were right. I now have an opportunity to look around the camp a little. I am feeling much better physically, if only it weren't for the damned hunger. Stefan tells me that sometimes they need men to carry potatoes from the outer barbed wire fence to the kitchen. This job offers a good chance for "organizing." At noon I arrive in the workshop with my pockets full of potatoes. Stefan bakes them for me quickly in the oven's firebox, so the SS won't find them when they come in. With my stomach full, the world looks quite different.

The Kaiserwald concentration camp is a very small place. It has only three men's and three women's barracks, a joint sick ward and a clothing chamber which has a tailor shop attached to it. The workshops are situated beyond the fence. They include a carpenter shop, a smithy, and a small workroom for the radio mechanics. Then there are the roofers whom I will join the next day. Also beyond the fence is a room where electrical appliances are disassembled into their original components for future re-use by the Wehrmacht [German army]. Most of the workers there are women. The women's camp contains a laundry and the kitchen. This is all of Camp Kaiserwald in which there are about 5,000 Jews.

Naehte, the chief roofer, reports to Labor Kommando Leader Schlueter that he has engaged another man. He gives my name and number; now I am a roofer.

Altogether we are five men — Naehte, his son Alfred Erich Pisk from Vienna, Manne Stern from Stuttgart and myself. We're all sitting around the tar-stove, because it is very cold early in the morning. Naehte says we can't go on like this. We need a shelter for the winter, or else the work on the roof is going to kill us. Manne says he saw some old barracks parts outside the camp which we could use to build a shelter behind the clothing chamber; it would be the most protected spot. We're all for the idea. Somebody suggests getting permission. But Naehte says, "Ask a silly question, get a silly answer. We'll just go ahead, they can't do more than tear it down again." Naehte reports he needs five roofers to fetch wood for the tar-stove; instead we go and bring the barracks parts into the camp. Soon a small hut is actually set up. We put a pipe through the roof, and one more stove is smoking in Kaiserwald. Although the hut has no door it is protected from the wind and, above all, it is removed from outside view. Now we are warm, though heat does not fill your belly. Naehte tells me and Manne to come with him.

A large number of calves feet have been delivered to the kitchen today; we'll see if we can't grab a few. Naehte gives the impression of a trustworthy working man; no one would believe him capable of "organizing." The head cook, a well-fed heavy prisoner, comes up and asks what we want. "We've orders to see where the rain came through the roof."

"Here," the head cook shows him, "and there."

They walk through the whole big kitchen. Calves feet are lying about everywhere; some of them have already been cleaned. Nobody pays any attention to Manne and me; we walk behind the two men, our eyes expertly on the ceiling. In unobserved moments we quickly shove a few calves feet under our jackets. We're in luck. The cooks are busy with the fires in their stoves, so nobody takes any notice of us. When we're back outside, we each have "organized" three calves feet. Manne even got a cow's foot. The tar-pot is quickly removed from the stove, water is boiled, and the calves feet are cooked. Naehte is an expert. He chops the feet apart and soon a strong soup is brewing. One of us stands guard and when an unwelcome visitor appears we quickly remove the soup pot from the stove and hide it in a hole especially dug out for this purpose. The tar-pot is quickly put back on again, and soon the smell of tar once more permeates the air.

Everybody in the camp is very surprised when Haar, the former police chief of the ghetto, turns up at Kaiserwald. All the other big shots quickly picked a good "outside camp"[5] when the ghetto was liquidated. Although these outside camps are run by the same authorities as the concentration camps, conditions are considerably easier there. Ghetto Elder Leiser and several other leading figures are stationed at the Lenta labor camp. Mainly artisans are living there; working conditions are good, and the commandant is called the "King of the Jews." Some claim the commandant himself is a Jew, but others say the Jews are so well treated there because they're rich and can afford to grease the commander's palm copiously. Schulz, the head of the ghetto Arbeitsamt, for whom many are waiting in the concentration camp in order to kill him, is in a camp where army uniforms are sorted and disinfected. All these gentlemen knew how to avoid the concentration camps. Only Haar has shown up and begins to play a fatal role. Apparently he came with a letter of recommendation from Krause because he immediately gets an armband "Camp Arbeitsamt." When Manne slowly crosses the assembly square, Haar jumps at him and asks him why he is hanging around here. "March off to work immediately!" he commands. Manne returns to the hut very angry, cursing Haar, and saying that all we needed was this swine.

Mr. X, formerly the Kolonnenführer of an Aussenkommando, is now in charge of the "interior service." Several interesting rumors are being spread about him. At the camp he is registered as a dangerous criminal and has to wear a black triangle. It is said that he was a professional car thief who already spent six years in concentration camps. He came to Riga via Buchenwald and Dachau and was made Kolonnenführer because of his outstanding achievements in killing Jews. In his Kommando, he threw the weaker Jews into the water, and when they came up again, he kept pushing them under with a board until they finally drowned. I'm told he played this game several times a week. Mr. X and Mr. Haar are now colleagues, but they don't get along too well. X considers Haar an unwelcome rival. When Haar bosses people around and shows off in camp, X feels outranked. One night the big shots of the camp throw a booze party, with liquor provided by middlemen through the Aussenkommandos. Everybody is having a high old time in the camp senior's quarters. Haar is also there. In the middle of the night, Haar and X go to the latrine together, but only X returns. The next day we hear that Haar "fell into the latrine" and was drowned.

X has human qualities and feelings, too. He loves pretty young Jewish girls. It is an open secret at camp that little Sonia from Block 2 is X's girl friend. She flutters about the women's camp in a light dirndl dress primping and adorning herself at leisure. She doesn't have to go on Aussenkommandos — X sees to that. But X does not stay long with any one girl. He takes one to his room today and another one tomorrow. The girls feel happy in the powerful arms of this Nero; they live for the day because nobody knows how long they've got to live anyhow. They take what they can get, even if the man's name is X and he murders people daily. Of course, X takes care that his little turtle doves do not lack for food — after all, the head cook is his best friend. Besides X, the camp senior is also in a position of power. He cannot possibly have been as well off when he was free as he is now in the concentration camp. There is no limit to the delights he is now enjoying. The rich Jews, all of whom he knows, pay him their tribute; thanks to his helpful informers, he has something on all of them. Woe to him who does not play ball and fails to come across with two pounds of butter or several cartons of cigarettes. Quite by accident, he will disappear to Dundangen. In the morning the camp senior usually takes a walk in the assembly square. With his arms crossed behind his back, his boots polished to a brilliant shine, his cheeks smoothly shaven, he struts about in his kingdom like a little emperor. The care of his physical well-being is in the hands of a servant who also does the heavy cleaning in the camp senior's room. He himself has no other occupation than to parade his powerful figure in the camp. Every now and then he punches someone in the face as a kind of morning exercise. From time to time he visits the clothing chamber and takes his pick of the clothes confiscated from the Jews.

One day he pays a visit to us in our roofer's hut. Nobody is stand-ing guard so we don't hear him coming. As if by accident, he tips over the soup pot on the stove with one hand, and he distributes lightning quick blows with the other. Most of them miss because Manne and I disappear immediately, but I still catch a kick in the pants. Then he continues his inspection tour, tipping his Kapo cap and bowing to the ground before every SS man. Standing at attention he receives daily orders from the SS, which he relays to the Jews through his subordinates X or Hannes, the blond German. Hannes, the senior of Barracks One, is not quite so brutal. Some say he is in camp for procuring; others claim he committed a bank robbery in Hamburg. The first suggestion seems more likely to me. His entire bearing and behavior is that of a Hamburg pimp. The last in this roster of dignitaries is Schlueter from the camp registry, of whom it is known beyond a doubt that he was a cat burglar and bank robber. Those are the principal figures entrusted with managing the Jewish prisoners. While there are a few subordinate creatures, they only do what the "big four" command.

A commendable exception is Jacob. I meet him one Sunday afternoon at Rosel's. He is likeable, intelligent and imbued with Marxist ideology. Jacob is the only real political prisoner in the camp. We soon start a conversation. He tells me he spent the past ten years in various camps, but all this time has not changed his political convictions; for him, all people are equal. "But you Jews have no pride left, you are all brown-nosers and toadies. You know, when I walk through the camp everybody steps aside for me. They holler, 'Make way for Jacob!' Nobody did a thing like that before. When a Kapo walked through the barracks, nobody made way for him. I don't like this servility — that's why I can't stand the Jews."

I try to explain that Jews have been degraded and enslaved throughout their history and five thousand years of oppression have left their mark.

"Anyhow," he continues, "you've caused all your misfortune yourselves. Why do you persist in raising your children in the Jewish faith? If your child and mine went to the same school and all religion were left aside, because it is nothing but nonsense anyhow, the Jewish problem would soon be solved, as it's been in Russia. Don't you think so too?" he asks me.

"No," I reply. "I can't imagine that Judaism is just a matter of education. I believe that specifically Jewish traits will develop in any Jewish child even if he's educated together with the others."

We cannot agree, but we become friends. In the end Jacob says to me: "Keep going just a little longer, my boy. Soon you'll see the Red Flag flying over Berlin and maybe then you'll find out what I'm saying is true."

Christmas 1943. We get half a day off at camp. Besides, we have a feast of sausages and potato salad. Yesterday they evacuated the sick ward again. Approximately 60 Jews went to their death. Today, the camp senior says he wants to hear music; it is Christmas and we should all be merry. On the assembly square a small band is playing all sorts of makeshift instruments. In any case a few men make a tremendous racket. The camp senior has all the Jews driven from their barracks: "Everybody listen to me!" he commands. Then he sings:

> "What more do I need than that you're mine?
> You're my only desire, my little girl.
> A room with a roof, and a girl like you,
> That would be wonderful, and I would have peace.
> What more do I need . . . "

Moshele from the third barracks always joins the refrain. Afterwards he sings one of his own compositions:

> "O Gott in himmel, hob rachmones
> Mit die Yiden in Kaiserwald
> Man shlugt un shlugt un newt karbones . . ."

[O God in heaven, have mercy
On the Jews in Kaiserwald.
They beat us and beat us
And we've lost so many lives . . .]

None of us feels like singing, but the half-drunk camp senior is having a ball.

January 1944. Large quantities of barley flour with husks and all sorts of other inedible additives have been dumped at the camp. This mess is served in many variations. Sometimes we get it as soup, other times as gruel, or even fried. It tastes bad, but contains some nourishment so we eat it, although reluctantly. Whenever we are very hungry, we cook some of the stuff from our own provisions. The sacks are stored very close to a window. One morning a window pane was broken while we were on the way to our hut. Now we have a supply of about 50 pounds. We won't be so very badly off this winter any more.

We have also "organized" a hundred-pound sack of potatoes. One Sunday afternoon I am in our hut with Alfred Naehte, the chief roofer; we are just about to wash ourselves thoroughly when the door opens and Hauptscharführer Platterspiel, a very nasty character, stands before us.

"Well, you sons of bitches," he says, "what are you doing outside the barracks on a Sunday afternoon? Get going over there, behind the kitchen; they're unloading potatoes. That's a more useful occupation for you."

Scantily dressed, we run outside to go to work. Bolek, a Polish prisoner who has been demoted from Kapo to plain inmate for theft in the clothing chamber, is busily shoveling potatoes. We know him well because he sometimes comes into our hut to get warm. We quickly come to an agreement. "Take as much as you can carry," he says, and that's the end of the affair for him. We quickly grab a sack, fill it to the brim and hurry off. In back of the hut we hastily dig a hole for our loot. Now for the next four weeks, we have potatoes, and the best ones, too, intended for the SS.

The carpenters have built new officers' quarters in front of the camp. We get the order to roof them as quickly as possible. But it is bitter cold, and you can't stay on the roof for longer than half an hour at a time. In addition, the tar paper is frozen and breaks easily. We know exactly at what time the commandant arrives in his six-cylinder Horch. When he comes, we're always busy working. As soon as he has disappeared from sight, we stop. In the hut, warm broth, made from calves feet that are still being delivered in bulk to the camp, awaits us. In a relatively short time we have finished roofing the officers' quarters, but only eight days later our chief, Naehte, is called to Commandant Sauer. "Here," Sauer says, pointing to his desk. "This is your lousy workmanship, you goddamn bastard," and he shows Naehte exactly where rainwater sits on his desk. Naehte tries to give the bad weather and the poor tar paper as excuses. "If you don't fix the roof properly, you'll wish you were dead, you old bonehead." Naehte is rather upset when he returns from the commandant and reports his interview to us. One clear day we do the roof over the commandant's room once more, and with that the matter is finished.

In the meantime I have formed several friendships in the camp. Little Rivka from Vilna works in the shoe department of the clothing room. I often go to her room to have her show me where the rain came through. We start a conversation, and she tells me about her father, who was a rabbi. He is no longer alive. Right away, when the Germans came, they took him off. Now she is here with her mama. At the end of our conversation she fails to notice that a pair of very beautiful boots accompany me out the door.

Large transports of Jews from the vicinity of Reval arrive at the camp. They have brought all their luggage, but everything is taken away from them. The men have to strip down to their underpants outdoors; later, they are thoroughly searched in the washroom for valuables. After that, they are given prison clothes. There is talk that within a short time all inmates will be issued prison clothes. So far we have only worn our numbers and a large Star of David on the front and back; the side seams of our pants are marked with white oil paint. The newly arrived Jews must have brought a lot of gold and valuables with them because I see them trying to bury pieces of gold in the sand. We take our largest ladder and place it against the barracks nearest the Jews, but we can't get close enough; the barracks are too closely guarded. When they're all dressed, we see an SS man with a rake working over the ground where they were standing. Every now and then he bends down — quite a profitable treasure hunt, no doubt. We hear that the Oberscharführer from the clothing chamber has been arrested for stealing some of the valuables. Later he is transferred. His place is taken by Oberscharführer Hirsch, a particularly brutal and vicious man.

The two radio technicians always come to bring us the latest political news. They listen to Moscow and we are informed about everything. The high command of the Wehrmacht keeps talking of successful "defensive action" in the vicinity of Leningrad, while the Russians say that this city has already been secured. One thing we know for sure: the Russians are advancing relentlessly. We often wonder whether we will live to see them marching into Riga. We are all quite pessimistic on this point. The Germans would have to be defeated very soon.

Some mornings I see a young Jewish girl of about eighteen going out on a labor Kommando by herself. I learn that this girl, who is from Cologne, is looking after Sauer's flat in Kaiserwald. Manne knows her. When he talks to her, I stand there and listen. She says Sauer is always very nice to her. Whenever she works in his place, he turns on the radio for her and shows her pictures of his children which he receives from Germany. "Sauer is really a good person," says the girl. Manne does not tell her differently.

In the dismantling center of the camp several children, mainly girls, are working. They all look considerably older than their age. Rosel Sachs from Liepaja has a younger sister of ten who wears extra long dresses and stuffs her breasts in order to look like a grown-up because the children at camp live in constant danger. Those still alive have successfully hidden out during the past Kinderaktionen [mass deportations and killing of children]. There is a small boy at Kaiserwald whom the SS call Itzig. It is said he managed to hide three times already. Many say X always protects him. The SS men play with him, they show him a loaf of bread, and when the small hands of the six-year-old try to grab it, they quickly withdraw the bread. In our barracks, too, there is a little boy with his father. The boy always goes along on the labor Kommandos so that he is not in the camp during the day. This has saved him several times.

The cold season has claimed many victims from among us. Many Jews who have to work outdoors all day long suffer from frostbite on their hands and feet. On top of that there is the increasing infestation of lice in the barracks. The lice get into the bandages and the frostbites become infected. It is disgusting to see the lice run around on the open wounds.

February 1944. We have very little work. Every day we walk on the roof of one of the barracks in order to be seen. Sometimes we sweep the snow from the roofs because it is impossible to work up there in this wet weather. Manne returns from one of his walks and says a Kommando has just returned to camp and he recognized Einstein in the car. About 30 Jews are standing in front of the registry, among them Einstein. We know we've been waiting for him for a long time. Many people have had memories of him from Salaspils. A few minutes later the camp senior walks toward the Jews, and stops in front of Einstein. "You are Einstein," he asks him, "aren't you? You once were camp senior somewhere, isn't that right?"

Einstein puffs himself up. "Yessir! I was camp senior at Salaspils."

"How many people did you have in your command?" the camp senior continues the conversation in a most jovial manner.

"That varied," Einstein replies.

It seems to me as if the camp senior has been waiting for just such a reply. Like a boxer he rushes at Einstein and shouts, "I'm sure it varied, you bastard, when you allowed all those people to starve! And you, swine, are still alive and fat like a pig." Several well-aimed left and right hooks land in Einstein's face. He falls down and is carried away by others. But that isn't the end of the story.

That evening the camp senior calls for Einstein. We hear later that he hands him a piece of rope and tells him he doesn't wish to see him alive the next morning. When Einstein returns to his block, several Jews attack him like furies, and he gets knocked senseless the second time that day. The next morning Einstein is still alive. X tells Hannes, the German, "You take this one into your Kommando." Eyewitnesses later report Einstein had to do hard labor until noon, when he received the order from Hannes to go and fetch something from the back. He was shot by a guard "while trying to escape." The head cook from Salaspils does not fare much better. Wherever he goes, he is beaten black and blue. As soon as he arrives at Kaiserwald, he is sent to Dundangen where he is said to have hanged himself. It seems to be true after all: justice prevails in the end.

Erich Pisk, from Vienna, has noticed how women in the laundry raise the skylight and hide clothing underneath. Since Naehte says that people working in the laundry always have a chance to get hold of more clothes, we decide to "organize" the laundry that is hidden under the roof. Instead of repairing the roof, we loosen a few boards so one man can creep through. He hands a whole basket full of laundry up to us. We don't know what to do with it since we are exposed to many observing glances up on the roof. We quickly get a tar bucket, lined with clean paper. The five of us got hold of a change of underwear each and several towels.

Every four weeks one of the blocks is given new underwear. Everybody has to take a bath first then the underwear is exchanged in the washroom. One day I act as Kolonnenführer and take the men to the women's section where the washrooms are. Without thinking, and being in a great hurry, I report to the guard as I march into the women's section: "Thirty men for washing."

"What, men?" he asks. "What do you mean?"

"Thirty Jews for washing," I correct myself.

"O.K., get going," he says.

After the bath the blond German announces that 50 extra sets of underwear have been issued; some people must have received double supplies. If the underwear is not returned by ten o'clock, there will be trouble. Nobody returns any underwear. Suddenly, at ten o'clock, Polish inmates storm the front and back doors of our barracks armed with canes and truncheons.

"Out of your bunks!" they shout, hitting everyone within reach.

At the exit the bodies pile up into mountains. I barely manage to jump out a window.

"Roll call! Everybody line up for roll call!" the order goes out.

During roll call bunks in the whole block are being searched by the Poles, who take whatever they can use. After roll call the fight continues in the assembly square. Several Poles try to drive some of the Jews into a corner so they cannot get away. Those bastards have developed great skill in this maneuver. The next morning there are several dead — badly wounded men who are taken to the sick ward.

March 1944. The German high command announces the German army is engaged in fierce defensive fighting near Smolensk against a foe superior in numbers and materiel. We see on our map that the Russian troops are advancing on all fronts. Beyond Kiev, which the Russians say they have retaken, they have crossed the former Polish border. These events make their influence felt on our situation. All the Jews in the Aussenkommandos are given prison clothes. We are given more and more work. A large number of Jews are now occupied day and night at the harbor unloading ammunition. When they return to the camp, they tell us large numbers of German troops are being shipped out. Big transports of heavy munitions are being unloaded in Riga. It seems as if the Germans are concentrating a strong force on the Leningrad front in order to stop the enemy from pressing forward from the east. Honig says that only six months ago he asked a German soldier where the materiel the Jews were loading was supposed to go. "It goes to Leningrad," was the reply. German troop transport trains stood at the Riga railroad station with signs, "On to Leningrad." But they never got that far. Late in March the German radio announces the Russians have entered Kowel; a few days later they say Kiev has capitulated. It really looks as if only the Baltic front is still holding out, although severe fighting has been reported from Lake Peipus. These battles, we think, will determine our fate.

Schlueter from the Arbeitsamt comes to our hut and says he needs two roofers immediately. Pisk and I happen to be on hand, so we follow him to the waiting car. We ride through beautiful Kaiserwald to the small seaside resort of Wilcaki. We greatly enjoy the scenery, the warm spring weather and the blue Baltic Sea which make us think of some wonderful vacation days. When we arrive at our destination, the officer in charge asks us whether we brought any materiel with us. We only have the order to make a few small repairs. Materiel is the responsibility of his military unit. He says he has to make a telephone call about this. Meanwhile, our car has returned to Riga with the order to come for us that night. The officer returns and says the material may arrive the next day. "Why don't you look around the neighborhood a little? But be sure you don't try to run away!" We promise him we won't. So we walk through the seaside resort, exchanging a few words with the natives. Some bring us eggs and bread without our having said anything. Others give us pieces of bacon. We eat and drink well. In the evening the car comes and takes us back to Kaiserwald. This goes on for several days without our lifting a finger. Apparently the place where the roof is to be repaired is the outside branch of the Communication Center, a two-story building. We've made friends with the officer. He is from Vienna. He never had anything against the Jews, he says. They never harmed him, and that's why he can't treat them badly now.

Finally, after eight days, the tar paper and two pounds of nails arrive. The small villa-like house has an old shingle roof. Every half hour or so we hammer in a nail so the officer can hear us working. The rest of the time we lie in the warm spring sunshine and get baked. I haven't had such a good time in years. Fortunately, the officer is afraid to climb the long ladder to the roof. Another eight days later he asks us whether the roof is going to be finished soon; he has a few other roofs to be repaired. He winks at us, as if he knew exactly what we're up to. Yes, I tell him, we're going to finish the villa in the next few days. After all, he must realize that with the food we get we cannot work so fast. We understand each other. Altogether, we spend about four weeks loafing around on the two little houses in Wilcaki. It is a very peaceful time, without the excitement of the camp. When we're finished, we say goodbye to our officer. He says, "Good luck, boys. I did what I could for you."

April 1944. Conditions at Kaiserwald are getting worse by the week. As soon as the Kommandos return from their "outside" jobs at night, they are put to work again inside the camp, carrying rocks or pushing carts on the run for the planned nursery section. Horn, the chief gardener of the ghetto, also has begun a small garden on an empty square behind the camp. For his project the camp has given him 20 female German prisoners, all morally depraved human beings. Horn says he cannot work with them because they do not take orders from a Jew. Every now and then Sauer appears and complains the work in the nursery is not progressing, but Horn says that whores make poor gardeners.

When darkness falls, work at the camp is finished. Everybody rushes to the barracks after roll call to devour his piece of bread. Exhausted, we soon fall asleep in our bunks, despite the bugs and lice.

More and more new transports arrive at camp. About 800 Jews have arrived from Vilna. They all have a lot of linen, bedding and other equipment with them. It is all confiscated at their entrance into camp. The men are standing in front of the office in their underpants while the women have already been dressed in prison garb.

Manne says we should try and see whether the guard at the gate won't let us go to our hut to work. Really, we're in luck. Soon we can mingle with the porters who are busy carrying off the luggage of the new arrivals. We are escorted to the clothing room by an SS guard. He remains standing outside the door to watch the Jews working until we return with the empty stretcher. The room in the clothing chamber has a window which the SS cannot see. Manne is standing there, waiting, while I continue carrying stuff with Erich Pisk. He takes all the loot we hurriedly hand him through the window and carries it to our hut. The knapsacks contain about 20 loaves of bread and much clothing. During the next few days we are no longer hungry.

Another time we place our roofer's ladder against the wall of the clothing room where the belongings of the new arrivals are being stored. Rivka, my girl friend from the shoe department, works there. She hands me two sheets. I don't know where to put them in my haste, so I quickly shove them under my jacket and climb up on the roof. Suddenly a guard from the watchtower calls to me and asks what I'm hiding under my jacket.

"Nothing," I reply.

"There is something white showing under your jacket," he shouts. "Wait till I get my hands on you."

I dash down from the roof and to the hut where I hide the stuff. Sure enough, half an hour later an SS comes from the office and searches our hut, throwing everything into a heap. He turns every tar-pot upside down, but of course he finds nothing, because we have dug a hole where we have hidden all the forbidden articles.

Cursing and shaking his fist at us, he finally leaves, after I've told him it must have been a mistake. "We can't trust you bastards," he says.

Meanwhile, the Russian advance continues steadily. They have long since crossed the Latvian border. It is only a matter of time until they reach the gates of Riga. What will happen then? We keep asking this question half anxiously, half joyously. Only dreamers believe we will be left in the care of the enemy. It seems unthinkable to me and to most of the Jews here that the Russians will force their way into the camp. Some think if there is enough time the Germans will transport us to camps inside Germany proper. But most believe that we will share the fate of the vast majority of Jews in the past few years — unless something unforeseen happens, like a German revolution, which would mean our salvation. I have the secret hope that with the approach of the Russians, a panic might break out and perhaps in the surprise and confusion we'll have a chance to escape. With this thought in mind, I look forward to the future. There are always the pessimists who say that five minutes before their final doom, the Nazis will finish us off. "Or do you really believe," one Polish Jew asks during a discussion, "they're going to let us live to testify against them?"

He is right, I think, because already they are beginning to destroy the traces of the mass graves in Riga. Frequently special Kommandos of ten Jews are picked up by the Security Service. Nobody knows where they're going and what they're doing. Only one thing is sure: their numbers are struck off the register. Rumors which later prove correct report that these Jews have to reopen the mass graves of murdered Jews to burn the corpses which are already half decayed. While they do this work the Jews are chained together. We also learn this command is under the Untersturmführer Roschmann from Vienna and that it is registered under file number 105. All the Jews in camp are very depressed, wondering when his turn will come. Usually, during line-up, the Rapportführer tells a prisoner in the first row to pick a row. Then the SS guards start counting off ten Jews from the row chosen and lead them to the office. One day this misfortune strikes a watchmaker. He and his haverim know exactly what's in store for them. He still has a gold watch. When X happens to walk by, the Jew asks him if he would let him stay in return for his gold watch. X leads him behind the office and beats him up; he then confiscates his watch and makes him join the other men, some of whom are crying. The Security Service car arrives, the men are chained together and driven off, never to return.

All my thoughts are occupied with plans to escape from this living hell. Once again Stefan comes to my rescue. He says he has learned from Arbeitsamt leader Schlueter the H.K.P.[6] is looking for a gardener. That same evening Schlueter hollers, "All gardeners step forward!" He writes down my number, and the next morning I am called up with two others. We are given prison clothes. Soon a car is taking us over the Dvina bridge in the direction of the Riga airport and from there to Spilva. A large iron gate opens before us and when we jump out of the car, Platterspiel stands before us with a letter in his hand. He is the same officer who sent Alfred Naehte and me to shovel potatoes from our hut. "Who is the gardener here?" he yells at us. My heart hammering, I step forward. Platterspiel waves me on with his arm and a load is off my chest. He did not recognize me as the roofer. "Those three go to H.K.P.!" he tells the guard standing beside him. The other camp is close by. We are immediately told to change back into civilian clothes. The camp senior, Wolf, is a beefy, middle-aged man who tells me right after our arrival that he doesn't know what a gardener is doing in a repair garage. In the evening, Platterspiel, who is in charge of this camp, too, appears for roll call and instructs Wolf the gardener is to remain in camp at his service. I feel very uneasy because I am no expert in this profession. But there is nothing to be done except wait and see what the Hauptscharführer intends to do with me. For the next few days I walk around the camp. It is very quiet here during the day except for the 600 Jews who are at work in the garage repairing automobiles. A non-commissioned Wehrmacht officer is in charge of the camp. He leads a very lazy life. Morning and night he has the camp senior report to him, and every now and then he complains about the dirt in the factory which has been converted into sleeping quarters. After roll call he usually goes back to his room to sleep. In this camp there is a famous physician from Riga, a Professor Minsk, of whom it is said he operated on the Tsar and also on Lenin. Unfortunately I haven't had a chance to talk to him as yet.

A few days after my arrival at Spilva a guard appears, by order of Platterspiel, to get the gardener. I quickly grab my lunch sack which is the only luggage we were permitted to take from camp and follow him to the street. In the other camp a woman working in the office tells me to report the next morning for work at the airport. She knows nothing about a gardening job. I march out to the airfield the next morning along with an endless column of others. Airplanes taking off from time to time make the monotonous work of loading the trucks a little more interesting. Everything else at the airfield is very unpleasant. Three men are busy with one truck and all day long we hear, "Hurry! Hurry! Hurry!" The whole thing has nothing whatever to do with gardening. The foreman, who is in O.T.[7] uniform, gives the command for the truck to move. He swears, shouts and beats us up if the trucks don't look full enough to him. After all this strenuous work we go without food at lunchtime. The O.T. foreman says he just has to build the runways — nothing else concerns him. Since we have no food, we lie down in the midday sun and sleep. We go on working like this for several days from seven in the morning until seven at night. The Germans are in a great hurry.

When we return to camp at night the place is crowded with Jewish women and girls. They look awful — without hair and wearing long grey dresses that hang down to the ground. About 2,000 of them have arrived to work on the airfield. I approach one of the groups.

"Where do you come from?"

"From Hungary."

"How long have you been traveling?"

"For two weeks. We were in Auschwitz. We were locked in a barracks for two days. They took away our fathers and mothers, and our little brothers and sisters. We went through selection and then we traveled for two days and two nights without food or drink. We froze because we had no other clothes except these rags, no underwear. They gave us nothing in Auschwitz. What is to become of us now?" they ask us.

"Everything is going to be all right," we try to comfort them. One man asks how long they have been in camps so far.

"Three weeks," is the reply.

I find it inconceivable that only three weeks ago these dejected, haggard women were free people. Crowded together, they have been put up in one of the large beer halls; some straw has been spread on the floor. We try to help where we can; one gives a pair of stockings, another finds a shawl among his things. It is dreadful to see these pretty young girls, who look so obviously Hungarian, shorn of all their hair. When they drape a shawl around their heads, they look a little more human right away. I see six sisters standing together, one prettier than the other. They start singing. It is a song from their home in the Carpathian Mountains. A large circle is forming around them, a circle of weeping despairing young Jews.

A long column marches to the airfield the next morning. We are taken off on the trucks and ordered to lay down metal strips, the Hungarian girls are put in our place. Free people only three weeks ago, they now stand on the airfield to fill the trucks with gravel. The women don't know how to hold the shovels. They aren't used to this kind of work. So there is screaming and yelling from the O.T. guards. It is bad enough when they torture us men, but what they do to the women is much, much worse. I, for my part, am resigned to this life, but the treatment of our women makes me realize how completely hopeless our situation is. How dehumanizing and cruel to beat these young girls who later huddle together, sobbing, not knowing what to do.

There are only a few days of this. Then one evening there is a call for general assembly. Several trucks have arrived. Five hundred women are picked out at random. Sisters are ruthlessly separated from each other; they are driven onto the trucks, and a short time later these girls are no longer among the living. This is repeated several nights in a row. All the Hungarian women are liquidated. Apparently, they were not fit for the work on the airfield.

Several times I have gone to see the Jewish woman in the office and asked her to talk to Platterspiel about my problem because there must be some error. The woman, who is very nice, promises to help. Then life continues in the same old way. Out to work early in the morning and back to camp late at night. Every evening they serve a broth of chicken feed and 300 grams of bread, occasionally a little marmalade or margarine as a supplementary ration for hard labor. That is our entire daily ration. But sanitary conditions are a little better in this camp. One frequently has the opportunity to take a warm or cold shower.

Then one night I am called to the office and told I will return to the H.K.P. the next day. The plans of the Hauptscharführer did not materialize.

Living conditions at the H.K.P. are considerably better. This camp is located in what was once a leather factory. There is even a small meadow within the confines of the fence where we have a chance to lie in the sun and rest on a Sunday afternoon. The harsh, military tone I experienced in Kaiserwald during the past few weeks is missing. Only Jews are here. There are no German prisoners as our foremen. When I enter the camp, Wolf says he has now found a job for me. The following day work is to begin at the army plant nursery for five Jewish women, me and one other gardener.

The next morning a truck arrives from the H.K.P. Kommando to pick up about fifty Jews and the seven of us who are to work in the nursery. A few have only a very short ride to their place of work. Others are taken to the H.K.P. repair. Then the seven of us are driven to the nursery, which is small and has a few greenhouses, where a Latvian gardener is at work. The non-commissioned officer in charge of the nursery assigns me to plant flower beds, a really enjoyable job. Working conditions are good, nobody is pushing, and I have the feeling that one could exist here. The other gardener is busy digging a field, while the Jewish women set out lettuce and cabbage plants.

May, 1944. Unfortunately things don't remain like this for long. Due to the worsening political situation and the continuing military reverses, our supervision has been increased. Almost every worker now has his own guard keeping an eye on him continuously. Sometimes I work with a soldier from the Sudetenland and we chat a little about politics. He seems particularly well acquainted with Die Stürmer,[8] but strangely enough that doesn't keep us from having some fun together at times. One day he tells me he read in Die Stürmer that the Jews are always the last to fight in a war so they can be the first to return home. I can't help breaking up with laughter, although I don't really feel like laughing. But then he joins in my amusement. We get along very well. He always sees me fill my pockets with tomatoes in the greenhouse, but he says nothing, although he knows it is strictly forbidden to take anything from the nursery. He also helps me to set out cucumbers.

"Tell me," he asks, "what are you going to do with me when the Russians get here?" I am not at all prepared for this question, but it shows me that he is considering this possibility.

"I'm going to let you live," I reply.

"You see," he goes on, "when they get here you're going to be the master and I'm going to be the slave. I'm afraid I'll never see my wife and children again. "

I don't feel sorry for him. Nobody has shown us any pity in the past and nobody gives a damn about us now.

At night, when I return to camp, a long line of Jews is already waiting at my bunk. They all want to buy tomatoes, radishes or lettuce. But it is impossible to bring vegetables for 600 people. One night I meet Professor Minsk in the line. He only has to pay five marks for two beautiful tomatoes; the usual price is six marks. I tell him that I'd like to come to his examining room later in the evening because I am not feeling very well. He starts to examine me; we talk about fertilizer and the raising of fruit trees. He asks me to bring him two tomato plants. He wants to set them out somewhere in the meadow. I see him repeatedly and sometimes we go for walks together, but every time I try to turn the conversation to the subject that interests me most, his operations on the Czar and on Lenin, I get no reply from him. Finally he tells me that posterity will learn about this either directly from him or not at all.

I'm doing very well in this camp. With the profit from the sale of my produce, I buy butter and bread and have enough to eat. But here, too, there is new excitement every day. Two Jews have escaped from the workshop. There are several roll calls that night; the whole countryside is searched, but they are not found. Their Kolonnen-führer is relieved of his command. He is dispatched to Kaiserwald and a few days later it is reported he has been sent on one of the "transports to heaven," because every Kolonnenführer vouches with his own life for the number of Jews under his command.

A few days later several oxygen tanks explode in the workshop. All the Jews working in this department are immediately arrested for sabotage. Kolonnenführer Bierhof is taken along because he tried to excuse the twelve Jews. All are sent to Kaiserwald and from there to their death in the usual manner.

These events hardly touch us anymore. They make gaps in our steadily thinning ranks, but are eclipsed by the undaunted advance of the Russian armies. The Russian radio reports extensive fighting around Dvinsk, about 150 miles from Riga. The German high command gives out bulletins about heavy fighting in Latvia. We have frequent air-raid alarms now, but they are caused only by reconnaissance planes which follow their course high up in the sky and are barely visible.

On our daily trips to work, I notice small signs that indicate our situation has changed. Every day when we pass the works of the A.E.G., I see endless rows of cars lined up in front of the gates. Sometimes we see their trucks, loaded with machinery, driving toward one of the suburban railway stations of Riga. This is the first sign the military and economic leadership is planning the evacuation of Riga. Not only the electricity works are being dismantled, everywhere on our trips through Riga we see moving vans standing in front of the houses. The Germans in the city are busy packing. These visible signs fill us with a grim pleasure. They give us the assurance there will be a change in our lives in the foreseeable future. Our slave existence must come to an end and we shall live, or the years of fighting for survival will have been in vain.

Every day on our return from work we are frisked at one of the camps by Eggers, a noncommissioned officer from Hamburg. He orders everybody off the car, arms held horizontally; then he pats us, one after the other from top to bottom. He is particularly keen on girls and women. He enjoys fingering them thoroughly and intimately. Eggers is in charge of about 80 Jews who are housed in barracks on this work site. Many trained car mechanics and engineers are employed there. So far, they tell us, Eggers has treated them with relative decency. But now he constantly tries to blackmail them. He knows from the Latvian Jews that some of them still own some valuables. If he doesn't receive a certain amount of money or several watches by a specified date, he sends ten people to Kaiserwald. And everybody knows what that means. Since our situation is becoming more and more critical, they give him whatever they possess, just so they can remain there and not be sent to Kaiserwald. That means certain death.

June 1944. When we return from work at night, there is a general roll call. An SS physician is coming from Kaiserwald we are told.

Sure enough, half an hour later a smart sports car drives through the gate. An SS officer accompanied by the physician, Untersturmführer Wiesner, gets out of the car parked in front of the guardhouse. Everybody has to line up in blocks on the right side of the assembly square, and to march past the SS officer to the left side of the assembly square. He permits most of the men to pass. Occasionally he says, "Come here!" and motions with his head where the prisoner has to stand. Of our block of 200 men, about 15 are already standing to one side. My heart is in my mouth when I march past him. I only breathe easier when I get to rejoin the majority. We all understand that one move of the head from this all-powerful man means the difference between life and death for us. The Aktion is taking place so quietly that one could imagine it was no more than the forming of a labor Kommando. Forty men have been selected.

Things become even more tense when the women are made to walk the same path for their lives. The SS officer lets the first five women go by. Then an older woman moves slowly past. He motions with his head for her to stand on the side. "Herr Untersturmführer, my only son is in this camp," she says to Wiesner in a clear, strong voice. But the officer only repeats his gesture coldly. Now the woman starts to plead and cry. "Please let me stay here. I've always worked hard, I'm still a strong worker. Please let me stay here." A gesture of Untersturmführer Wiesner has summoned the guard, who drags the woman away. "My son, my son," she whimpers. Her son is standing in one of the lines and does not move. He knows he can't help his mother; he only has the choice to die with her. One after the other the women walk past Untersturmführer Wiesner. Every now and then comes the death-dealing motion which most of them accept with stoic calm. Thirty women and forty men have been selected from among five hundred of us. They stand aside on the assembly square heavily guarded. Everybody else is permitted to fall out. Half an hour later two trucks arrive. Calmly and matter-of-factly, as if it were the most natural thing, the Jews climb into the trucks that take them to their deaths.

A few days later we learn that Linas Hazedek, once the Jewish hospital in the Riga ghetto, has been converted into a crematorium. Some prisoners driving past saw the trucks with the Jews arrive and later others saw the trucks depart empty. We therefore assume the Jews are being gassed and cremated there. Other Kommandos passing by saw whole trucks filled with clothing leave the hospital. We remember that during the period of the ghetto this building was used to disinfect clothes. Apparently it did not require a big change to exterminate Jews there instead of lice.

Beside me in the three-decker military bed lies Sasha Shadchen. Sasha works with me in the nursery. We get along very well; he is a German Jew and comes from Stuttgart. We discuss the events of the previous night. Sasha thinks this will now be repeated every night, and when the Russians reach Riga no Jews will be left among the living. That is the Nazi reaction to the changed war situation. It is quite logical, Sasha says. The closer the Russians get, the faster the Jews will be exterminated. A Latvian worker told me today the Russians are already close to Vilna, and if they succeed in their advance in the direction of Tilsit, this whole territory will soon be encircled. He also said that German transport ships have been sunk in the Gulf of Riga. I don't know whether these stories are true, but this is what I hear. Yet one fact stands out, the A.E.G. has shipped off all its Jews from the Riga railway station today. A worker on the railroad said the transport went to Thorn. So it appears the A.E.G. took its Jews along. This is a good sign for us. It means there is a chance we, too, may be taken back. "Perhaps," Sasha says, "but I have very little hope because these bastards are unpredictable." Then we fall asleep exhausted from the events of the day. In spite of all these worries, our will to live is unbroken. On Sundays one can see the Jews play ball in the little meadow. Teams from the various blocks are fighting for the basketball championship: others are lying in the grass and enjoying the sunshine on this Sunday morning. Professor Minsk's two tomato plants thrive beautifully although he has planted them much too low. I often see the older man standing in front of his shrubs and admiring the many fruits hanging on the vines.

On Sunday nights they usually have a concert in one of the large shops of the factory. There is an old upright piano, badly out of tune, several violins, and even an accordion the Jews have salvaged. The small orchestra is made up of former professional musicians. They play Beethoven, Haydn, Mozart, Rimsky-Korsakov and other modern Russian compositions. These concerts are always overcrowded. Everybody applauds enthusiastically and the worries of the past week seem forgotten. At the end the orchestra plays "Mosiva Mya, Lubimaya" and other Russian songs. Everybody joins in, their eyes shining, for those are the songs of the rapidly advancing Russian armies who one day will perhaps be our liberators.

Sometimes the camp senior protests against the noisy singing. But he is shouted down with the powerful Russian melodies that stir the blood and make the heart beat faster.

July 1944. New rumors are making the rounds in camp. One foreman says the entire works, including all the Jews there, are going to be evacuated to Germany! We can't quite believe it, although many plants in Riga are busy dismantling their machinery.

When we drive to work early in the morning, the streets are already crowded. People shove and push in the narrow sidewalks, crowds accumulate and disperse as soon as a German uniform appears. The atmosphere is restless and nervous as if there might be an explosion at any moment. We are told a bomb went off in the railway station yesterday and that they had a fire at the post office. If you listen carefully, you can sometimes hear the distant thunder of heavy artillery. Cars heavily laden with household furnishings move past us, in between marching soldiers and civilians who are trying to rescue their last possessions from the city. Riderless horses are galloping around and herds of cattle are driven past us; everything gives the impression of headlong flight. We all look upon these scenes with ill-disguised delight. What has happened? We wonder. Did the Russians break through and how close to Riga are they? We have only one thought: maybe we'll be lucky and after all these years of slavery and murder we will be liberated. "Look, just look," I say to one of my comrades. "Look how they run. The Russians must be quite close."

"It's possible, Josef," says Sasha, who has stepped up to us and heard our conversation. "Otherwise there wouldn't be such a confusion here, but I have my misgivings. There's something in the air. I think the situation is especially critical for us now. You know what they do when they have no way of removing their prisoners. Don't laugh!" he shouts at me. "You've never been as close to death as you are right now."

Meanwhile, we have arrived at the nursery and begun our work. Our conversation is interrupted by a guard who has come to supervise our work. This nursery is on a road leading out of Riga, thus we are able to observe everything that goes on in the street.

"Sasha, what do you think? I believe it's time to scram. Maybe now there's still a chance, but nobody knows what will happen later. Tomorrow we may not be able to get out of the camp anymore. Maybe this is our last chance to escape. Just look at the confusion in the street."

From early morning on, endless lines of cars move along the street. One car applies the brakes just in front of our nursery, when a cow runs in front of it. The whole line comes to a standstill. All the horns start honking. It is music in my ears, as if the horns were calling, "Onward, onward, to the west!"

"It's no use, Josef," says Sasha, "as long as we don't know the position of the Russians it's useless to run away. It doesn't make sense," he repeats, "to run into the blue. If the Germans should stop the Russians somewhere, or if some river blocks the advance of the Russian armies, we are lost. You know as well as I do the Latvians aren't going to help us and how long can you go without food?"

"All right, Sasha," I agree. "Let's ask around at the camp tonight so maybe we can get a clearer picture of the situation."

Our guard comes closer again and watches the planting, then turns and goes to supervise the women at their weeding.

Thus the day passes quickly. Our eyes are riveted on the street and the ever-growing turmoil. At five o'clock the guard calls the end of the working day. We clean our tools, wash up, and at five-thirty sharp the truck stands at the gate to take us back to camp. The expression on everyone's face is serious: we are pleased but also worried by what is happening all around us. We realize there is about to be a change in our lives. But the three guards in their steel helmets, guns at their shoulders, make us realize immediately how hopeless our situation is. Several women are standing at the back of the truck and crying softly.

"Now come on and be calm — everything's going to be all right, Soni," an older man says to a pretty young girl. "You know that something has turned up every time so far. Something is going to turn up this time also." He gently strokes her hair while she keeps her face buried in her handkerchief and sobs quietly. Suddenly, as if she had an unexpected thought, she raises her head and looks the older man squarely in the face.

"You know as well as I do, Daddy," she says to him, "that in reality we're dead already. You just want to comfort me. You yourself don't believe what you're saying." Then she dries her tears and tries to smile at him. "Give me a kiss, Daddy," she says affectionately. "We don't want to think of what's going to happen."

The father kisses his daughter tenderly on the forehead. "You're a brave girl, my little Soni. I know."

The car stops at the gate to the camp. We line up in rows of five men and women and march in step into the camp.

"The place is much more closely guarded, Sasha," I whisper to him as we enter. "I don't think a mouse could squeak out of here."

Meanwhile we have been counted three times, and finally we come to the sleeping barracks where groups of people are standing around, debating.

"My foreman told me the Russians have broken through at Mitau," says one man. "Maybe we'll be liberated this very night! There are no more natural obstacles," he continues, becoming very excited, "after they've crossed the Aa River."

"Oh, what do you know?" someone interrupts him. "If it were true that the Russians are only 20 miles from here, Riga would have been bombed long ago, and we would have been evacuated. Or do you believe they're going to leave us in the direct line of advance? No, you don't believe that yourself," he says.

"Maybe the Germans were caught by surprise," another answers him, "and the Russians broke through their lines. Maybe Russian tanks are already close to Riga."

"You're a real armchair strategist," interrupts yet another, "one can tell it is just wishful thinking with you. Don't imagine things are going to be that smooth. Only one thing is sure: something's in the air."

The group dissolves, I walk over to another, listen in for a moment, and then go to another — I still cannot form a clear picture. The whistle blows. "Everybody to bed!" comes the order. "Quick! Quick!" with more urgency than usual. "Get going, or else!"

For a long time Sasha and I lie awake in our bunk pondering what to do, but we cannot decide. Soon we can hear the deep, quiet breathing of our comrades, though their sleep is not to last long. The shrieking of air raid sirens rends the air and immediately afterwards there is an ear-splitting noise of crashing and bursting as if the world were coming apart at the seams.

"The Russians are laying their eggs," Sasha says. "Let's get out of here."

Through the window we see the searchlights fingering the sky. Riga is illuminated to brilliant daylight by the Russian flares. At short intervals we hear the detonation of bombs and shells. Once the whole house seems to be shaking. A bomb must have exploded in the immediate vicinity.

People from everywhere push toward the air raid shelter. It is pitch dark. We cannot see one step ahead. People shove, push and stumble over objects lying in their path. Occasionally the flashlight of an SS guard lights up, and he drives us on with his rubber truncheon. Scantily dressed, we stand in the damp cellar, squeezed closely together while more and more people are pressed inside by the SS. The air in the small cellar soon becomes unbreathable; some people faint. They are carried outside but are immediately chased back by the guards who beat everybody with their gun barrels. We are not permitted to step out to relieve ourselves during the alarm because "you bastards might give light signals," the chief sentry says to our camp senior. The air raid alarm lasts for several hours and an incredible mess develops. The ack-ack is shooting madly and we can clearly hear the hum of the Russian bombers. For five hours we stand pressed against each other in the stinking air and the freezing cold of the damp cellar. We long for the morning, at least daylight, even though we don't know what it will bring.

Finally day breaks. As on any other morning, we are called to report for work. The truck comes as usual to take us to our various work sites. The closer we approach the Dvina bridges, the thicker the traffic becomes. The streets are congested with military vehicles, and we can watch what is happening around us. The bridges are heavily guarded, while several SS stand at the entrance, checking the papers of vehicles and travel permits. Military personnel with steel helmets and rifles are everywhere. On the other side of the bridge German soldiers are marching, some without shoes, some without rifles, their coats torn and dirty. A captain marches at the head; proud and erect, he leads his defeated detachment to the western bank of the Dvina. The exhausted soldiers just drag along. They must have been in battle for a long time.

At the sight of these defeated troops, our spirits rise again. Maybe we will make it, after all. Things seem to be coming to a head. New hope enters our hearts.

At our work site nobody is interested in working anymore. We just sit around and make plans for what we're going to do when we will at last be free. We wonder whether this one or that one is still alive and imagine how wonderful our life is going to be. As so many times before, we have been too optimistic.

Shortly before noon, a truck stops at the gate of the nursery. Three SS, armed to the teeth, jump off, and before we realize what's going on, we're already on the truck and moving off to God knows where. I'm not even surprised that they sent three guards for seven Jews. What dangerous criminals we must be! We pass through the streets of Riga at a brisk speed; the town looks like a disturbed anthill with everybody running about excitedly. The trains are crowded and people with horses and carriages or hand carts are trying to leave as quickly as possible with their possessions. We drive along the Dvina and then turn to the left. Only then do we realize where the car is taking us.

"Do you know where we are, Sasha?"

Sasha only nods his head curtly.

Two minutes later we stop at the gate to Camp Kaiserwald. The usual counting and checking, then we march in step into the camp.

The faces we meet tell us immediately something is wrong here. They avoid our eyes; they hardly dare talk to us, and walk by silently. Only now and then a sympathetic glance reaches us as we line up at the clothing center. Now we begin to realize why their faces are so serious, for opposite us, at the office, we observe a strange spectacle. A truck is parked, loaded with people, all pressed tightly together. Some have bandages around their heads or on their hands. Oberscharführer Hirsch stands in front of the office in his brown shirt, sleeves rolled up, and amuses himself by kicking and hitting the Jews coming out of the office. If he wore a white apron he would look like a butcher.

Jews are constantly being pushed and kicked onto the truck by the guard standing nearby.

"Get up there, you swine, or I'll make you fly!" and a fist lands right between the ribs.

"Move faster, goddamn you! D'you want to screw up the whole works, you bastard?" A man in his forties who, because of years of starvation, cannot climb onto the truck fast enough is seized by two guards and thrown like a sack on top of the other Jews. The guards laugh.

"They have to work fast, before people realize what's going on," flashes through my mind. "You don't need to think deeply to know where the truck is going."

Thus, one after the other goes to the office, gives his number and is dispatched to the top of the truck with kicks and blows. Now we realize why people looked at us with such pity. Probably we are to be included in this Aktion.

That would mean good-bye to life forever. At this thought my knees grow weak. It is simply impossible to believe that on such a lovely day everything is going to end. The sun is shining so nicely and warm, it cannot be possible. But in front of us the tragi-comedy is proceeding according to plan. One man after the other goes to his death, one truck after another takes its living load to destruction — just as if it was the simplest and most normal affair to murder thousands of innocent people.

On the opposite side a path has been cleared through the Jews standing there; they shrink back as Oberscharführer Hirsch slowly approaches. At this crucial moment, arousing Hirsch's displeasure by our looks or some other trivial cause means certain death. Beside him is Eggers from Hamburg, the non-commissioned officer in charge of the small H.K.P. camp. "Seven Jews from the H.K.P. nursery," a guard reports. The report is ignored, as if it had been spoken into the air.

I think my heart is going to stop. The eyes of the Oberscharführer move over every one of us; they come to rest on a man whom he motions forward, then on a second and a third man who both get the same fatal motion. "The others go back to camp and get prison clothes, understand?"

"Yessir!" the guard replies. The three "selected" men, their heads bowed, go over to the registry on shaky legs. "Get on up, you swine, or do I have to make you move?"

Hirsch walks up to the three, hits them in the face and kicks them, because they cannot climb up on the truck fast enough since so many people are already squeezed tightly together there, leaving no more room. The truck moves forward, turns around and slowly drives past us. One haver holds out his hand toward us, cupping the other to his mouth. As loudly as he can he cries out the Hebrew words "Al ha-met!" [We are going to our death]. We stand there and wave until the truck turns the corner at the registry and disappears from sight.

"What are you still hanging around here for, you bastards?" the well-known voice of the camp commander suddenly brings us back from our thoughts. "Get moving to your barracks, and step on it!"

Again a guard counts us. This time, unfortunately, there are only four men — three have been taken away from us. I walk as in a trance. The place beside me where Sasha used to walk is empty. I cannot accept that I am forever separated from the man with whom I made such hopeful plans for the future. I cannot eat anything that night. I feel as though the eyes of the Oberscharführer are still resting on me; my nerves are overwrought from the experiences of the afternoon. I keep seeing Sasha standing before me, his eyes shining at the thought of our liberation. Now they are closed forever, and I shall never again hear his convincing voice say, "Josef, if we can only gain some time, everything will be all right." All that is over, snuffed out by a merciless, unfathomable fate.

The atmosphere at Camp Kaiserwald is unbearable. People walk about with vacant eyes, staring at the ground. Everyone is trying to think of a solution to this intolerable situation. Work for the inmates has diminished considerably because so many factories have been evacuated from Riga. Only some of the prisoners are still used on "outside" Kommandos. Jews who had been put up outside the camp have now returned because the factories have been dismantled. The place is overcrowded. Some of the Jews are occupied in the army's dismantling center, in back of the camp; another Kommando is building air raid shelters with rifle ports so the SS have a clear field of fire if a riot should break out during an air raid.

The camp looks quite different now. Flowers have been planted around the barracks, vegetables are growing between the blocks, and at the entrance to Kaiserwald there is a large tomato field. All this gives the camp a very pleasant appearance, though the initiated know every tomato vine and every head of cabbage was planted with the blood and sweat of Jews. The red roses at the registry are blooming in arrogant mockery, a reminder of all the blood that has been spilled for them.

I can no longer work as a roofer and am occupied in the dismantling center. Hundreds of Jews are squeezed together in a small area here. Very little work is being done, but a lot of discussion is going on. The topic is the Russian advance and the possibility of hiding somewhere in the camp. I look under every barracks building to see whether it is built on a concrete slab or on posts. In the latter case, perhaps one could push the sand aside and crawl under the building in time of danger. Even these chances are very small. No doubt the Kapos will know how to find us. Then again I study the barrack's small attic, but it is impossible to climb up there unnoticed. I realize there is no way of escaping my fate. The number of guards watching the camp has been increased; they all wear steel helmets and are armed with hand grenades, ready to snuff out any rebellion at the first signal.

One evening there is another general roll call. Even the kitchen personnel, which until now have been excused from such assemblies, must report. All children are to report. We line up in five rows. In order to facilitate scrutiny of the inmates, the first row is ordered to advance two steps; the second row remains standing, while the third row takes two steps back. The fourth and fifth rows also move back. Spurs rattling, the gentlemen of the SS march through the rows of

Jews, tearing gaps into the solid lines. In the row ahead of me stands Gunther Horn, the son of the gardener. He is twelve years old.

"Are you still here, you son of a bitch?" one of the SS guards yells at the child, pulling him away from the hand of his father, who is standing beside him.

"Daddy! Daddy!" Gunther sobs. "Help me, Daddy!" and he stretches imploring arms to the man who remains standing motionless in the line. Slowly, the boy walks ahead of the SS man and joins the other children on the opposite side. In back of me stands the father who always took his boy out on Kommandos with him. An SS guard comes to tear the child's hand from his father's, which the boy is clutching fearfully. The father is heroic. Tall and strong, with the boy holding his hand, he walks through the rows to stand with his son and the other children. Like a king he stands among them, proud and unbowed, fearlessly facing whatever may befall.

At the same time, we can see the "selection" in the women's camp. There, too, several little girls have been isolated. A skinny woman is standing with them; later, we hear she is Horn's wife, and that she chose to die with her husband and her son Gunther.

After the assembly the children are flung on to the trucks like so many rag dolls, among them little Itzig, who had escaped three such Aktionen before. This time, on the specific order of Sauer, X pulled him from the barracks floor where he had been hiding. Sauer said after the assembly he no longer wants to see a child in the camp, or else the entire camp will go.

Several trucks, with their load of crying children that were thrown helter-skelter on top, drive toward their grim destination. Rosel Sachs' ten-year-old sister saved herself with her long hair and stuffed breasts.

There are new orders every day. Four weeks ago all the Jews were ordered to have their hair shaved off. As soon as their hair had grown about three quarters of an inch it had to be cut again. Now comes the order that a swath has to be shorn through the newly grown hair from one ear to the other and from the forehead to the neck, in order to distinguish the Jews more clearly. This creates four separate tufts of hair on our heads. We take this matter from the humorous side: we don't care how funny we look as long as our heads are still on.

We learn the camp senior has been removed because of an infraction of camp discipline. A few days later he is replaced by a similar figure from Strassenhof, a neighboring camp. The new man now struts about the camp like a peacock. Unfortunately Honig crosses his path. The camp senior leaps at him like a hyena: "Honig! Honig!" he hollers. "Now I finally got you, you dog! Now I can kill you if I like!" all the while hitting him with well-aimed punches and blows. When Honig has barely recovered from his first shock, the new camp senior asks whether he remembers him. Honig says he does not. Again he gets a series of punches and blows. "You bastard!" the camp senior shouts. "I bought my furniture at your store in Lübeck and you had it repossessed when I was out of work. Now do you remember me?" Honig remembers. In the meantime X has appeared on the scene. "You can take over now, X," says the camp senior. When X is through with him, Honig is only a helpless bundle of flesh. He is carried to the sick ward where he recovers fairly fast. Later he tells me he is glad to have gotten off so easily. But he is still afraid the camp senior will send him on a "transport to heaven."

The dismantling center is operating night and day. I've decided to work the night shift because I feel I may be less exposed to the danger of being sent on an Einsatzkommando [mobile killing unit]. So I work from seven at night until seven in the morning, when the day shift comes to relieve us. During the night the lance corporal, who looks like Hitler, cannot watch our work so well because the camp's outside lights are often dimmed to lessen the danger of air raids. He mostly sits in his room with some Jewish girl and has a good time. It is so cheap under these conditions.

I, too, have met a nice Hungarian girl. Her name is Tubi. While we're working outside at night, I use every opportunity when the guards are not around to go talk to her at her barracks. She comes from the Carpathian Mountains. She left her parents and three sisters behind in Auschwitz when she was brought here. It is touching to listen to her speak about her former life. In her thoughts she is still at home, because she has been at Kaiserwald for only three months. When the air raid alarm sounds, all the lights are extinguished, and while the shrapnel rains onto the barracks roof and we hear the guards shouting, I sit with Tubi and hope the alarm will never end.

But early the next day we are called back to reality with a vengeance. At six in the morning I see X and some Polish inmates, armed with rubber truncheons, storm Barracks One. A few seconds later several Jews, barely clothed, come running out of the block. Several trucks are parked on the assembly square, and before the men can gather their wits they are already on top of the trucks which take them to their doom. The whole Aktion comes off so quickly that some of the Jews in the barracks don't know what has happened until they find one or the other of their friends is missing.

Outside the camp they are getting together a large supply of gasoline. This leads to new rumors and conjectures. Some claim to know the gasoline will be used to burn the corpses. There are stories that a transport of Hungarian women was standing at the railroad station for several days. Among them was a female German prisoner who was supposed to be a camp senior. This German inmate has been returned to camp. We assume the Hungarian Jewesses were gassed. There had been a plan to put these people into the newly built camp of the A.E.G. at Thorn.

Our Jewish grapevine claims the Russians are close to Tilsit, so that our entire region is surrounded. Since the Germans cannot remove the Jews any longer, they simply liquidate them. We don't know which of these rumors is true, though one thing we know for sure is that after having spent three days on a railroad siding, the Jews were collected in trucks and taken to an unknown destination.

The outlook for our future is grim. At night during assembly, Schlueter, the prisoner in charge of the office, reads an order to the effect that, beginning tomorrow morning, all those who are able will have to work in Riga harbor. Two Kommandos are formed: one for the day shift, the other for the night shift. They'll change every week, he says. The work at the harbor is very hard, but still most of us are glad to get out of the uncertain atmosphere at the camp.

The whole day we have to unload bombs and ammunition. The cargo arrives in large transports and is immediately sent on waiting freight trains to the front. This goes on day after day, night after night. The food at the camp has improved a little. They frequently serve well-prepared pea soup with plenty of bacon and half a loaf of bread a day. Apparently they're willing to preserve our strength for the unloading of ammunition. Others say the Germans cannot move the large army food supplies anyway; that's why they give us more to eat.

In the evening, after assembly, everybody hurries from the day's hard labor to the blocks in order to lie down and get some sleep, as much as it is possible to sleep in these dark, overcrowded rooms. Because the "outside" camps have been closed, we are now lying four abreast on a bunk about six feet wide, not to mention the lice and bedbugs which disturb our rest and make everybody itch and scratch. No fresh breeze moves the foul air; so the night, too, is turned into hell. The shrapnel rattles on the roof during the air raid alarms. The thought never occurs that it might crash through the thin roof and kill me, although other blocks have reported prisoners wounded by splinters of flak.

One day only a small number of harbor workers is needed, so I remain at the camp with several others to get some rest from the hard labor. We are sent to work in the dismantling center and are sitting around a table when a Kapo enters and says he needs ten Jews to fill sacks with straw. It is a warm July day, and I have hung my jacket over the back of the chair. The Kapo comes to our table and points to all the comrades sitting around me. "You all come with me," he says. "But you," he says, pointing at me, "stay here because your number is not properly sewn on. Get going, the rest of you."

They never come back. Outside, they are received by the Security Service; the blankets they grabbed as they left are taken away from them, with the comment that where they're going they won't need blankets any more.

Once again I have escaped death in a mysterious, incomprehensible manner.

Another time people are needed, supposedly to gather potatoes. About 100 men came forward in the belief they would be able to eat their fill. The next morning they are shipped off to Poland and never seen again; their numbers are struck out at the registry.

Levi and the other remaining Jews from Baloschi have arrived at the camp. Levi doesn't seem quite normal anymore. Schapiro, who was at Baloschi up till now, says Levi was made to work eight days and eight nights in a field; his wife brought him food. He suffered mental damage, Schapiro says, from the beatings and other cruelties of Big and Little Willi.

Another general roll call. The count is wrong; it turns out Levi is missing. I can hardly believe my eyes when I see him being dragged by the collar over the assembly square by the Hauptscharführer, his feet in the wooden slippers clattering over the ground. He is taken directly to the waiting truck. So Ernst Levi, too, is gone from us.

Then the chief sentry tells an inmate to name a row, and ten men two rows to the right of me go to their death. I keep wondering when my turn will come. Can it go on like this forever, with a guardian angel holding his invisible hand over me? There is hardly time for thinking such thoughts in Kaiserwald. The whistle blows. "Everybody line up with their coats in front of the barracks! March! March!" We were already lying in our bunks when this order came. So we get up again and get dressed quickly. Everybody is running around, shouting, not knowing what is going on. We don't understand why we should take our coats along in the middle of summer. One man lost his socks in the confusion; another one cannot find his shoes in his haste. Behind us, at the door, we already hear the screams of Jews who are being beaten by the Kapos with their rubber truncheons. We aren't getting ready for them fast enough. Some jump out of the window, but in front of the window the Kapos are also waiting to beat them, for it is forbidden to climb out of the window. So at least the Kapos have grounds for brutality. At the door two real heavyweights are standing; everybody has to pass by them in order to get through the door. With satanic pleasure they whip the helpless people. This pastime of the Kapos costs us several dead and badly wounded.

We line up outside in the dark, our coats over our arms. "March to the railroad station!" comes the order. Ten trainloads of gravel have arrived which we have to haul in our coats on the double. The trains are urgently needed elsewhere. Some of us are given shovels; by order of the Lagerführer [SS camp commander] every coat has to hold eight shovelfuls. Nothing must be lost, and SS and Kapos are posted on both sides of the road, about 30 yards apart. They watch us to make sure we're running and drive us on to greater haste with their whips and truncheons. Men who cannot run any longer are beaten until they drop. Then they're carried to the sick ward by other inmates. Everybody wants to help take the casualties away; it's a way of getting a few minutes of rest. Old Jews who can hardly walk any more are running bent over their heavy load, the SS jeering at them. To the right of the road an air raid shelter has been dug out for the guards. One SS guard is having fun pushing old people into the excavation, which is about ten feet deep. It is very hard for them to climb back out again; as soon as they have reached the edge, he pushes them back in. He repeats this terrible game several times until the men collapse and are dragged off. Another SS carries a very thin stick in his hand. He only hits people in the face, "so that you dogs feel something," he says. So we run with the heavy gravel until one o'clock in the morning, always under blows and threats. This interlude costs us 20 dead and many injured. Several others lay moaning and whimpering in their bunks. The doctor from Dunaburg who shares the bunk with me has also been injured. He lies there crying and groaning. I fall into an exhausted sleep. When I wake in the morning he is dead. The doctor comes and says he must have suffered internal injuries and bled to death.

August 1944. Russian sources report the Red Army in a steady advance on the Baltic front. The Russian troops have liberated countless towns and villages and are now on their way to Riga. German Army headquarters, too, report heavy fighting in the Latvian theater of war.

Sometimes, when I have a chance to read the news from the front, I think how interesting it would be to follow the Russian campaign on a map somewhere out in the free world. But in Riga it is hardly comfortable. I am trapped, and my nerves are on edge because I never know whether I shall live to see the next day. We are all tense, nervous and irritated, and suspect danger in every call to a Kommando. We are living on a powder keg. We hear of a big Aktion in neighboring Camp Strassenhof; all Jews over the age of 35 were taken away. At the same time the gasoline stored outside the camp was loaded on, so we seem to have guessed correctly. Inmates from another "outside" camp are returned to the main camp. The 100 inmates are not even being registered. Right after their return to the camp they are locked into a block which they may not leave any more. Aware of what fate is in store for them the Jews try to free themselves — they break the windows, try to lift the locked doors from their hinges, tear up the floor boards in an attempt to crawl their way to freedom. Only a few succeed in escaping from the block and mingling with the other prisoners. The next morning about 20 younger men are chosen from among the doomed and exchanged for 20 older ones from the camp. X chooses those who are to survive. As soon as he has picked one, 20 others surround him, but fate is inexorable. Finally, with the help of Polish Kapos, he manages to load the condemned Jews onto the trucks, three SS guards mount after them, and the last ride begins.

Not all rides go smoothly. We hear that on some trucks the Jews tried to overpower the guards, and in one case, it is said, ten escaped. Another time six men managed to get away, while four were shot attempting to escape in one of the most crowded streets of Riga. Therefore the SS have ordered greater security measures for these transports. A larger number of guards with their guns at the ready always ride along now. They no longer use open trucks but only those with canvas tops so that Jews can no longer jump from the sides.

During the last few days I have been assigned the night shift at the harbor. The ships which arrive are mostly loaded with 300-pound bombs. It's no easy job to juggle these block busters all night long.

When we return to camp the next morning, an endless row of prisoners, their blankets tied around their backs, is already lined up at the gate.

"We're being sent back to Germany!" they call to us as we march past. "You can join us, if you like."

The camp commander announces they're still looking for volunteers to join the transport to Germany. I decide quickly I'm not going, although I see Honig and many of my friends in the line. In my opinion, the later I get back to Germany the better. Many people try to make me change my mind. "You know what happens to those who remain behind," they tell me. During those few minutes I have acquired the unshakable conviction that it is wrong to volunteer for this transport. So I say farewell to my friends, particularly to Honig. Today I know that joining this transport to Germany was the only mistake of that cool and calculating thinker. I later learn he died in Buchenwald, as did most of those who joined this first transport from Riga. We are told that those remaining behind will be sent off a few weeks later.

There is wild confusion in the women's camp. Most of the
women do not want to go with the transport, though they are
forced to. They are pushed into the two-yard gap between the
barbed wire fences separating the women's and men's camps. They
have to give their numbers and form five rows. I see Tubi, my Hungarian friend, between the fences. She asks me what she should do.
Unfortunately she has no voice in the decision. I say good-bye after
she has lined up in one of the five rows. The transport is put aboard
a freighter which sails that same night, returning many Jews who
had been deported to Riga back to the Reich.

The Russian telegraph agency reports the Red Army is battling
for the town of Tukums, about 30 miles west of Riga. A few days
later the Russians announcethey have penetrated several miles
beyond the Gulf of Riga and have reached the beaches around the
port city.

Life in camp has become quieter. Only several hundred Jews are
left; the food is good, better than ever before during my three years
of imprisonment. Our spirits are high; we are all excited because
every day we imagine we hear the distant rumble of the guns more
distinctly. Often we see Russian planes flying over our camp, low
enough for us to recognize their markings.

One night a roofer is needed. I am picked for the job. Many
roofs are in need of repair due to shrapnel damage, particularly over
the SS kitchen, where the rain is coming through. I tell Schlueter
I need an assistant. I work well with Shmuel, a Jew from Lodz; we
repair the roof over the SS kitchen together, and then we both strut
through the camp like two very important people. I always carry a
small hammer in my hand and Shmuel a yardstick. Thus we walk
on the flat roofs of the blocks and gather the many pieces of shrapnel which are lying there. Sometimes X passes by, and we give him
the largest pieces. He always takes them to Commander Sauer in
order to present him with his finds. Once when I'm on top of the
women's barracks, I see a young Jewish girl in the door of Block
One crying bitterly. By chance Rosel is just passing by, and I ask

her what happened to this charmingly dressed little girl. "Don't you know?" says Rosel. "This is X's latest girl friend. X has to leave today. Hannes probably also. Now they are considered good enough to defend their imperiled fatherland. She is crying because her protector is leaving." Dramatic farewell scenes are reported to have taken place later, but all other Jews remaining at camp breathe easier when this sadist has finally disappeared.

A new Rapportführer has arrived; he seems to be quite a jolly Bavarian. Shmuel and I pass him in camp, and I take off my cap as per regulation. He waves us off. "No, boys," he says. "For me you don't have to take your caps off."

"For heaven's sake," I say to myself, "a new wind seems to be blowing," and the Rapportführer seems to have noticed it, too. Only six months ago not taking off your cap before an SS guard would have left you eligible for the sick ward, and today he acts as if he were my comrade.

September 1944. All Jews from Kaiserwald, with the exception of a few artisans, are working at the harbor. They are mostly occupied with unloading army food supplies and ammunition. When the labor Kommando returns to the camp, everything can be bought that the heart desires. We have chocolate, cigarettes and cookies, all kinds of delicacies — despite strict control, everything is being "organized." A few days ago half of a Kommando was nearly stripped bare, but nothing was found on them, because the Jews had thrown everything away in the dark. The SS are overjoyed when the Jews return to camp with their pockets bursting. They are then thoroughly searched by experts, with an SS guard standing by, and everything found is distributed by the guards among themselves. Nothing is ever reported to the commander; the gentlemen of the SS are pleased to obtain cigarettes again in this way.

Every day the German newspapers in Riga print announcements by the army commander asking all civilians to report voluntarily to collecting points for evacuation to Germany. Large German transport vessels are leaving the port daily carrying Latvian and Russian prisoners of war to Germany. They can only take a few possessions with them. Many Latvians have no intention of going to the Reich. Whole sections of Riga are searched by the army for hidden civilians. All those found are taken straight to the harbor. We hear there have been skirmishes between Latvian partisans and German troops.

During these raids several hidden Jews are caught, among them Bischofswerder, a Jewish doctor and his wife; they had escaped from one of the camps during a severe air raid on Riga. The Bischofswerders are returned to Kaiserwald, their clothing marked with black circles in front and back, and are no longer allowed to leave on an "outside" Kommando. When the next 10 people are assembled for a "transport to heaven," the doctor and his wife are among them.

Every day the thundering of the heavy artillery becomes louder. The air activity over Riga, too, increases from day to day. With breathless intensity we follow developments. My constant dream is that I shall wake one morning and the Germans will have disappeared. German newspapers are no longer obtainable in Riga. The Russians announce in their army bulletins that Tukums has been captured and the Red Army has advanced further toward the Gulf of Riga.

In addition to the Jews in Kaiserwald, varying numbers in several "outside" camps are still occupied with dismantling and packing army supplies. Schlueter of the prisoners' Arbeitsamt says approximately 3,000 Jews are still in Riga.

Our situation is becoming more uncertain and there are many among us who regret not having taken the first transport back to Germany. In the end, they say, no ships will be available for us, and then we'll be lost.

The two radio technicians who always listen to Radio Moscow tell us the Russians are only 20 miles from Riga. They could arrive any day. At this report the deep depression some of us live with changes to happy anticipation. We have become so used to the thunder of the guns, we no longer pay any attention to it. Every day is the same.

5

Stutthof, Poland

Fall 1944

Fall 1944. Suddenly, one afternoon, we get the order to report in front of the clothing room to receive new prison clothes. We're also given blankets and when dark falls, we leave Camp Kaiserwald for Riga harbor. In the harbor an endless line of Jews, all in new striped outfits with numbers on chest and pants, is already waiting to embark. They wait until nightfall to be allowed to board the ship that is to take them to an unknown destination in Germany. The Jews assembled here are the last from the East — the survivors of hundreds of thousands, maybe millions. The sight is absolutely incredible. Jews whose lives weren't worth a damn are now being transported back to Germany. "What is the meaning of this?" I ask myself. It would be so much simpler for the gentlemen of the SS to finish their murderous job right here in the East. Why transport us back to the Reich when the freight space must be urgently needed for other purposes? These and similar thoughts pass through my mind, going back to our arrival in Riga.

"You remember when our transport from Hamburg arrived at Skirotava?" I ask Stefan, who is standing beside me. "We were then about 1,200 Jews. How many of us are going back today?"

"We were talking about it the other day," says Stefan, "and we counted all our acquaintances from the Hamburg transport. About 30 are left. Maybe one or two others might show up someplace, but there certainly aren't many more."

We start to feel very sad. At that time, every one of us left with his family, sisters and brothers. Today, out of whole families there may be a single survivor; in most cases, all are gone. And what lies ahead for us in the West? Nothing good — all of us lucky enough to leave Riga alive are quite agreed on that point. Stefan says they definitely have a purpose in shipping us back instead of simply shooting us down like rabbits. We can do nothing about it. Until today I always thought that there would be some chance for escape, but even this last ray of hope has been extinguished. Shortly before our march from camp they said 30 men were to remain behind to dismantle the Riga barracks, but the order was countermanded and everybody had to leave. How I would have loved to see the Russians marching into Riga! I would have been spared all the hardships that lay ahead of us. But nobody except me wanted to remain behind, not even Stefan, or Robert Popper, the glazier. They think the Germans would have done the same thing they did in Salaspils, where they murdered the last remaining inmates.

We have been standing in the heavy rain for several hours with blankets spread over our heads and shoulders. Despite the danger of air raids the ship is brightly lit. The head of the line starts moving and the first prisoners board the vessel. Also things start happening at the wharf. One car after the other drives up. The highest-ranking SS officers get out and immediately board the ship via a gangplank specially prepared for them. Their cars are loaded as well. Now our line begins to stir; we all climb up the ladder on the run; they say we're going to leave this evening.

Up on deck we are received by several SS who tell us which holds we are to go to. Here, also, they cannot manage without the usual "Quick! Quick!" One after the other we climb down the long ladder to the bowels of the ship. It is pitch black down there; you can't see your hand in front of your eyes. There is no straw, nothing but the bare iron which seems to grin at us scornfully.

"How long do you think we have to stay here, Stefan?"

"Three days," he says. "If we ever get out at all," he adds.

"But that isn't possible," I say. "You can't even go up on deck. We can't possibly stand here for three days and three nights. Nobody can endure that."

"Who says you're supposed to endure it, Josef?" Stefan says. "If you can't endure it, they'll probably throw you overboard. Besides, it's impossible to lie down here and let the others step all over you. Go ahead, lay down if you like. Me, I'm going to stand here like a post."

"But over there, in the corner, Stefan, we could perhaps sit, and then maybe sleep for a while."

"If you'd paid attention, Josef," Stefan replies, "you would have seen that someone just pissed there." Indeed, the corner gradually turns into a toilet. How long we stand, I don't know; at any rate we do nod and sleep for a short time. When I wake up I feel sick to death, as though I will throw up any moment. The sea must be very choppy, because the boat pitches and tosses and we are thrown from one side to the other. It is a scene of mad chaos. Some vomit without interruption, soiling those standing near them; others shout and complain — many are on the floor, wailing and groaning without anybody taking notice of them. One man lies in a corner calling out, "A drop of water, please, why don't you give me some water." He seems to have gone out of his mind.

Suddenly, the hatch is opened. Some fresh air reaches down to these depths. It revives us somewhat, and in spite of seasickness some start eating their pieces of dry bread, which they have wisely taken with them from Riga. At the top of the ladder men are hanging like monkeys, all trying to get a drink of water, but the SS guard who is distributing it amuses himself by throwing most of the water into the faces of the exhausted people. Through the hatch we can see the blue sky. How wonderful it must be, I'm thinking, to be up there and look over the vast expanse of the blue Baltic. Meanwhile, latrine buckets are handed down to us. People willing to empty them out up on deck can catch a breath of fresh air for a moment. In spite of the unpleasant contents, I bring up one bucket, stand on deck for a moment and feel the beauty of an ocean voyage. We are sailing in a convoy. Fast gunboats are fighting the stormy sea.

I count six steamers sailing in a line ahead. On each side I see two gunboats. When they have reached the head of the convoy they return to the rear. I'm not sure whom they are really protecting, certainly not us Jews. A Kapo roughly orders me back into our dungeon. All I'm supposed to do is empty the bucket and disappear, he hollers at me. While he is chasing other Jews off the deck, he himself can remain there. Each one of us is longing for when we can leave this floating prison. We are lying about and dozing or discussing our uncertain future; from time to time someone yells when another steps on his belly in the dark. But he soon quiets down again.

Suddenly a murmur goes through these lifeless figures on the ground; everybody rises, for above, on the first deck, a Jew is standing with a prayer shawl over his shoulders and a prayerbook in his hand. Softly he starts to pray. A few candles eerily illuminate the dark hold. The monotonous sing-song of the praying Jew resounds from the iron bulkheads and is repeated in chorus by the other Jews. A solemn mood takes hold. Old familiar melodies are heard; we are humming along softly. Pictures from my childhood arise; for a moment my thoughts are at home. I see my mother and my sisters and brothers on Rosh HaShanah [Jewish New Year]. I always used to write my mother with a list of wishes, at the end of which I promised to be very good during the next year. The pitching and tossing calls me back to reality. It is Rosh HaShanah now, too, but I am on a ship that is taking me to an unknown destination and uncertain future.

We shake hands with our comrades and go from one to the other, wishing each other a happy New Year. Suddenly we are all one big family. It is a miracle how common destiny and common faith can forge human beings together as one. "L'Shana tovah [Happy New Year], and good luck in the New Year. This will be the year of our liberation." These words are heard everywhere. A festive mood has taken hold; all is peace and harmony.

In the meantime a group of musicians has gotten together and gives a concert with all kinds of improvised instruments. Artists from all parts of the East tell their stories. Everybody is laughing. One man sings in Hebrew about Rachel. The beams of several flashlights are focused on him, as he leans at the railing around the steerage: only the outline of his figure is visible in the darkness. He could be standing on a stage — he sings with great feeling, softly accompanied by a violin. Everybody cheers and applauds when he finishes his performance. Another man tells anecdotes about his shtetl [village] in Lithuania, singing in conclusion, "I want to go home" — he wants to see his home once more, his little room, and the small ghetto street where he lived his childhood. Everybody joins in the refrain.

The song is interrupted. The hatch is hurriedly closed, and we are again surrounded by deep dark night. Suddenly the boat shakes, and then firing starts from all its guns. An earsplitting noise of bursting shells fills the hold; the ship seems to rear up under the force of the firing. During the lulls we can clearly hear the humming of the Russian planes. Our hearts stop. If we're hit, we'll all be lost. Then the humming recedes; the attack seems to be over. A few minutes later though the guns start up again, and the ominous hum of the airplane engines resumes, as the second wave of attack strikes our convoy. We sigh in relief when it is over. When we arrive in Danzig we learn the last ship in our convoy was sunk during the attack.

Afterwards we all sit closely together. Some have fallen asleep from exhaustion, others are talking quietly. We are all very pessimistic about our future, but we're also convinced this is the last year of our enslavement. One Jew sums it all up — next year, we will either celebrate Rosh HaShanah in freedom, or the last European Jews will have been destroyed.

Then the hatch opens. An SS guard calls down to us to count how many men are in the hold. They're going to give out bread. We give him the number, and one of us skillfully balances the bread ration for 350 people down the ladder. The 300 grams of bread is the only nourishment we receive on our three-day journey.

Meanwhile, the sea has become very rough. A sailor on deck is supposed to have said we are having a gale of intensity nine. We constantly roll from one side to the other or are thrown back by the force of the waves hitting the bow.

The Oberscharführer standing guard at the top of the ladder says one Jew may go fetch water for us. It is a little relief because our mouths are dried out by the foul air in the hold. Several say they heard we'll reach Danzig in six hours, but since it is going to be dark by then we will be piloted into the harbor only the next morning. After that we are supposed to get off the boat immediately.

This night, too, passes. Very early the next morning we receive the order to get ready to disembark. Soon it is the turn of our hold, and we enter the territory of Danzig in the most beautiful sunshine. We are hustled off like criminals. Every five yards a guard stands with his gun drawn. We are marched to the collecting point, which is situated close to the Westernplotte, a former German fortress, as the natives explain to us. A few British prisoners of war wave to us when they see from our Stars of David we are Jews. We remain in the assembly square all day long, heavily guarded by SS from the Stutthof concentration camp, who have taken the places of the guards from Riga. The Nazis provide us with ample guards on German soil, but as so often in the past, they forget about nourishment.

We expect to be sent on by train, but soon find out differently. Toward evening several open Vistula barges which are used to ship sand and rocks arrive. Each barge carries a load of 500 people. A tugboat appears, and around midnight we slowly sail through Danzig harbor. We are part of a long train of barges, linked together by cables, crammed full with men, women and children who so far have been fortunate enough to escape the murderers.

The whole scene is like a fairy tale. The moon shines brightly in the sky, its mild light mirrored in a million reflections in the dark water over which we are slowly gliding. Out of the darkness the silhouettes of boats at anchor suddenly emerge and almost instantly sink back into the night. The whole setting is unreal, dreamlike. Occasionally I hear in the distance a few bars of accordion music or the cry of a seagull. But a nighttime peacefulness surrounds us; the only sound is the monotonous murmur of the water lapping the side of our barge in even waves. Sometimes we glide past giant dockyard installations where cranes stretch their long necks toward the starry sky.

We cannot sit or lie down on our barge; we can only stand, as we have been doing for hours and hours. My feet are hurting. Meanwhile the late fall night has turned very cold. Men and women move closer together. There seems to be no difference between the sexes anymore; everyone just seeks the warmth of the person who happens to stand beside him. Suddenly the tugboat pilot announces he has to remain at the next bridge overnight, as the next sluice will not be opened until morning. So we spend our first night on the water. Many people have collapsed with fatigue; others have squatted down next to them and covered them with our grey blankets to keep off the cold morning fog. Conditions are so crowded that people are lying on top of each other, a tangle of human limbs. Through the center of the barge runs a narrow gutter which collects the water seeping through the bottom. We take half-hour turns bailing it out.

When the sun rises, our caravan gets moving again toward our destination of Camp Stutthof,[1] which by now we fervently await. Our sole desire is just to have a roof over our heads and to sleep.

"In six hours you'll be there," says the tugboat pilot, but later we see that he miscalculated by thirty hours. When we pass under bridges, people stop and stare. They apparently have never seen such a procession.

In the early morning hours we have our first mishap. The last barge, which I am on, suddenly breaks off from the cable while passing under a bridge. The vessel smashes into a wooden post. There is a loud scream. With the sudden jolt, everybody falls down; there is a pile of shouting and gesticulating women. Some hit the floor too hard and are bleeding. Others are crushed and bruised. Many women are crying, I don't know whether from hunger or pain, but crying women are dangerous because their crying is contagious and can cause panic. We try to comfort them as best we can and apply improvised bandages, but the prolonged hardships of the voyage without sleep or food have found their ultimate expression in this one hysterical scream.

After a while our barge has been reconnected and the trip continues. Hungry, freezing people stand wrapped in their blankets, having gone without warm food for days.

It seems as if some of them no longer had any feeling of shame, as if the most primitive instincts were coming to the fore. The women let themselves go more than the men. The men still preserve a semblance of civilization, but the women and girls act as though they were quite among themselves.

Finally we pass under the drawbridge, are towed through the locks and float slowly out on the Vistula River. It is a beautiful wide body of water bordered by lush meadows and fields. Dappled cattle are grazing on the shores, and mares with their foals are scampering about in joyous freedom.

Bridges span the river in high arcs; several excursion boats steam toward us. The passengers leaning against the railing shake their heads in astonishment at the strange freight they see passing by. We glide on and on. Then we leave the Vistula, and are carried through a network of narrow, never-ending canals out to the fresh-water lake. With amazement I remember that I haven't eaten anything in two days, but I feel no hunger. It is as if my stomach has shriveled up; I feel only weak, terribly weak. Once again dusk falls; evening mists rise from the water and quickly change the meadows and fields into an impregnable milky scene. The tugboat pilot docks our barge at the shore; he says he has to stay here for the night, and without further explanation he walks back to his own warm tugboat.

The moon has penetrated the grey walls of the fog; its clear light illuminates the peaceful calm and solitude around us. The prisoners have become apathetic. We move even closer together, spread the damp woolen blankets over our heads, and try to find some rest. The only sound is that of the men constantly bailing out the gutter. I find it increasingly hard to lift the full bucket over the low side of the boat, but if we don't keep up the bailing, it won't be long before we will be standing in water.

High up in the sky a bird of prey follows its majestic path. Suddenly it dives from the heights, pounces on its victim and immediately wings back up with its prey. It looks like a goshawk to me.

In the middle of the night a woman becomes delirious. She stands up wrapped in her grey blanket, her hair blown by the breeze, a little above the others, like a figure on the stage. In the background tall, slim spruce trees are growing to the sky; against the moon and stars, the whole scene is dramatic and unreal.

"Schnucki," [my pet] the woman calls. "Schnucki, please come here, Schnucki. Can't you see I'm in distress? Please come and help me." And then, a little softer and pouting, she adds, "I promise I'll always be good from now on, Schnucki."

Ghost-like, these calls echo in the night. Somewhere a dog barks in reply. Finally a nurse who has worked in the hospital at Riga manages to calm her down. She fishes a sleeping pill from her lunch sack and gives it to the stricken woman, who finally falls asleep.

I hardly know how the night passes. From time to time I nod, but I am immediately awakened by the icy air, or by somebody stepping on my foot because he can't see in the dark. There is no thought of rest or of getting any real sleep under these conditions. For six nights we've been without sleep — how much longer can this last?

Suddenly a woman leaps over the side of the barge and disappears in the water. Two boys immediately jump after her and with great effort manage to pull the already unconscious form back into the boat. Several women show some human compassion again. When the woman regains consciousness they help her put on some dry clothes. I am assailed by doubts whether it was right to pull her from the water, whether it made any sense to save her life only so she can continue suffering. It becomes increasingly clear to me that the way things are we have little chance of surviving our tormentors. All one's energy is useless here; the whole battle for physical survival makes no sense.

With the first gray of dawn our caravan starts moving again. The barges are again detached, each one sluiced through separately. Then we go at a fast clip through the rapids and past old fishing boats until we reach calmer waters.

Each one of us yearns for the dubious paradise of Stutthof. Even a concentration camp appears like a haven after such a journey.

Our string of barges passes through narrow canals. On shore several women in prison garb are standing with potato hoes in their hands, waving to us as we pass by. They revive in many of us a will to live. We start dreaming of work on a vegetable farm; it all boils down to the image of a large pot of mashed potatoes.

Stutthof

It is late afternoon when we arrive at the village of Stutthof. The woman are taken off first, and things move briskly, but nevertheless it is pitch dark when we finally leave the barge after the three-day journey. The usual roll call takes place, and then we march off, to the less than friendly shouts of the local populace. This is the first indication that we are back on German soil.[2] Later I see a sign in a brightly lit storefront in already faded letters: "You are buying from a German store here." With mixed feelings we totter through the village. Some of our people are so weak that they can no longer walk. We take turns carrying them. Only now do I notice the SS guards accompanying us are holding dogs on leashes.

After a short time the camp comes into view, illuminated by countless lamps. That is the first impression: lamps and barbed wire, electrically charged. It reminds me of the story a German comedian told on the stage somewhere in Germany: One day, he said, he went somewhere by train and passed by a concentration camp that was guarded by so much barbed wire, so many lights and so many watch towers, that he thought to himself, "People really had to be very smart to be able to get in there."

It really isn't all that hard to get into a camp like that. Another roll call, and with some apprehension we march into this dubious paradise. Stutthof certainly does not have a comforting reputation: we already heard on the barge it is supposed to have a crematorium where smoke rises from the chimney all the time.

"Listen, everybody!" We are suddenly called to attention, after we have lined up before the delousing center. "Leave your valuables, watches, rings, and so on right here at the entrance, so you won't have to carry them to the office later on."

The Oberscharführer is speaking to us in an almost polite, friendly tone. But he is not going to get very far with us this way; we are old and experienced camp foxes. Apparently he has noticed this tone of voice does not have any effect on us, because he continues a little more brusquely:

"So then, all your junk, including soap and towels, everything, is to remain outside. I don't want to see anyone bring anything into the washroom except shoes. Understand?"

"Yessir!" comes the reply from several hundred throats. But nobody intends to follow these instructions. We all think that no matter how hard they're going to try to take our last few pieces of clothing and the shaving kits some of us carry in our lunch bags, we're not going to surrender them voluntarily. We might as well try to smuggle them through the delousing procedure. If you're caught, you might catch a few fists in the jaw.

The first 50 men are sent into the washroom. One of them hides his shaving kit in his shoes, another has managed — God knows how — to hold on to his papers. Two men paste their money under their soles, while several others form a screen around them. When an SS guard comes near, a hiss goes from mouth to mouth.

Everyone is trying in his own way to save his last valuables. Some very clever people had their items sewn into their shoes in Riga; those are the luckiest here because if they can manage to hold on to their shoes, they will not suffer any hunger during their first months in camp.

Things seem to be lively in the washroom. We can hear the Oberscharführer shouting; apparently he has found something on somebody. One man with very long hair is trying to hide his wedding ring in his mane. "They're going to get it," he murmurs. "I'd rather throw it away." Indeed, several people throw their watches and rings into the latrine. Others bury their stuff in the sandy ground. They cautiously dig a little hole with their feet and then hide everything there, hoping to be able to return to this spot someday. I am convinced here, as in Riga, an SS will rake the ground after the delousing. At any rate, things are moving pretty fast today. Into the washroom! Two SS guards at the door examine you. One makes you open your mouth and spread your fingers, while the other one empties your shoes, though in my case he only finds a few small passport photos. He takes them away. It is lucky they're in such a hurry, so they can only make random checks. For ten seconds we stand under the shower, and then we're outside again, our bodies wet, in the middle of the night.

A few Stutthof inmates in striped clothes press clothing into our hands. In a short time we are newly dressed, not for the coming winter, but for the heat of summer. It is now past midnight. Finally we get the order to march off to the barracks. "Sing!" the escorting Scharführer commands. We look at each other, bone weary, hardly able to walk, but the Herr Scharführer has told us to sing. "I want to hear you sing, you swine," he says, "I said sing."

"We don't know any songs," one of us remarks.

A fist smashes into his face. "I'll teach you to sing, you lazy bastards!" the Scharführer shouts.

Up front in the first row one man makes up his mind. He starts singing "Das Wandern ist des Mullers Lust" [Hiking is the Miller's Joy"]. Several others join in, and so, laughing out of one eye and crying out of the other, we march towards the barracks of Camp Stutthof.

October 1944. Barracks Three is for the new arrivals. Whether there are a hundred or a thousand doesn't matter. Everybody has to go into Block Three. We find triple-decker army bunks, each bed a little over two feet wide, four men to a bed. This is the place for which we were longing so desperately. I am squatting on the third deck of the bunks with Stefan, Robert and a Jew from Kiel. The air is unbearable up here; you can hardly breathe. All the smells of the fully dressed people below us rise upward. You have to be careful not to hit your head on the ceiling. I'm perspiring from every pore. I decide it's better to sit on the floor between the beds than up here in the foul air. I find a small empty place. With my feet under the bunks, my head on the prison jacket, I quickly fall asleep.

A bugle sounds and a Kapo yells: "Everybody up! Everybody up!" It is five o'clock. I have slept some four hours, I figure, but there is little time for figuring here. "In five minutes you're out!" the Kapo hollers. A few seconds later there is a mad scramble at the door. Several Kapos have stormed the block with rubber sticks and truncheons, just as in Riga, hitting everybody in sight. "So you won't listen to orders? Get going! Out with you! You, there!" They beat anyone within reach mercilessly. There is a headlong rush to the door. Somebody must have stumbled, and others are falling on top of him. Most of the men climb right over without paying any attention to those stretched out on the floor. Without a second thought I climb out of the window, but unfortunately an SS guard is standing outside and sees me. He calls me over immediately and then, without another word, goes to work on me with his fists. But others have taken the same route as I, so he now must turn his attention to them. Later we stand at assembly for two hours. After that, we are ordered to fall out, but despite the pouring rain we are not permitted to go back to the barracks.

At ten o'clock they serve us our first warm food. We eat outside, standing in front of our block. There aren't enough bowls or spoons. One man waits for another to finish eating, so that about 30 men eat out of the same dish. It is soup with potato peels, beet chunks and a few threads of meat swimming in the greasy brown water. The cook is very smart. He ladles the broth off the top so that all the thick vegetables remain at the bottom, to be given to his own people later on. After this "meal" we're properly hungry; it seems to have stimulated the stomach nerves.

It is difficult here to relieve oneself. Toilets in our block have been stopped up for a long time because of overuse, and the doors are locked. The "Aryan blocks" don't allow Jews to use their latrines. Whenever they find a Jew in their toilets, the Polish inmates beat him half to death. I run around for hours until I find a place.

The washroom, too, is most often locked. It contains three round basins; some of the faucets dribble a bit of water. This has to be sufficient for 800 men, says the Polish block senior.

The whole camp has Polish leaders for the inmates. These Poles are bastards. They are virulently anti-Semitic; most are hardened criminals serving time for serious crimes. They suddenly realize that human beings are living among them, namely, the Jews. We are fair game. Anybody here can beat or torture a Jew with impunity. There are different classes of inmates here in Stutthof. First are the so-called "prisoners of honor," former diplomats who live in a special block to themselves and lack for nothing. Next in the pecking order are those who enjoy certain privileges because of their good conduct — they probably excel in the maltreatment of Jews. They are permitted to buy food for certain sums in the canteen. The various block seniors and camp police fall in this category, too. After that come the non-Jewish inmates of various nationalities; they, too, are treated more or less decently. The lowest of them all, the most downtrodden of the downtrodden, veritable pariahs, are the Jews.

In the afternoon we are registered. We have to state what kind of work we do, which transport we belong to and whether we're of Aryan or non-Aryan descent. Then we are given our numbers, with the yellow and black Star of David.

Several days later a small Jewish transport arrives from Liepaja, and the Ghetto Elder Leiser is among them. From the minute he enters the camp, things are tough for him. He appears only a shadow of his former self; all his arrogance and swagger are stripped from him like an old shirt under the force of the blows he catches from all sides. I, too, had planned to clobber him, but now I find it impossible to lay a finger on this miserable wretch.

The days follow each other in endless succession. Assembly at five in the morning, then two hours of standing outside in the cold until seven. After that, fall-out. Before roll call we quickly grab our breakfast, consisting of 100 grams of bread. In front of the block stands a prisoner from the kitchen with a bucket of coffee. If we're lucky, there is a cup, but mostly the 50 mugs that serve 800 men are all in use, so that most of us go without a hot drink in the morning. The piece of bread is gulped down and right away we start figuring how many hours it will be until we get something to eat again. We starve until lunch time, after which our stomachs are just as empty as before, as though we had hardly eaten anything at all. At five we again get the same amount of bread, sometimes with a dab of marmalade on top. Then again, two hours of standing on assembly, and then to "bed." That is the usual course of the day in the Forest Camp of Stutthof, which is the official title of the camp.

Now and then we hear rumors regarding our labor Kommandos which later prove to be false. Somebody claims our transport is to be sent to Buchenwald, another says that 500 of us are to be put to work in a machine factory. Thus all kinds of rumors, which never come true, abound. Hardly any political news reaches us, but we do learn Riga capitulated eight days after we left.

A whole company of Frenchmen arrived at camp. They were deloused, disarmed and put into striped garments. Only their long hair is left intact. It is said they had been sent to the Western front, but refused to fight. Now they're marching through camp, singing their French songs.

Around eleven o'clock in the morning, some strange vehicles pass through the camp on the road to the crematorium. The four-wheeled carts are crammed with women who are barely alive. They are pulled by several of their campmates; other women, wrapped in shawls, follow on foot. Two female SS guards drive them on with long whips. It is said that these women will be gassed and then cremated.

The chimney, it seems to me, is spewing particularly dark smoke. It is smoking day and night — I'm sure thousands upon thousands have gone through this chimney already.

We become quite used to the sight of the women walking to their death, and the chimney, too, no longer bothers us.

During the past few days we repeatedly went on "outside" jobs. In the forest Kommando we have to lug tree trunks on the run. As soon as one tree trunk is carried from the forest, we have to run back for the next one. The Jews, as usual, are given the hardest jobs and the worst Polish Kapos. The B.V.[2] of the forest Kommando whacks us like crazy if the work does not proceed fast enough for him. On top of that he inspects our bodies and takes everything he finds in our pockets. He takes away even the pieces of bread we have saved from breakfast.

From time to time an SS guard arrives who helps the B.V. give the beatings with a thick rubber truncheon. We are at their mercy. Whom should we complain to? To the block senior who steals our bread and exchanges it for tobacco, or to the "interior service" which is in cahoots with him? If we have to stay here much longer, none of us will get out alive. But all the transports from the East have been sent on "outside" work so far, and so we long for the day when we, too, will leave this camp again.

Sometimes I see a man on a bicycle ride up the road to the camp. He is smartly turned out in a leather jacket, matching leather pants, and brown boots. He looks dressed for a hunt. Later I'm told he is the camp senior.

Occasionally I observe the diplomatic gentlemen, the "prisoners of honor," walk about the camp in measured steps. They are identified by yellow armbands.

One night, when I have just made myself comfortable on the floor, we suddenly get the order to report for assembly. Again there are several wounded, and then we stand outside, facing a brightly illuminated gallows. A Polish prisoner is hanged for trying to escape. I turn my head away. It is not pleasant to see somebody hanged just before going to sleep. As soon as the sentence has been carried out, we are allowed to go back to our block.

The next morning all Jews have to assemble on the camp road. An SS guard stands on the right side of the road, and all the Jews have to run past him as fast as they can. After the assembly we hear that all the Jews were declared fit for work.

In the morning after assembly we all try to hide in every conceivable nook or cranny. Everybody refuses to work under these horrible conditions. A hunt starts in the camp. The Polish Kapos with their canes and truncheons begin rounding up all the Jews. Do those poor unfortunates catch it when they're discovered and driven to the assembly square. The inmates of other nationalities are spared such manhunts, but everybody enjoys watching us Jews in our misery.

I once try to mingle with the prisoners who are exempt from work, but I'm caught, and am given a good beating amid the cheers and jeers of the inmates standing in a circle around me. After that I have to report for work. We go to the army clothing center and have to move furniture. I get to see the large buildings under construction at Stutthof. A giant prison kitchen is being built where the food is going to be prepared for 100,000 inmates, the cheerful Kapo explains to us. Broad highways lead to the SS shelters which former Norwegian policemen are engaged in building. Enormous graded sites indicate the future size of the camp.

"You are pretty lucky," our Kapo tells us. "When we first started building this camp things were different here. Those SS barracks over there had to be put up in short order. In the morning 500 men set out to work on the building site. The Kapo had orders to bring back only 400. The other 100 were killed at the site. That's how things stood with us," he said. "Many of our comrades are pushing up daisies now."

"Now get," he urges. "Lend a hand, move faster than you usually do." The pieces of furniture have to be carried quite a distance. On the way back we always have to run. We pass the crematorium. It is an area enclosed by a wooden fence; all that is visible to the world outside is the tarpaper-covered roof of the building next to the chimney.

Frequently we have to report to the Arbeitsamt after morning assembly. People are constantly picked for small work Kommandos; some are used as artisans in Camp Burggraben. One day 500 Jews are chosen for work in a machine shop. It is said they are going to Brunswick. No German Jews are taken along. Whenever German Jews mingle with those chosen to go, they are ordered to step aside immediately. Thus I sneak into the transport three times, only to drop out again at the last moment when the Arbeitsamt clerk starts crossing out each number on his list.

Every one of us has only one desire — to leave this hellish place, no matter where to, as long as we can get away.

6

Schichau Dockyard, Poland

November 1944-January 1945

November 1944. One morning we are called to the office. The various occupational groups have to line up, and are ordered to turn left and go directly to the delousing center. From there, without being permitted to return to the barracks, we are marched on board a Vistula steamer which takes us to Danzig. Our destination is the submarine building section of the Schichau dockyard.

We sigh with relief. We're all glad to have left that madhouse behind. Nothing can be worse, we think. No food, no sleep and constant mistreatment — none of us could have stood it much longer. A different wind is blowing outside the camp; it seems to carry a faint scent of freedom.

We are taken off the steamer directly on the wharf. An Oberscharführer takes charge of us. We march past giant construction shops to the meeting room of the plant. Work is assigned here for the following day; then we march through Danzig for the first time. Our route leads past old patrician mansions, past old churches to the railroad station. People stare at us in astonishment, some also in pity; no malicious words are heard, as so often happened in Germany. It seems to me people become very grave at the sight of us; they pause, shake their heads and walk on, seemingly deep in thought.

Again we are greeted by barbed wire fences, lit by countless lights. At the camp gate each of us is given a plate, a mug and a spoon. The facilities are tolerable, everyone has a bed, and although the straw sack is hard, we will finally be able to sleep again. We get no food, because the camp has not yet been issued our rations. It hardly makes any difference any more whether we eat or not; our bodies getting thinner and thinner.

At half past four we are awakened. Outside the camp a special train is waiting to take us to Danzig. The train is unheated. There are no windowpanes; the icy air whistles through the compartments, and all we have on our bodies are our light prison garments. Later our wooden slippers clatter through the empty streets. The gate opens and we are assigned our places of work.

I had registered in Stutthof as an assembler, just to be able to get out of the camp. Now I am assigned to a foreman in U-boat construction. I have to bend oil pipes and of course have no idea about the work; my foreman realizes it immediately and he explains patiently, without scolding, how to do it. As soon as I'm up on the scaffold, he tells me he is a member of the Nazi party and doesn't consider Germany's military situation hopeless. I reply that if Germany's situation is not hopeless, my own is even less so. He keeps me busy bending pipes. In the morning he hands me a pipe and when he returns at noon I'm still standing in the same spot, pipe in hand. With such workers building submarines you certainly can't win a war. There are Latvians, Russians, Frenchmen, Poles, Ukranians and Serbs; everybody stands around without lifting a finger. And now we Jews, who have no intention of doing any work either. The Russians say, "Nyet kushet, nyet rabotti [no food, no work]." The Frenchmen keep a polite grin on their faces, and the Poles tell us newcomers, "Germanski kaput." My foreman is a very decent fellow; he sees that I don't want to work and he leaves me alone. This way we get along fine. But not all the foremen are like him. Many fanatical Nazis drive and beat their workers, though most of them know they're losing the war.

Still, the days are very strenuous. We have to work for twelve hours in these vast, cold machine shops; the hours seem endless, and the stomachs growl. At noon we receive about a pint of very clear hot broth, which has been prepared from some artificial substance. It tastes awful, but it warms our innards a little.

At night when we return to the camp, we receive our daily ration, a quarter of a loaf of bread, and another pint of watery soup. On that we are supposed to work for twelve hours.

It is very difficult to get any additional food. We have nothing left to trade and can only steal wherever and whenever possible. The storerooms are broken into again and again; one night the clothing chamber is cleaned out. For this reason the Oberscharführer lectures us one Sunday afternoon. "Listen, you've got to stop the stealing, or you're all going into the ovens. I know your lives are tough, and I'll try to get more food. When we've won the war, you'll all be free and can go to Palestine."

This speech restores my good humor. It is very nice of the Oberscharführer to promise us permission to go to Palestine.

Another habit has developed among the Jews. Most of them cannot be found at their places of work but in the beautifully tiled washroom, where they sleep sitting on the toilets or on the floor. It is the only room that is heated.

We're soon found out, and every ten minutes a guard comes to chase us out. One who walks with a limp excels — you only have to open the door to the toilet, and already he is there and starts beating you. But one day we pay him back. One of us is hosing down part of the factory while he is standing watch. Every now and then he comes into the shop to go to the toilet and to drive the Jews out. Our boy just waits for the door to open and accidentally hits him with a hard jet of water. He is soaked through from top to bottom and swears like hell, but even his comrades have a good laugh at him. Then he starts beating up our boy, but we're all used to that.

This camp is run by Jews. A Latvian Jew by the name of Glücksmann is the camp senior, his assistant-in-beating is a Jew from Cassel named Österreicher. There is no difference between them and their counterparts in Stutthof; they are just as brutal and vicious as the Polish Kapos. Österreicher and Glücksmann make it a habit to search our beds and drawers for forbidden food. Whatever they find they keep.

Occasionally potatoes are unloaded close to the camp. The Oberscharführer says that if the night shift will work for several hours to help unload them, we can have as many as we can carry. I return to camp stuffed with potatoes — I have "organized" close to 50 pounds, for which I sacrificed several hours of sleep. When we return from the night shift the next morning, dreaming with anticipation of a large pot of potatoes boiled in the jackets, we're all bitterly disappointed. Glücksmann and Österreicher have searched the beds and drawers and taken all our potatoes. Our own Jews have seen to it that we should be too hungry to sleep.

Glücksmann carries on like mad. He is dressed up like a hunter. On Sunday, his valet polishes his boots for him, and in this getup he struts about the camp. Every now and then he stands at attention before the Oberscharführer to receive his orders. After Glucksmann a Polish underworld figure named Chamek plays a dangerous role in the camp. He is a block senior, and it is said of him that he worked in the gas chamber at Auschwitz where he is supposed to have murdered many Jews. From there he came to Stutthof, and now he is with us to continue his murderous trade. One blow from him, and the victim does not get up again. Besides Glücksmann, he is the most savage figure in the camp. After the liberation he is immediately shot by the Russians; Glücksmann manages to escape — he lives in Hanover and is suffering from persecution mania.

Many Jews often collapse from starvation and the long working hours and soon die. At night we carry our dead back to camp. It is a ghastly procession that moves through the streets of Danzig. Worn-out, ruined figures, clad in oil-stained rags, we clatter through the narrow streets. The dead are carried at the rear of the column; behind them march Jews with freshly cut planks for the coffins. Our guards march on the sidewalks beside us, their rifles at the ready. Many of us link arms because we feel too weak to walk alone. Sometimes a pile of coal lies in the railroad station. We all try to pick up a few pieces in passing, for there is no fuel in the camp. The people in the streets hardly notice us any more. Once a woman called out to her husband in fright, "My God, Max, look at those poor people!" when she caught sight of us.

My comrades say they saw her weep. Occasionally passers-by even hand our people sandwiches, but these are rare acts of kindness.

Several Jews are building air raid shelters for the workers. They are badly treated and exposed to heavy snowfall all day. They suffer the most casualties, but this Kommando is constantly being replenished from the so-called Umschichtung [replacement].

Management has decided to train Jewish prisoners as specialists. They are trying to make welders, smelters and plumbers out of us to keep the German war machine going. Sometimes I think of Salaspils: it is a long road from there to here, from the destruction of thousands of our people to the attempt at training the survivors of these infernos as specialists to keep up war production. They hope to win the war with the help of their worst enemy. This thought makes us all feel better; it is obvious that this war cannot last much longer.

The whole submarine production is a flop. Machine parts are missing everywhere, factories producing essential items have been destroyed by bomber attacks, and it looks as if nobody is taking a real interest in the work anymore. We hear that a submarine built on our wharf sank during its trial run — we suspect somebody pulled the plug. Our Kolonnenführer announces the impending inspection of the works; everybody is supposed to be working hard when these gentlemen pass through. Several high party functionaries appear, cross the shop with measured steps, and stop here and there in order to watch a worker at his job. Their chests covered with medals, they stand near a Jewish welder who seems to be their last hope of winning the war. They even try to climb the scaffolds, take a peek into the interior of a U-boat, notice a few Jews hanging around and walk on, turning up their noses.

The spirit of solidarity in our block is no longer as it should be. Sometimes we are given a whole loaf of bread which is supposed to last us for four days. It often happens that a piece of bread rationed with great self-discipline disappears from our cupboard, so we have to go without food for several days. But the thief who lives in our midst is rarely caught. Most of us start carrying our bread, though that tempts us to eat it all at one time and then we have to go without bread for a long time.

Once a whole bucket of marmalade is stolen during the unloading of the supply truck. All the blocks are searched, but the 25 pounds of marmalade are not found. Unofficially we learn that the kapos got it all.

Some items of clothing have arrived from Stutthof. I manage to get hold of a sweater which I sell several days later to a Russian for a pound of tobacco. The tobacco is resold at camp, rolled into individual cigarettes at half a slice of bread for each cigarette. In place of the sweater I wrap my blanket around my chest under the prison garment. It's hard to move like that, but the blanket keeps me warm and serves the same purpose as the sweater.

In this way we drag on from day to day, from week to week, without a change in our situation. The night shifts in the cold assembly shops are almost unbearable — from six at night to six in the morning is a very long time. The shop is lit by many lamps; however, they only light up the immediate area surrounding them. Cold air penetrates through the open doors into the interior and mixes with the heat of the electric welding machines. The rhythmic hammering on iron is accompanied by the screeching and creaking of the cranes lifting finished parts to the outside where they are fitted into the ships. My foreman on the night shift is from Danzig. He doesn't talk much, but sometimes when he thinks nobody's observing him he starts to rave about the time when Danzig was a free city. "You could get everything then," he says. "We lacked for nothing until Danzig became German. But soon it'll all be over," he says, "and Danzig will be independent again."

He often takes me to the forge where it is warm because of all the electrical equipment in use there. I am permitted to leave the huge assembly shop in his company, walking behind him at a respectful distance, carrying several pipes. In the forge the foreman tells me to wait until the pipes have been properly bent. That takes about two hours; then he picks me up again and we go back to the assembly shop. The rest of the night I usually spend on the toilet. Every now and then I am awakened from my light slumber by the furious voice of the shopmaster who throws everybody out of the toilet, but as soon as he is gone we all go back and continue sleeping until dawn, when the relief shift arrives. During the night we cut up several boards intended for scaffolding and smuggle them under our prison coats out of the gate so that we can use them to warm our shelter a little.

December 1944. Only the complete military defeat of the Germans in France keeps our spirits alive. The Allies have advanced to the German border in the west. Fleets of bombers in numbers never known before are destroying the German cities. Danzig is overcrowded with German refugees fleeing from the East; a section of our camp has been vacated as an emergency shelter for them. We realize to our regret that in a very short time we will have to flee from our liberators. That was the reason I had such misgivings about Danzig — we all knew it, too, would be just another temporary stop. How long before the Russians are near and we will have to endure a second evacuation?

And then I get sick. Stefan and Robert carry me back to camp from work and take me immediately to the sick ward. The thermometer shows a temperature of 102 degrees. Probably typhoid fever, the doctor says. I am put into an isolation ward, together with several other men; every morning and night they take my temperature. That is my only treatment, since there are no medicines. I lay there for two weeks with a high fever, getting no better. One day the Jewish doctor takes a blood test which is sent to a medical institute in Danzig. A reply arrives, addressed to the Jewish inmate doctor, which begins, "Dear Colleague." We have to laugh: the professor at the institute considers himself a colleague of our Jewish concentration camp doctor. But we are impressed with him, because there is no doubt it takes great courage to address a camp

Jew in this manner. Still, we have to smile at the colleague out in the free world who probably has no idea of the chasm that separates him from his "colleague" here.

Every day several Jews die in the typhoid ward. They are carried out and buried in a mass grave near the camp. For several weeks I lay there with constant fever and diarrhea, getting no better. We are completely isolated from the world; nobody can visit us because of the danger of infection. The medic hardly speaks — it is as if we were already dead. A patient sometimes goes mad in his delirium and starts throwing any object he can lay his hands on around the room until the medic comes and ties him down. The next morning he is dead and men come to carry him outside.

In one corner there is a Jew with spotted typhus. This disease is particularly contagious, but we all have to use the same toilet. When he dies, several people actually feel relieved — the danger of contagion was too great.

Death has become a friend to me. Sometimes it truly seems to be a blessing. But then I want to live; I dream of wonderful hiking tours and picture myself sitting in a little boat on a lovely summer evening, slowly drifting out to sea with the current. Often I wake up bathed in perspiration and see a man lying next to me groaning in pain. News from the outside world reaches us even here. The carpenter who repairs a bed that collapsed tells us the evacuation of Danzig has begun. It is only a matter of days until we'll have to leave the camp. They say we'll have to march since there are no other means of transportation. We in the typhus ward don't feel good about these reports. Though the doctor says I have passed the crisis, I'm much too weak to march.

The doctor comes into the ward with a list and puts down the names of all those he considers unable to march. He tells me and a few other men that he can't assume the responsibility for leaving us behind here. We should decide for ourselves whether or not we wish to stay. I believe that to remain means a sure death, and I cannot anticipate the hardships of the march. Thus five Jews are released from the ward so they can do walking exercises to prepar

January 1945. For days we've been waiting for the order to march. They say that when the Russians reach a certain point, we will have to leave the camp. Every day we see endless columns of refugees in the streets; some are inmates from Stutthof, plodding westward on the icy roads under heavy guard.

My health is very bad again. The high fever has returned, but I don't dare to go back to the sick ward since I'm afraid they won't let me join the march. The last thing I want is to be left behind. There is only one thing to do: pull myself together — we are so close to our probable liberation. I have dreamt of freedom through too many tortured years to give up now.

The camp is rather quiet. Every now and then we are called out to work, sweeping snow from the streets so that the waves of refugees fleeing homeward can roll smoothly on. Sometimes we shovel the snow from the railroad tracks, which is very dangerous work because the trains to Danzig, loaded with war materiel, run constantly. Rumors are rife that the Russians are already near Danzig. We are encircled, a railroader told one of our men; there are all sorts of other stories, but unfortunately never any truth to them. The food has become much worse since the factory no longer sends hard labor rations to the camp. We cannot imagine how we're going to march a whole day in our physical condition; most of us are so weak we can barely walk.

Every day sick people are brought to us who collapsed on the road, but the camp is already so overcrowded we don't know where to put them. The Oberscharführer orders that all new arrivals are to be put on the mess hall floor. It is only natural that the sick people lying on the cold cement die very quickly; every day we have twenty of them. They bring us mostly women, but also some men who tell us of big raids in Danzig — everybody who does not have proper identification papers or has been absent from critical war work without excuse is immediately taken to a concentration camp. All of Danzig is being evacuated, we are told. The streets are over-crowded and nobody knows where to put all the refugees.

These reports give us some hope that maybe we won't have to set out on the march into misery. It would be the salvation of many of us, but the SS isn't going to give us our freedom that easily.

Today a new company of guards has arrived at camp, all black-uniformed SS with skulls on their caps. They look very dangerous; the entire camp is under intensified guard. Even the barracks are patrolled by SS men with automatic rifles. We learn the guards have been given the order to shoot anyone who comes near the fence. Late at night they call the roll. Everyone has to run in single file past the Oberscharführer for "selection." Those who run well are sent to the left, the others have to line up on the right. Everyone tries to create an impression of robust health because we're all afraid to remain behind. We have had ample occasion to find out what they do to sick and weak people. Those found unfit for the trek are sent to the sick ward. They plead with the Oberscharführer to take them along, but he brusquely refuses. We're not so sure whether it is a good idea to go on the march. We've learned from a guard that according to a new order, every Jew who collapses on the road is to be shot. On the other hand, we don't know what they will do to those who remain behind in the sick ward. It is a gamble with death.

At ten the next morning we get the order to march.

7

Death March in Germany

January-March 1945

January 1945. This is the second time we're fleeing from our liberators. Fortunately the weather isn't too cold, so it is quite comfortable walking in our wooden slippers. One has to be careful not to step into the many puddles that the mild weather has created from the melting snow. There is no halt the whole day, nor is there any food, so that even on the first day it takes great physical stamina to keep up with the column marching at a smart pace. Toward evening it starts to rain; and the mushy snow sticks to our wooden slippers so that we're all relieved when we reach the village. The Kolonnenführer says we're going to spend the night here. Since he can find no other quarters for us, we're locked up in the village church. We have to lie down on the stone floor because all the pews are occupied by other refugees.

This night is one of the most horrible nights of my life. I am stretched out on the cold stone floor, totally exhausted and shivering with fever. The blanket offers no protection from the iciness under me nor from the freezing air coming through cracks in the door and the windows. We move close together to warm each other. I am bathed in perspiration; I feel I won't be able to march any further and that my will to live is leaving. I ask Stefan, who is lying next to me, to give my love in case he should survive to my brothers and sisters who are scattered all over the world. He tries to comfort and encourage me, but the fever is stronger.

"Don't be silly, Josef," he says. "Tomorrow morning you'll feel better. You don't want to give up now, so soon before our liberation." But my resistance is gone and my mind escapes into feverish dreams.

I remain lying in the church the next morning. I am confused and don't even know where I am. A few kicks from the guard recall me to reality. Two Jews come, drag me behind them through the church — they're too weak to carry me — and put me down in the snow outside. I don't know how long I've been lying there, when an old woman hands me a cup of hot milk and a sandwich. I think I must be dreaming. "Here, take this," she says, and puts the bread, which I did not touch, into the pocket of my prison coat. She takes the empty cup from my hand and runs away quickly. Two men arrive with a cart. One grabs me by the head, the other by the feet, and they throw me on like a piece of junk. After a while heavy iron doors open, the two men seize me again by head and foot and drag me into the village jail. A warden undresses me and brings several blankets. I'm just beginning to get warm and to enjoy the prison, when the door opens. Two guards stand outside. The warden has to dress me all over again in my wet prison clothes. I'm tossed on a cart, my head resting under the driver's seat, and off we go over the bumpy road out of the village.

I am again seized by feverish chills. What do they want from me? Why don't they let me die? All I want is to die, to die and to be buried somewhere on the road. I press my handkerchief into my mouth and some rags into my nostrils. I don't want to breathe anymore and imagine I can suffocate like that. But I don't suffocate. I start banging my head on the floor of the cart, and am pleased when I am shaken by the deep ruts. Maybe I'll die that way — I cannot die. In the meantime they have picked up other Jews from the road; the cart is filling up and we move closer together. I hear the two guards who accompany us. "I'm sure this guy is dead," one of them says, and kicks my feet with his boot to see if any life is left in me. When I don't make a sound, he throws his bread sack on top of me. "This one's finished," he says to the other guard.

Suddenly I am struck like lightning: maybe I'm not supposed to die. Maybe I'm going to live. It is like having a revelation. I'm suddenly convinced I'm going to live, that everything else was only a bad dream. I start moving again. The guard takes his sack off me and remarks to his comrade, "So he's alive after all." Yes, I'm alive, and

I'm going to live — this is an unshakable certainty which will not leave me any more until my liberation.

At night we arrive in another village. We spend the night standing up in a barn, because there is no room to sit or to lie down. The next morning we move on, dead tired. The cart remains in the village, and the sick have to rejoin the march. Very early the next morning a guard shoots two Jews who are too weak to continue walking. When I turn around I see the guard kick the bodies into the ditch by the side of the road.

Shortly before Rieben, in Pomerania, our column is divided; one half marches to the left and the rest proceeds straight ahead. Our column has become so long the guards are no longer enough; still, it makes no sense to escape because we don't know where the Russians are. In addition, our striped prison clothes are so conspicuous, the villagers would certainly be afraid to give us shelter.

In the late afternoon we reach a vacated labor camp, which is now used to shelter prisoners. Our guard decides we're going to spend the night here, but since there is no room in the blocks for Jews, we 500 men are locked into the cellar beneath the kitchen. The floor is damp, there are puddles everywhere, and more water from the melting snow penetrates into the dungeon where we stand pressed close together. This is our third night without sleep and without food on the march. My knees are weak, my limbs are heavy with fatigue, and my eyelids close. Stefan, who is standing beside me, puts his head on my shoulder. I lean against him, and thus we fall into a dreamless slumber for several hours.

The next morning I stumble up the cellar steps to relieve myself. Since I don't know where the latrine is, I look around the kitchen corner to find it. A few yards away is a guard.

"Come here!" he calls to me. "What do you want?"

"I want to go out," I reply and try to stand at attention.

"Did you arrive yesterday?" he continues, because yesterday only Jews arrived.

"Yes," I reply.

"When I hit you, you'll fly ten feet," he says, and motions to me with his forefinger to step closer. The next moment a right hook lands on my chin. I do fly several feet and lie in the snow.

"Come here, my friend," he calls to me and makes the familiar motion with his forefinger. I rise painfully and come towards him, fully aware this can't be healthy for me, but neither would it be to disobey his command. He repeats his game several times and finally leaves me lying in the snow. Meanwhile, other Jews have emerged from the cellar on the same quest as I.

They get a severe beating from the guard; then they are sent on from one to the next — the guards stand at ten yard intervals and get their a chance for some early-morning exercise. Later many Jews are lying outside in the mud. We can hear their wailing in our cellar, which I have managed to return to, though none of us dares to go outside to assist the unfortunate men.

On the order of the camp commander, a storage barn is cleaned out for the Jews. Some straw is scattered on the floor and a sign reading "Jewish Ward" is put on the door. Our first typhus cases are put in this ward. The sick are left without any care, because there are no medicines. They waste away and die one by one. There is no way to save them. The number of sick grows day by day due to the lack of food. Desperation seizes us; we all feel this camp is going to be the final station on our long and arduous road of the past few years. This is where we will meet our destruction just before liberation.

There is no food for the new arrivals, the well-fed head cook tells our Kolonnenführer. "We didn't count on you here. We have to take care of our own people first," he says with a sarcastic grin.

For three days now we haven't had any bread. At two o'clock all those still able to walk have to assemble in front of the kitchen. We are given one ladle of clear horse broth, with scraps of horse meat and a few potato peels. As soon as we've received this brew, we are driven to our cellar where we drink it standing. The Kapo stationed at the door does not let anybody out, to make sure the Jews won't get a double portion. We are hungry all the time; our thoughts are occupied only with food.

How will it be possible to keep from starving to death? It is again a matter of mathematics, just like in Salaspils. If the food situation does not change, I will starve in a short time. It is a gruesome sight to watch the figures staggering about in their grey blankets, and to be able to calculate: this one, or that one, is not going to last more than two days. The husky electrician from Kaiserwald limps past me. His face is completely emaciated, and his staring, starving eyes indicate he is not going to live much longer. In the evening someone finds him in the latrine where he fell asleep, and drags him through the mud to our block. The next morning he is dead, without having regained consciousness. When I wake from my dreamless sleep, I'm so weak I can barely rise. With tremendous effort I pull myself together to report to roll call. Holding on to the wall, I cautiously walk step by step in order to get my feeble legs moving again.

Weisel, the former head cook of the SS kitchen in Riga, is the camp commander here. He is a real sadist and takes pleasure in keeping the skeleton-like men, already marked by death, waiting in the cold for a long time. Meanwhile he stands in the entrance to the SS barracks cozily smoking a cigarette. Every now and then he tells the newly-named camp senior that the line of the column is still not straight enough, adding casually he has plenty of time.

A snowstorm is howling about us; we stand there, shivering with cold. Some collapse and are dragged to the ward. A young Jew from Lodz goes insane. "Mama," he screams incessantly. "Mama!"

A blow from Chamek, the Pole, shuts him up; he is dragged away.

After the counting I usually go right away to the typhus ward and lie down on the bit of straw, although it hardly keeps the cold off the floor. It is best to lie down because this way you use up the least energy. Sometimes, several Jews secretly creep to the guarded garbage heap next to the kitchen and pick out potato and turnip peels, which they then cook on the small iron stove in the typhus ward. There is always a fierce struggle for the place next to the stove. Stein, the man who heats the stove, demands his tribute in the form of a portion of the fried peels, but nobody wants to share anything with him. With the pushing and shoving in the crowded room, the flimsy stove, which is only temporarily installed, threatens to fall over. Stein hollers he is not going to chop wood for the stove any more if he doesn't get his share of the peels. The men lying here are members of the human race only in outward appearance. They have lost all civilization or humanity. Here everybody fights everybody else for a place near the stove, for a piece of potato peel, or for the last possessions of a comrade who has just died. The pockets of the dead man are quickly searched, the lunch bag is snatched from under his head and ransacked, and the blanket is torn from his body. It no longer matters how one lives, as long as one survives.

Several times I, too, creep to the garbage heap and get hold of a few horse bones. I put them on the stove and let them roast; then I slowly gnaw them. At least my hunger pangs are somewhat appeased, and sometimes I even find some marrow in the cooked bones.

Everybody in the typhus ward now has diarrhea. Most of the men are so weak they can no longer walk over to the bucket to relieve themselves. The straw is soiled, the people are covered with filth and crawling with lice; they are ruins. I have never seen so many lice in my life. People scratch their bites open, and large, suppurating sores are formed which are terribly disfiguring. I, too, have a couple of sores which keep me from lying on my back. Wherever you touch your body, you get hold of lice which multiply enormously in this filth and stench. For the thousands in the camp there is only one water pump, and that is reserved for kitchen use for several hours of the day. So we no longer wash because nobody has the strength to stand in line for an hour for a chance to wash from the mugs we are given. Of the 500 Jews brought to this camp, 100 are dead two weeks later and about 120 are ill; the rest are barely able to walk. We're all agreed it is just a matter of time until those still alive will be piled into the mass grave dug by the Polish inmates.

February 1945. The certainty of our approaching death brings renewed thoughts of escape. Those still somehow able to do so make plans to cheat death and then try to put their plans into operation. After evening roll call an alarm is sounded from every corner of the camp. About 20 Jews have tried to break through the chain of guards. Twelve are shot during the attempt; the others apparently succeeded in escaping. There is another roll call. The SS wants to determine exactly how many have escaped. Tension in the camp is worse than ever. Most of the Jews are ready to put an end to this situation even if it should cost them their lives, rather sooner than later.

The SS, in steel helmets and with fixed bayonets surround us. The Jewish block senior is called. The Obersturmbannführer in charge of the camp tells him that if another attempt at escape is made, all Jews at the camp, without exception, will be killed. This is his last warning. Our block senior tries to describe conditions at the camp, but the Sturmbannführer interrupts him after his first words.

"You keep your mouth shut, you swine," he says. "Tell your people to move off, that's all."

We've been in this death camp now for almost three weeks; three times we received a slice of bread weighing about 100 grams, and 10 grams of margarine. Every morning when we get out from the block, we receive half a cup of coffee, because the kitchen is not equipped for such mass feeding. Every few days, an old nag that like us can hardly walk anymore is led to the camp and slaughtered. It is intended for our midday soup.

Our conversations are often concerned with whether the bread truck is going to come today or not. If it does, we have a chance to get a slice of bread again. We always watch the gate to see whether the truck is finally arriving. Mostly we are disappointed. Sometimes a truck with potatoes drives into the camp, heavily guarded, and is unloaded in front of the kitchen. And when the truck with bread really arrives at last, we stand at a respectful distance and count the loaves being unloaded. Some of us figure out how much bread each one will get, but we always make mistakes because here, too, half of the bread is grabbed by the Polish Kapos.

Our own Kapos act no differently. Several buckets of soup are brought for those Jews no longer able to walk and lying in the typhus ward. It is the Kapos' job to distribute the soup fairly. I am lying close to the door so I can observe the goings-on in the adjoining room where the soup kettle has been placed. The Kapos have assembled and first take heaping ladlefuls of soup for themselves as reward for their important job of beating the Jews out of their barracks. During the next half-hour everybody's eyes are on the door and impatient voices are heard demanding soup. After a while a strong Kapo appears and counts the wretched figures on the floor. In this way he determines how many Jews have died since yesterday. Because he has received rations according to yesterday's numbers, he can now figure out how many portions he can keep for himself and his friends.

Then, slowly, they start dishing out the soup. The first ones to get it start complaining. They were given only half a ladleful.

"Chamek, dip deeper into the bucket," one sick man calls. Another starts to cry when he sees the small portion of soup for which he waited all morning in desperate hunger. A few hastily swallowed spoonfuls of hot water and the day's meal is finished. It is hard to believe we will have no more food until the next day.

"Did everybody get served?" asks the Kapo dishing up the soup of a Jew who passes it on to the figures lying on the floor. "No! no!" some start screaming. "We didn't get anything." Two more portions of soup are brought. "Here, this one didn't get anything," somebody says, pointing to a Jew lying next to him. The Jew serving the soup kicks the man's leg, but he no longer moves.

"This one's dead," he says. "He doesn't need soup any more. You wanted to get a double ration, eh, gonif [thief]?"

After the mass feeding the Kapos have their second meal. It makes my mouth water when I see them dig deep into the bucket and come up with ladlefuls of potato peels and meat scraps which they gobble up with relish. I have known for a long time that only the worst and most brutal kind of person can survive here. Everyone else is fated for the mass grave.

Several days later some German army officers come to the camp. We learn they need workers for building tank ditches, and that they have asked the commander to release inmates for this purpose.

The next morning the Obersturmbannführer calls up all the Jews to report for work. Only those lying in the typhus ward are spared. It is off to Tuchler Heath without breakfast. The Germans hope to stop the Russians even here in their advance.

Already on the way to work some collapse with exhaustion; we are too weak to carry them so we drag them by the arms behind us through the high snow. At the work site we simply drop them; by evening, most are dead.

A special detachment of SS, some with police dogs, accompanies us on the way to our labor. We are a pathetic column of starved men dragging over the lonely heath, dirt and mud clinging to our wooden slippers. Sometimes our slippers get stuck in the deep snow; I have a lot of trouble digging mine out again. We're all used to wet feet, but our thin clothing offers no protection from the icy wind blowing over the heath. From early morning until late at night we stand exposed to the weather in the open field, praying we'll soon be delivered from our misery. Already a pile of people are lying in the snow. I hear the Polish Kapo ask the Kolonnenführer for a vehicle to transport the starved, frozen men back to camp.

"Are you crazy?" the Kolonnenführer shouts at him. "You think we're going to drive these swine yet?"

At night the death column moves slowly toward camp. Every few steps we have to rest; our dead are too heavy. It is especially difficult to negotiate the uneven ground. Sometimes the carriers break down beside the dead. A column of horror, far removed from the eyes of civilized men, we stagger through the desolate landscape toward camp. At the entrance we have to form a line, stand at attention and raise our shovels while we're counted. We leave our dead outside the gate. The Kolonnenführer counts them to verify our number, and calls the burial Kommando to bury the dead.

In the evening after roll call they tell us that beginning the next day we will get a supplementary hard labor ration. And in fact, when we leave the camp again, we receive about 150 grams of bread at the gate. Unfortunately we get this extra ration only once. The next morning we are told at the gate we'll get our ration when we return from work. When we get back, dead tired, and ask for our piece of bread, the camp commander turns us away with the words, "The demands from you Jews never stop." Thus we are cheated out of our hard-earned bread. As a consequence more Jews remain in the camp, unable to work. Suddenly the SS storms our block, armed with rubber truncheons, and drives us outside like cattle. "We'll show you swine! You'll work until the juice boils in your assholes." And they beat us, not caring where their blows land. Some are not quick enough to get up; they are trampled to death by the mass of people stampeding outside. Moaning and groaning, one Jew lies in the mud directly in front of the block. An SS guard tells him to get up. Several Jews step in to assist the sick man, but the SS man drives them off. The man can no longer get up by himself. So the SS man draws his revolver and shoots him before the eyes of the assembled Jews.

On top of everything it starts to rain. In a short while we are wet through, the heavy clay soil sticks to our shovels, the rain seeps into the ditches we're digging, and soon we are standing in water up to our ankles. An SS leader arrives and chews out the guards. The work has to go faster, he shouts at them. We don't have forever; there are other jobs to be done.

Several vehicles bring fir trees which the tank ditches are to be camouflaged with. From now on the Jews who collapse lie on the ground on top of the fir trees. Every day we drag more and more of them back to camp; the column is being replenished with Poles and inmates of other nationalities. These inmates receive different rations and are therefore better able to work than the Jews, who are about completely starved. But there is no mercy. Our clothes are in shreds; we have tied the wooden slippers to our feet with string. We are out in this weather day after day without warm underwear or gloves, waiting for death which to many of us would mean a blessed release.

In the evening, when I lie down on the barracks floor (there is enough room now, since half of the Jews are dead), I dream of a means of escape. I see before me a large potato storage pit which we pass every day on the way to work. Maybe I could hide there, build a cave and live on the potatoes until the Russians arrive. But I lack the courage. My legs are too heavy; I cannot run anymore. The situation appears hopeless.

A new rumor is making the rounds in the camp. An inmate who fetched a load of potatoes for the SS says he heard from a peasant that we are encircled. This time the truth is guaranteed. It will only be a matter of days, and we will certainly be liberated.

Our courage is revived. I give the good news to Stefan, who is lying beside me. He says, "If your news had always been true, we would have been liberated ten times already." But in spite of everything I begin to hope again. It is not too late yet; I am still alive. There is less of me day by day, but I can still last a few more days. I can encircle my thighs with my hands. I cannot sit on a bench any more; I am only skin and bones.

A new order has been posted on the blackboard: all inmates have to be deloused. All shirts and underpants are to be rinsed in a solution, and then we have to put them back on wet so that the lice on our bodies will be killed also. Icy cold these last days of February, and we are asked to put our underclothes on wet. I decide it is better to go around for one day without underwear, dressed only in the prison pants and jacket. By evening I have a bad cold. My resistance is gone, and I would so much like to live. But inwardly I prepare for death. In my thoughts I say good-bye to all my loved ones scattered throughout the world, each in a safe haven. I would have liked to tell them about the fate of our dear mother. I would have liked to see my hometown again, to show myself and say, "Here I am again. A kind fate, against which even the cruel German murderers were powerless, has spared me. I want to return good for the evil they have done to us." But these are only dreams. In reality I'm lying here in stench and filth awaiting my death. For four days we have received no bread, only the thin horse soup. I just live on charred horse bones.

Next to me, the conductor of the Riga Opera died this morning. Last night he still told me about his plans for the future. He wanted to go back to the opera, make music again, and take over the direction of the Riga Conservatory which he lead until his arrest. But he has starved to death. I still find a little soup under his pillow which he had saved to eat for breakfast.

Opposite me lies Professor Weil. He used to give the Faust lectures in the ghetto; before that he was a professor at the University of Vienna. Now he lies there and sobs constantly. Again and again he tries to get up, but he is too weak; his legs won't carry him any more.

Since he knows he is going to die, he calls Stefan and asks him to look up his wife in case he should survive. Then he takes a medallion he wears on a chain around his neck, hands it to Stefan and asks him to give it to her as a last greeting. All the while he talks he is crying softly. The next morning he is carried outside. There is a tinsmith from the Riga ghetto; he used to be like a tree, but one cannot recognize him anymore. His will to live has left him; for several hours now he has been sitting outside in the snow, his head bent forward, sleeping. Several Jews try to carry him into the barracks, but they no longer have the strength; they let him sit where he is. A few hours later he is dead. One by one our fellow Jews leave us. When will it be my turn? I keep asking myself the same anxious question. Shall I outlast this race with death?

Then they carry out my dear Stefan. I did not realize death was so close. My heart is about to break. From the start on our road of suffering we always met again at some point and were happy to see each other. We would shake hands and rejoice that we were still alive and believe in our lucky star. It was Stefan who visited my dear mother a day before her sudden death and gave her my love. Dear Stefan, you truly were a pure soul; you never harmed anyone but gave away your last piece of bread. I shall never forget you, my true friend and comrade. If I live, Stefan, I shall shout from the rooftops the injustice done to us, so that everybody will hear, for the world cannot block its ears to our suffering. I will say the Kaddish for you as if you'd been my brother. Your parents whom you mentioned so often are buried somewhere in the Hochwald near Riga. You had no brothers and sisters, so who will look for you in the free world? But if I should live, I shall honor your name and light a candle in your memory every year on February 28.

So life with its misery goes on. Sometimes Polish inmates come to the typhus ward where I'm lying and seek out the patients who are still able to walk. I am among them. We have to bring fir branches to the camp from the nearby forest in order to camouflage the barracks. Several half-starved figures sway along the path, always on the lookout for something edible. Our guard is a Volkssturm [People's Home Guard] soldier from Berlin. He is fairly tolerant, one can talk to him. I ask him a few simple questions, trying to find out what is going on in the world, and how far away the Russians are. But I don't learn anything about that; he just says "if this stupid war does not end soon we're all going to throw away our guns." He is fed up, he says. We pass a few farmhouses and he lets us go inside. We beg for potatoes, but we have to hurry, because the guard is afraid his comrades or his superior might see us. He starts beating us with his rifle butt to drive us out of the potato barn.

Outside, a real battle develops among us. In the haste several prisoners did not get any potatoes, and they attack those who they think did. But who is going to give up a potato here without a struggle? These people who are hardly able to stand on their feet are fighting and wrestling with each other; there is nothing human left in us anymore. The potato has become the greatest treasure we can still possess. I carry eight precious potatoes in my pants pockets; every day I shall cut one up in slices and roast it on the stove. I decide that I will give one slice to Stein, who heats the stove, so I shall live on my potatoes for eight days. But where am I going to keep my hoard? I cannot possibly carry them on my body, and in the ward they will be stolen, because we no longer respect each other's property. So I roast one potato after the other, with Stein watching like a hawk to make sure he gets his promised share of each potato.

When I lie awake at night I always imagine I hear the thunder of the guns; it cannot be very far away, many of us think. Every night the camp is completely blacked out; all the lights are extinguished. A notice on the blackboard says that leaving the block during the night is strictly forbidden. The guards are instructed to shoot on sight. A rumor is going around the camp that we will be evacuated in the next few days, but nothing happens. The work parties march out, as usual, only the atmosphere at the camp seems more restless. Many cars are parked in front of the administration building; there is constant coming and going. The rumbling of the guns has become much more distinct — to us it is the music of freedom.

Still the labor Kommandos march out. Some Jews say the tank ditches can be used equally well as mass graves for us. "Ha, ha, ha, freedom!" they mock. "Five minutes before the Russians arrive, we will all be under the earth." But the distant rumbling and thundering come closer and closer; they cause some to go mad with joy and others to tremble with fear. Then suddenly, at twelve o'clock noon, we get the order to report for the march. The camp is being evacuated. Only the patients in the Jewish sick ward will remain behind. I no longer could or would want to march. I shall survive, or else the struggle of the past years was in vain. It is a hard decision to make to remain lying in filth and mud when all those still able to walk are leaving the camp.

Everybody reports for the march at the camp gate. Commander Meisel, on horseback, rifle slung over his shoulder, gallops past the line of inmates. The camp senior reports to him: "Six-hundred and sixty prisoners ready for the march." "Ready, march!" Meisel commands. Slowly the column moves out the gate, escorted by about 50 guards in battle uniform.

Immediately after the departure of the walking prisoners new life awakens in the deserted camp. Many inmates have hidden. As soon as the column is out of sight, they emerge from their hiding places and immediately begin to raid the kitchen. But we're still not free, the camp is still being watched. Only inside the camp there are no guards anymore.

The starved men in the barracks begin to stir. Everyone still able to crawl moves slowly and cautiously toward the kitchen, dish in hand. Then they all fall on the soup buckets. This soup was intended for the "outside" Kommando, but it could not be taken there any more because of the sudden departure. People hurl themselves at the food. Everybody pushes their dishes into the buckets; those without a dish use their hands to fish out a few potatoes. It is as if a horde of starved lions had been let loose. Some of us are more clever. We start to break open the SS storage chamber. To the right of the door stands a full sack of sugar, which everybody reaches into immediately. As soon as one man has grabbed some food, another one greedily snatches it from his hand. I have seized two cans of peas with one hand and clutch a calf's foot in the other. Before I know what is happening, everything has been wrenched from my fingers. One man is trying to carry his bowl with sugar to safety, but all of a sudden the hands of many inmates are in his bowl. Most of the sugar is spilled and trodden into the ground. I am glad to get out of the room with no broken bones. I see a few inmates sneak off happily with several bags of ersatz coffee.

The camp is now ruled by a starved mob. The door to the potato cellar is broken open; everybody fetches as many potatoes as he can carry. Potatoes are being roasted everywhere, but there is no bottom to our stomachs anymore. I eat and eat and feel no fullness. Again and again I start eating; I'm afraid it is all just a dream. I fetch more potatoes, place them beneath the bread sack under my head and check every few minutes to make sure I still have my treasure.

Exhausted by the excitement of the afternoon just past, I lie down again on the dirt straw. In the meantime darkness has come on, though our camp is still under guard. The sound of shooting comes closer and closer. Inbetween we can hear pistol shots, sometimes the rat-tat-tat of machine gun fire. We all feel we're facing the most crucial moments of our lives. I have roused myself and stand at the small barn window. From here I have a view of the road leading past the camp. I see running, fleeing soldiers; some have thrown away their guns, one looks back as though the Russians were right at his heels. Then again the hammering of the machine guns. Things begin to happen in rapid succession. The guard in front of the gate lines up and marches off. German reconnaissance drivers speed by, followed by a German motorized column that doesn't want to lose contact with the last of the retreating German troops. Suddenly our door is flung open, a Jew rushes into the block and shouts he has seen the first Russian tank at the edge of the wood.

"Soon," he cries, "our brothers will be here!"

There is shooting everywhere—the boom of heavy artillery mingles with rifle shots; hand grenades fly past us; the earth seems to tremble. Outside a real battle appears to be raging, flares light up the night sky; we are surrounded by thundering air. The barracks are reverberating from the explosions. It is as if the earth was opening up around us to give birth to a few people, to return them to life again.

We hear the rumble of tanks outside. A few moments later the door swings open and a Russian tank driver stands in the frame — a messenger of freedom. Several Jews fall on his neck and kiss him, crying and laughing. Suddenly everybody is shouting, "Hurrah, hurrah, our liberators are here!"

8

Liberation and Lübeck

March-April 1945

March 8, 1945. One tank after another rolls up in the assembly square. Many Russians burst into tears at the sight of us. Immediately Russian ambulances are on the spot, and while the battle is still raging, the sickest among us are carried away. Doctors and nurses arrive and lead us out of the filthy typhus ward into the former SS accommodations. Under my bed I see a trunk marked "Oberscharführer Meisel." I rummage around among his possessions and find clean underwear; my heart rejoices when a few seconds later I lie down clad in the Oberscharführer's vest and shorts and enjoy the happiness of my new-found freedom.

The next morning we have everything a man could want. One Russian arrives with a large sack of flour; another brings butter and sugar. They say we should bake cakes. And really, those with enough energy start kneading dough at the dawn of the new day and bake cookies in the oven, which are distributed among the rest of us. In the early morning hours a Russian general appears. He makes a speech which a Latvian Jew translates into Yiddish. He says the brave Red Army has come just in time to save at least a small number of us. "If we had come a little later," he says, "we probably wouldn't have found anybody alive any more. Those among you who are now twenty-five years old," he continues, "should believe you are only twenty years old, because you will now start a new life." Then he goes outside. He walks to the Jewish sick ward where those who died during the past few days are still lying unburied, for we had no more strength to carry them outside. The general stands among the corpses; he takes off his cap and pays his respect to our dead. We cry with grief for them and with joy at having been restored to life.

All day long Russian units have been driving past our camp. Some of them are led by big, robust women with carbines slung over their shoulders. Cossacks on their horses gallop past, searching the fields and forests for hidden German soldiers. A never-ending procession of troops passes our camp. Sometimes we stand by the side of the road and wave at them. As soon as they see us in our striped prison suits they start throwing food at us in passing — bread, butter, bacon, sausages. Soon we all have so much food we could live on it for months. But again and again we go outside to receive new gifts. It all still seems too unreal; it is like a dream from which we fear to awaken.

At night, before we fall asleep, our door suddenly opens, a German sergeant-major and several German soldiers enter the room where I'm lying with Walter, a Jew from Hanover. Behind them is a Russian guard.

"Comrades," the German sergeant-major says to us, "we have orders from our captain to see that you are looked after properly."

I think I don't hear right. "Comrades," he calls us. Only yesterday we were sub-human and were being starved and exterminated. Today he is concerned about our welfare. All the pent-up fury, the whole desperation of the past years wells up in me.

"You goddamn filthy bastard!" I shout at him. "Will you get out of here?"

"But, comrade." the sergeant-major interrupts me, "it wasn't our fault."

Now all the vocabulary I learned from the SS rains down on him. Our situation is now reversed. For the first time I realize that I can scream at them and vent my wrath on these beasts, something I have yearned to do for years. The German prisoners and their Russian guard leave our room. I cannot fall asleep now. My heart pounds so hard it threatens to burst my chest with excitement. "Comrades," he called us, I keep thinking again and again. I am not his comrade.

April 1945. After weeks of bed rest the Russian woman doctor permits me to get up and sit in the sun in front of the barracks. After that I start going for walks, at first just around the camp because my legs still don't quite want to behave themselves. The next day I walk a little further. Slowly, very slowly, I feel my strength returning.

In the middle of what once was the assembly square, German refugees have dug a mass grave where our dead are buried. The Russian camp commander erects a red wooden pyramid with a hammer and sickle as a lasting memorial. A few days later the survivors leave the Rieben death camp to be taken to a larger collection camp.

A short time later we are called up to work again. The Russians drive the cattle from the neighboring farms in order to send them to Russia. Together with Russian soldiers, we tend the cows in the fields and guard the cattle. Usually I stand guard together with a Mongolian. Since our conversation is anything but fluent, he tries to teach me his mother tongue. He points his finger at the moon and says, "Lung." I repeat it after him and he is pleased. Usually he disappears after having stood watch for a short period and leaves me behind, alone. Once a Russian officer drives past. A few minutes later the Mongolian returns, the same one who gave me such good instruction in his language, and with his gun pressed into my back he drives me to the officers' barracks. There he locks me up in the attic. The next morning the Russian commander appears with the Mongolian; both of them are laughing and send me away. These people are unpredictable.

Early in May we are taken to Neustadt in Pomerania. We ride through the beautiful countryside on trucks, with Russian soldiers at the head and the rear of the column. There are barriers at every cross point, and we are being counted again and again before we are permitted to pass. Sometimes we see large posters in the streets showing a Red Army soldier waving the Red Flag, his boot on the stomach of a German soldier lying in front of him. Our procession to Neustadt becomes a victory parade; the streets are lined with laughing, friendly people whom we pass to the accompaniment of Russian songs sung by Jews from the East. For a short time it seems that the brotherhood of nations has become a reality.

But in Neustadt I already realize my mistake. A Pole gives a short speech. "Estonians, Latvians, and Lithuanians," he says, "will go back home in the next few days, and the German Jews," he continues sarcastically, "will return to their fatherland."

A few days later I stand in front of the Russian commander of Neustadt to have my new papers verified. We have received new ones from the Neustadt magistrate; they are to guarantee an unhindered return to our hometowns. From numbers we have changed back to people.

"What do you want?" he asks me through a translator. I hand him the papers of the 20 surviving German Jews requesting to undertake the journey home. I tell him it is already three-thirty and the one daily train for Danzig leaves at four. But the commander is in no hurry. He takes a cigarette from his case and hunts for matches. When another officer enters the room, he takes the commander's cigarette from his mouth. He puts another cigarette in his mouth; this, too, is taken by an officer. When he has finally lit his cigarette, he starts rearranging the papers and searching for his stamp. He opens all the desk drawers, but the stamp is nowhere to be found. Finally he puts his hand in his pants pocket and withdraws a handkerchief, from which he unwraps the rubber stamp. He soon finds the stamp pad and in a few minutes all my papers are sealed and signed. Now quickly to the station where the small group of men and women is already waiting.

In Danzig we run into the first obstacles. The Polish guards at the barrier let us pass, but at the exit of the bombed-out railroad station there are Russian guards who again check our papers. We men are wearing old German Labor Service uniforms, because no civilian clothes were available. I show the Russian guard our papers, give him our number and say "Stutthof." I ask each one in our group to walk past him. But then he changes his mind and makes us all line up on the left side of the station exit. Then he comes to me, asks: "Stashe [sergeant]?" I nod affirmatively. "Kommandantura [orders]." In a minute we are surrounded by Russian guards and are led over the station square to the Russian headquarters. Once again a gate is closed behind us.

I am taken to the commander. One man tears the knapsack off my back, and curses, "Germanski, nix Ivreh. Ivreh kaput [You are German. Not Jews. We Jews are all dead.]" He starts to search the knapsack and finds some underwear and provisions. Then he inspects the luggage of several others and orders us taken back to the station. But we did not get our papers back, and without them we all feel vulnerable. We stand in front of the administration building and wonder what to do next, when a window above us opens, the head appears, and a few seconds later our papers flutter to the ground.

Danzig, where we spend the night, is completely devastated. The next morning an open freight train takes us to Schneidemohl. We are told that a train is leaving in the direction of Berlin the same evening. We can't get on board. The Poles do not allow any Jews on the train. Everywhere we're greeted with vile insults. We decide to ride on top of the compartments. One man climbs up and starts collecting the knapsacks we hand him, when quite suddenly the train starts up and rolls off with Ignatz and some of our luggage.

Several hours later a freight train arrives and takes us slowly to Kopenick, about 25 miles from Berlin. Finally we reach Berlin by streetcar. For hours we run through the bombed-out streets, looking for a place to stay overnight. The Berliners whom we ask about a Jewish organization shake their heads in surprise. There are no more Jews here. Berlin without Jews!

We sit down to rest at the Doehnhofplatz. I remember a large air travel exhibit here a long time ago. We debate what to do, where to go. Opposite us on a bench sits an old woman; I start talking to her and ask her whether she knows any Jews who might give us information regarding Jewish assistance organizations. She only shakes her head, but suddenly she remembers that somewhere on her street lives a "mixed-marriage" couple. Soon we're on our way. The former Jewish hospital in the Iranien Street is now the haven for homeless Jews. We are welcomed with great joy. Rosel Sachs from Liepaja is here and, to my incredible surprise, so is the young girl who gave me some bread when I was in the bunker in the Riga ghetto. She comes towards me with outstretched arms. We are both overjoyed; a miracle has happened. She tells me she intends to go to Fürth and look for her relatives. A year later Irene and I get married in Lübeck. I shall always be grateful to her, for she gave me courage in one of the darkest hours of my life.

At the hospital we are given board and shelter. The rooms are clean, the beds have white sheets. We are supplied with cl hes and have soon put the hardships of our travels behind us.

After a few days of rest in Berlin, I continue my journey with a Jew from Hamburg. Our goal is Lübeck. We ride first on a heavily loaded freight train, then in small carriages with the Russians; after that we hike from village to village, from town to town until we reach a small place in the vicinity of Schwerin, the borderline between the Russian and British occupation zones. The Russians don't want to let us cross the border, although I repeatedly shove my permit, with the Russian commander's stamp, under the guard's nose. "Kommandantura," he says, only "Kommandantura." He is adamant. There is nothing we can do with him. We move on and come to a small village, about two miles from the border. A farmer takes us in after we've told him we want to go to the "other side."

We drive out to his potato field and start to work while he describes the exact layout of the land and the position of two bridges crossing the river that forms the border. At night he returns to the village alone.

We lie in a cornfield, waiting for darkness to fall. Around midnight we get going, sneaking along the cornfields, crossing ditches, stumbling over the roots of trees lining the edge of the field. It is a moonlit night; in the distance we hear the pounding of horses' hooves, then the shouts of the Russian guards who are somewhere in the darkness, invisible to us. We wait for half an hour, and creep on. Branches crack under our feet and birds are frightened out of their sleep. We become nervous and wonder whether we've taken the right road. Suddenly we see a small river and, a few yards to our right, the bridge the farmer spoke of. Soon the forest offers us shelter. We rush from one tree to the next, cross a road, jump over a wide ditch and heave a sigh of relief, because according to the farmer's description we are now in the British occupation zone.

In the morning we are in Schwerin. A British soldier gives us a ride on the Lübeck Boulevard, and two hours later we walk through the old castle gate into the inner city. I feel nostalgic and proud at the same time. In my mind's eye I see the long column of Jews being deported. I see my mother, and I see the brown hordes rushing through the streets, breaking windows and demolishing stores. I remember the ghetto song: "The same old streets, the same old streetcars," but I know now I no longer want these streets.

People take little notice of the repatriates. Only the butcher with whom we used to do business for many years gives me an extra quarter-pound of sausage when he recognizes me.

I go to the police department to register, and find the same clerk who took my keys from me so long ago sitting at the desk.

"But Mr. Katz," he says, "where have you been all this time? You never notified us of your departure."

A year later, my wife and I sail across the ocean toward a new home. Speedboats are circling around us, the sun shines brightly, people are waving, and sirens are shrieking as the boat slowly passes the Statue of Liberty to enter the harbor. A new life begins.

Epilogue

August 1972

It has been a long journey. We left Frankfurt about four hours ago. The train has just stopped in Hamburg and we should soon be in Lübeck, the old town close to the Baltic Sea where this story began nearly half a century ago.

It was a hard decision for me to return to the city of my birth. Looking back, I feel that I never had a normal childhood in Lübeck. My concerns were always focused on the growing power of the anti-Semitic movement. But that is past history. This is another Germany, I am told, a country which is trying to forget and in a way to atone for the many crimes committed against the Jewish people.

"Please take me to the synagogue at St. Annenstrasse," I tell the taxi driver. There is no answer, only stony silence. The radio announces a memorial service held for the victims of the Dachau concentration camp. As soon as the driver hears the mention of "Dachau," he abruptly turns off the radio, somehow not wanting to be reminded of the past.

"Three marks eighty," he says as we stop in front of the synagogue. No further word is spoken and he takes off at once. I do not believe he liked his passengers.

A few children play on the steps of the synagogue. An old man, cane in hand, walks slowly to a bench at the side of the building where he sits down, holds his face in his hands and looks around. There is not much to see.

"Always the same," he says. "There is not much I can do anymore." He explains he has been sick since his liberation from Bergen-Belsen. "There is not much to live for here either," he continues. "No more prayer services because only a few are left — not enough for a minyan. I will be the last to be taken to that old cemetery just outside of Lübeck, the former ghetto. Everybody else is moving away," he tells me. "There will be no more Jews here in a few years."

"Where can I find the key to the Synagogue?" I ask him. I am told that Rosneck, who lives next door in the former building for the Jewish aged, can let me in. Today this building is occupied mostly by non-Jewish people who also live upstairs in the remodeled parts of the synagogue, where our rabbi used to live.

Slowly I cross the playground of the former Hebrew school. The dust swirls under my feet — dust, and ashes — all that remains of the once thriving Jewish community. The heavy door creaks on its hinges as Shmuel, a survivor of Auschwitz, opens it. The floor under my feet echoes back from the walls of this lonely place. Gone are the heavy candelabras and the beautiful ornamental covers of the Aron Hakodesh [Ark of the Law]. There are some empty prayer benches, a few prayer books which are never used, and some pictures at the entrance telling of the proud old history of this congregation.

I decide to leave quickly. The air is filled with memories and there is no sense in my staying here any longer. Walking down to a waiting taxi, I begin to realize that at this very moment, on other continents, new Jewish communities are being founded to continue the traditions practiced here for many centuries, traditions which I pray will last forever and always.

The car enters the Muehlenstrasse. I do not look back, knowing that an era of Jewish history in this country is coming to a close.

Notes

Lübeck, Germany

1. (P. 3) SA. Sturmabteilung, known as storm troopers or brown shirts. First led by Ernst Röhm, the SA had a significant role in destroying opposition to the Nazis in the early 1930s.
2. (P. 4) Rishus. "Wickedness," a Hebrew term popularly used to denote anti-Semitism.
3. (P. 5) Herschel Grynszpan. Shot and killed Ernst vom Rath, an official of the German embassy in Paris; this act served as a pretext for the Nazi Kristallnacht pogroms throughout Germany and Austria in November, 1938. Grynszpan, learning that his Polish-born parents would be deported from Germany, had planned to kill the German ambassador to arouse Western public opinion against the Nazi persecution of Jews.
4. (P. 8) Haverim. "Comrades" or "friends," a form of address in Hebrew among members of Zionist organizations.
5. (P. 8) German Kibbutz group. Young people preparing to emigrate to Palestine as a group and found or join a kibbutz (collective agricultural settlement) there.
6. (P. 8) Rabbi Leo Baeck (1874-1956). Spiritual leader of German Reform Jewry, who was to survive the war in the Theresienstadt ghetto.
7. (P. 8) Hatikvah. "The Song of Hope," anthem of the Zionist movement, now the national anthem of the State of Israel.
8. (P. 8) Oneg Shabbat. "Sabbath delight." Gathering held on Saturday afternoon for lectures and cultural performances.

Jungfernhof and Salaspils, Latvia

1. (P. 14) Rabbi Joseph Carlebach (1883-1942). At the outbreak of the war Carlebach, a native of Lübeck and member of a distinguished rabbinical family, was Chief Rabbi of Hamburg and Altona. He was eventually transported to Riga, where he was killed by the Nazis on March 26, 1942.
2. (P. 15) SS. Schutzstaffel, elite military unit of the Nazi party, led by Heinrich Himmler. The SS Death's Head units were in charge of Germany's concentration camps.
3. (P. 16) Rudolf Lange. Commander of the Nazi party intelligence service, the Sicherheitsdienst (SD) in Riga, Latvia. Known as the "Bloodhound of Latvia," he was largely responsible for the extermination of the Jewish population of Latvia. The Einsatzgruppen A killed over 250,000 people in less than six months. Reportedly killed in action in Poznan, Poland, in February, there is some question about whether he committed suicide.

4. (P. 19) Kolonnenführer. Jewish concentration camp inmate acting as foreman of a labor detail.

5. (P. 20) K'ria. Cutting a tear in clothing; a symbolic act of mourning performed by Jews following the death of a close relative.

6. (P. 21) Kapo. Inmate appointed as overseer (see Glossary).

7. (P. 23) Oil Lamp. The Hanukkah candles symbolize the miracle that came to pass when the Jews rededicated the Temple following the victory of the Maccabees over the Greeks. In rekindling the Everlasting Light in the Temple, only one small cruse of oil was found which would ordinarily have been enough for just one day; however, it lasted for eight days.

8. (P. 26) Lagerälteste. Camp senior: Inmate in charge of all camp quarters.

9. (P. 31) Sh'ma Yisrael. Jewish declaration of belief in One God, recited as part of the daily liturgy and also before death: "Hear, O Israel, the Lord our God, the Lord is One." (*Deut. 6:4*)

10. (P. 32) Blockälteste. Block senior, inmate in charge of a block of inmate dwellings.

11. (P. 35) Hochwald. Forest near Riga where many Jewish deportees were murdered.

12. (P. 37) Mah Nishtanah. The Four Questions. Asked at the Seder by the youngest person at the table, beginning with "Why is this night different from all other nights?"

13. (P. 37) Haggadah. The special prayer book from which the Seder ritual is conducted.

14. (P. 38) Minyan. Quorum of ten men necessary for Jewish religious services.

Riga Ghetto and Liepaja, Latvia

1. (P. 45) Organize. In camp parlance, to "organize" was to take food or clothing wherever it could be found.

2. (P. 46) Karl Wilhelm Kraus. Ghetto Commandant who succeeded Lange, he held absolute power over the camp. As Bernhard Press writes in *The Murder of the Jews in Latvia, 1941-1945*, (Northwestern University Press 2000), "Krause was so cruel and bloodthirsty that only words like 'incomprehensible' or 'unimaginable' could approximately describe him. Murdering an innocent human being with a shot in the neck was for him a wholly everyday occurrence, a routine matter."

3. (P. 51) Arbeitsamt. Office of ghetto administration that supplied workers for Nazi forced labor.

4. (P. 51) Judenälteste. Elder of the Jews, the Jew placed in charge of the ghetto.

5. (P. 53) Reichskommisar. High Nazi occupation official.

6. (P. 55) Dr. Aufrecht. A German Jew who local Jews suspected was collaborating with the Gestapo. In *Zwischen Tag und Dunkel [Between Day and Darkness]*

(Frankfurt am Main, 1984), H. Sherman refers to him as a lackey of the SS. In 1920, for example, he signed a newspaper advertisement that called for deporting Polish Jews from Bavaria. At the end of the war, Bernhard Press writes, he was executed by the Russians for "hard-hearted treatment of the Jews."

7. (P. 55) Linas Hazedak. Originally the Jewish women's clinic, financed by foundations of Jewish merchants and funds from the American Joint Distribution Committee (see p. 138 on its conversion into a crematorium).

8. (P. 59) Yom Kippur. The Day of Atonement, a solemn day of fasting, prayer and repentance.

9. (P. 63) Selektion. Selection of camp inmates for work or for death in gas chambers (see Glossary).

10. (P. 63) A. Kehlmann. He and his assistants were responsible for various administrative areas, primarily Economic Authority which supplied food for the ghetto.

11. (P. 63) Aktion. Mass herding of Jews for deportation (see Glossary).

12. (P. 65) Ten for one. Ten will be shot for each individual attempting to escape.

13. (P. 68) Skeden. A town on the Baltic coast north of Liepaja. In mid-December 1941, Jews of Liepaja were transported in trucks and on sleds to Skeden, while others were forced to make their way on foot in the freezing cold. Men and women were ordered to disrobe completely and in groups of ten were forced to run into previously dug pits where they were shot by groups of Germans and Latvians. The terrible bloodbath that began on December 15 and ended three days later claimed some 2,800 Jews.

14. (P. 69) S.D. Sicherheitsdienst. Nazi party intelligence service.

15. (P. 72) Yekke. Pejorative term used by East European Jews for German Jews. Probably derived from the Jacke, or short jacket worn by "modern" Jews in Germany as opposed to the long coats worn by Jews in the East.

16. (P. 74) M. Weinreich. Dr. Weinreich had headed the hospital in the Liepaja ghetto. "One of his most dreadful memories of that time was the visit paid to the hospital by the notorious murderer H. Cukurs. Cukurs, bent on finding able-bodied men and women who might be hiding in the hospital, had forced his way into the women's ward, where he discovered a newborn baby. Births were forbidden in the ghetto. Cukurs snatched the baby by its feet from its mother's bed, smashed its head against the wall so that the skull broke, and tossed the lifeless body to the ground. When the Liepaja ghetto was liquidated, Cukurs spared the lives of Weinreich and [a Dr.] Sick, who had once been his own doctors, and sent them to Riga together with a few other Jews. Both of them survived the war." Bernhard Press, *The Murder of the Jews in Latvia, 1941-1945.*

17. (P. 87) Sidewalk. Jews were not permitted to use the sidewalks.

18. (P. 89) Hakhshorah. Center where prospective immigrants to Israel receive training in agriculture and other pioneering skills.

19. (P. 92) Aussenkommando. Labor detail working outside the ghetto.

Kaiserwald, Latvia

1. (P. 108) Mr. X. Xaver Apel, a professional criminal who was one of the brutal Kapos the SS recruited to terrorize fellow inmates. Bernhard Press (*The Murder of the Jews in Latvia, 1941-1945*) refers to Josef Katz's accounts and quotes several other survivors who told of inmates that Apel beat so severely that they fainted or even died, women he raped, and feeble people he threw into the Daugavea and drowned.

2. (P. 110) Rapportführer. SS guard whose main assignment was to count the camp inmates.

3. (P. 112) A.E.G. Allgemeine Elektrizitots-Aktiengesellschuft: General Electric Corporation.

4. (P. 113) "Think not..." The famous Partisan Song that came from the ghettos and concentration camps of World War II.

5. (P. 115) Outside camp. Camps where the Jewish inmates were also quartered while they worked there.

6. (P. 130) H.K.P. Heereseraftfahrpark: headquarters of military motorized communications agency, where Jewish labor was used.

7. (P. 131) O.T. Organisation Todt: Nazi agency in charge of construction projects.

8. (P. 134) *Die Stürmer.* Julius Streicher's anti-Semitic publication, featuring obscene and grotesque cartoons of so-called Jewish types.

Stutthof, Poland

1. (P. 169) Stutthof. Nazi concentration camp about 22 miles east of Danzig [Polish: Gdansk]. Set up in September, 1939, it received Jews from the Latvian camps and Auschwitz in the summer and fall of 1944. By the end of World War II, a total of 52,000 prisoners had passed through Stutthof. Of these, about 3,000 survived.

2. (P. 172) German soil. While Stutthof is in Poland, it was German territory, like Danzig (Gdansk) during the occupation.

3. (P. 178) B.V. Beserufs-Verbrecher. Professional criminal; non-Jewish concentration camp inmate serving time for a crime, as distinct from a political prisoner.

Glossary of Ghetto and Concentration Camp Terms

Aktion. Mass herding of Jews for deportation to concentration camps or, in the camps, for death in the gas chambers.

Arbeitsamt. Office in ghetto administration that supplied workers for Nazi forced labor.

Aussenkommando. Jewish labor detail working outside the ghetto.

Blockälteste. Block Senior. Inmate in charge of a block of inmate dwellings.

Judenälteste. Elder of the Jews. The Jew placed in charge of the ghetto.

Kapo. Trustee or overseer in charge of labor details or concentration camp departments such as the hospital or kitchen. The origin of the term is uncertain. Kapos were concentration camp inmates appointed by the SS officers in charge of the camps. They were responsible for carrying out SS orders. Initially, Kapos were selected from among German non-Jewish inmates imprisoned in the camps on criminal charges, but in all-Jewish concentration camps there were Jewish Kapos. The Kapos received special privileges, including better food rations than the other inmates. Some Kapos were helpful to their fellow inmates, but most of them spied on the other inmates and were generally hated and feared for their cruelty.

Kolonnenführer. Leader of column. Camp inmate acting as foreman of workers.

Kommando. Jewish labor detail or work party.

Lagerälteste. Camp Senior. Inmate in charge of all camp quarters.

Lagerführer. SS officer in command of a concentration camp.

"Organizing." To take food or clothing wherever it can be found.

Postenführer. Chief sentry.

Rapportführer. An SS whose main assignment was to count the concentration camp inmates. His total was checked with the records of the camp commander.

SS. Schutzstaffel. Elite military units of Nazi party. SS officers and men served as a special police force in the concentration camps.

Selektion. Selection of concentration camp inmates for work, or for death in the gas chambers. In Selektions the inmates would be lined up before the camp officers. Inmates considered fit for work were told to move to one side, usually to the right; those arbitrarily classed as unfit for work, and therefore to be exterminated, were ordered to move to the other line.

Sicherheitsdienst (SD). Security Service. Nazi party intelligence service created by SS Chief Heinrich Himmler.

Stubendienst. Room Orderlies. Inmates assisting Blockälteste.

SS Ranks with Army Equivalents

SS Mann	Private
SS Sturmmann	Private First Class
Rottenführer	Corporal
Unterscharführer	Lance Sergeant
Scharführer	Sergeant
Oberscharführer	Sergeant Major
Hauptscharführer	Warrant Officer
Untersturmführer	Second Lieutenant
Obersturmführer	First Lieutenant
Obersturmbannführer	Lieutenant Colonel
Standartenführer	Colonel
Oberführer	Brigadier General
Brigadeführer	Major General
Gruppenführer	Lieutenant General
Obergruppenführer	General
Oberstgruppenführer	Colonel General
Reichsführer SS	Commander-in-Chief of the SS

Biographical Note

Josef Katz was born in 1918 in Lübeck, Germany, the son of a leather merchant who died when the boy was two years old. Despite great economic hardship, his widowed mother managed to give her five children an orthodox Jewish education. Hitler came to power when Josef was fifteen years old. His experiences from the years 1933 to 1945 are reported in this record which he wrote immediately after liberation.

Shortly before immigrating to the United States he married Irene — a fellow survivor whom he had met in the Riga ghetto. The young couple landed in New York on August 31, 1946, thanks to President Truman, who permitted 50,000 Jews to enter the United States without an affidavit.

At first Katz was employed as a shipping clerk and his wife as a garment worker. In time he established himself in a textile concern in Los Angeles, where a daughter Jeanne was born.

In the original edition, he wrote of his life after the dehumanizing brutality and terror during World War II:

"I would like to say that our life in the United States has been like the lives of other immigrants who arrived on the shores of the New World. For me this country fulfilled the promises inscribed in the Statue of Liberty — the right to be free of religious and political persecution, and the ability to advance economically.

"For me and my friends of the same background, the scars of the Hitler period remain. I cannot forget, nor do I want to. The past is ever present, as tension and insecurity linger on. But there is one ray of sunshine. My daughter Jeanne, growing up with unlimited educational opportunities in this free society, is looking forward to a fruitful, normal life, always aware, however, of our traditions and the troubled past of her parents."

Josef Katz died on August 14, 1990